MANDELA

MANDELA
A Critical Life

TOM LODGE

OXFORD
UNIVERSITY PRESS

OXFORD

UNIVERSITY PRESS

Great Clarendon Street, Oxford OX2 6DP

Oxford University Press is a department of the University of Oxford.
It furthers the University's objective of excellence in research, scholarship,
and education by publishing worldwide in

Oxford New York

Auckland Cape Town Dar es Salaam Hong Kong Karachi
Kuala Lumpur Madrid Melbourne Mexico City Nairobi
New Delhi Shanghai Taipei Toronto

With offices in

Argentina Austria Brazil Chile Czech Republic France Greece
Guatemala Hungary Italy Japan Poland Portugal Singapore
South Korea Switzerland Thailand Turkey Ukraine Vietnam

Oxford is a registered trade mark of Oxford University Press
in the UK and in certain other countries

Published in the United States
by Oxford University Press Inc., New York

British Library Cataloguing in Publication Data

Data available

Library of Congress Cataloging in Publication Data

Data available

Typeset in Bembo
by RefineCatch Limited, Bungay, Suffolk
Printed in Great Britain
on acid-free paper by
Clays Limited, St Ives plc

ISBN 0-19-280568-1   978-0-19-280568-3

1

CONTENTS

PREFACE

This is hardly the first serious biography of Mandela. There are already two 'authorised' biographies, both by friends of his, writers belonging to the same generation as their subject. Fatima Meer's *Higher than Hope* was researched and written in the late 1980s and published in 1988.[1] Anthony Sampson's *Mandela* was published in 1999.[2] Martin Meredith's equally perceptive and detailed treatment of Mandela's life appeared in 1997.[3] This book draws upon these writers' work substantially, as well as using the same kinds of primary sources: correspondence, Mandela's own writings, interviews, and memoirs, court documents, and contemporary press reportage. My first acknowledgements should therefore be to Fatima Meer, Anthony Sampson, and Martin Meredith. Their work will continue to represent essential foundations for any future assessments of Mandela's career.

How is my treatment of Mandela's life different from theirs? It is different in several ways. First of all, my understanding of Mandela's childhood and youth is, I think, more complicated than in the other narratives about his beginnings. Mandela's childhood was unusual because of his early departure from his mother's household and his subsequent upbringing as the ward of a royal regent. Mandela's emotional self-control as a personality, as well as his receptiveness to new ideas, is, I think, attributable to his upbringing in highly institutionalised settings. Both at court and at school, Mandela absorbed principles of etiquette and chivalry that remained important precepts through his public life. They were principles that were reinforced by a sophisticated literary culture that fused heroic African oral traditions with Victorian concepts of honour, propriety, and virtue. From his boyhood, Mandela's life was shaped by ideas or values that were shared by rather than dividing his compatriots, black and white. In this context, the absence in his early life of intimidating or humiliating encounters with white people is significant, and, to an extent, distinguishes his childhood from many other black South African childhoods.

Understandably, Mandela's role as a primary agent in enabling the achievement of South African political reconciliation is a key theme in later projections of his life. Mandela's autobiography, published in 1994, emphasises his own experience of empathy and even kindness across South Africa's historic social and political fault lines, experience that could reinforce a project of new nation building. The tactful omissions in his own testimony when it is compared with other histories of his life should remind us that autobiography is not always good history and Mandela's own words about his own life should be read as critically as any other source. Even so, my book does cite plenty of contemporary evidence to suggest that Mandela's willingness to embrace all his compatriots as citizens was sustained by professional protocols and codes of behaviour. Even in the increasingly polarised climate of South Africa in the 1950s, these ideas about social conduct could transcend racial identity and they reinforced the decorous manners and patrician conventions that Mandela had maintained from home and school.

I find less of a contrast than other writers between the young Mandela and the older veteran of imprisonment. Generally in Mandela's career there are no sudden turning points; rather key decisions develop out of lengthy incremental processes of thought, and are often influenced by Mandela's recollection of precedent. One especially significant instance of the continuities in his political beliefs was his conviction that reasoned discussion would eventually broker what he himself would eventually describe as a 'legal revolution'. Legal training and practice had a crucial impact upon Mandela's political development. In general, historians of anti-colonial movements have paid insufficient attention to the influence of colonial legal ideas on African nationalist leadership. Mandela's life is an especially striking demonstration of the ways in which ideas about human rights and civic obligations were shaped by his professional training. Most importantly, the structured world of courtroom procedure itself shaped Mandela's political practice, restraining it even in its most theatrically insurgent phases, and reinforcing his respect for institutions, traditions, and history.

The language of theatre is used quite commonly among Mandela's biographers, but in this book one of my particular preoccupations is with Mandela's political actions as performance, self-consciously planned, scripted to meet public expectations, or calculated to shift popular sentiment. Birth, upbringing, emotional self-sufficiency from an early age, social grace, imposing appearance, and elite status combined to encourage in Mandela an unusual assurance about his destiny as a leader, a 'sense of his power' to shape his own life that seems to have been shared by those around him. For Mandela, politics has always been primarily about enacting stories, about making narratives, primarily about morally exemplary conduct, and only secondarily about ideological vision, more about means rather than ends. In the South Africa of the early apartheid era, Mandela was one of the first media politicians, 'showboy' as one of his contemporaries nicknamed him, embodying a glamour and a style that projected *visually* a brave new African world of modernity and freedom. Mandela's ascent as a politician and as a member of black Johannesburg's high society occurred at a time of more general upward mobility among black South Africans and early sections of this book explore in some detail the social setting in which Mandela became a public personality.

Mandela was especially sensitive to the imperatives for acting out a messianic leadership role during his short service as a guerrilla commander, a phase in which he and his comrades deliberately set out to construct a mythological legitimacy for their political authority, and in which they could engender hopes among their compatriots that salvation would be achieved through their own heroic self-sacrifice. From this perspective, their strategic and tactical decisions become more explicable. It was an approach that was rewarded several decades later when both Mandela and the movement around him exploited his iconic and celebrity prestige to endorse political compromise that may otherwise have been popularly unacceptable. In this book, I maintain that Mandela's prestige, his moral capital as it were, was the consequence of an exceptional public status that began to develop very early in Mandela's career, well before his imprisonment.

His moral standing as a leader was enormously enhanced by his imprisonment, of course, although the reasons for his ascendancy as an international public hero during his years on Robben Island are by no means straightforward. In my own treatment of Mandela's life in prison I underline the extent to which the prisoners became an organised community—here I was helped by Fran Buntman's superb monograph[4] as well as a rich range of memoirs from Mandela's fellow prisoners. Within this community, Mandela was accorded a particular status. He was accorded this status by the prisoners and also, as importantly, by the officials who governed the prison. This highly structured world of the prison may have been a crucial environmental setting in helping Mandela to preserve his commitment to orderly political process, a commitment that contrasted sharply with the more apocalyptic perceptions of many of his contemporaries during the 1970s and 1980s.

Imprisoned leaders can be supplanted by fresh generations of politicians at liberty, however, and what was remarkable about Mandela's authority was its endurance over generations and, moreover, his incorporation into an international iconography assembled by young people at the beginning of the 1990s. I do not find organisational explanations for Mandela's continuing influence very persuasive, those explanations, for example that focus on the channels of communications between the Robben Islanders and their followers elsewhere. Instead, the sources of Mandela's appeal were then, and to an extent remain today, charismatic and cultural, to do with his apparent immortality despite or even because of his removal and absence, a product of the stories enacted by him and told about him, and the particular power of these stories to reach a multiplicity of audiences inside and beyond South Africa. His especial accessibility to a transnational English-speaking following was the consequence of his own personification of the secular liberal values instilled in his 'English' schooling. Also, perhaps more importantly, it was an effect of his marriage to a remarkably talented leader in her own right who helped keep his authority in currency. In prison, especially, popular projections of his life become intertwined with Winnie Madikizela's story, and the couple's very public exemplification of romantic love and sexual intimacy accentuated Mandela's appeal outside South Africa.

As his former wife's contribution to Mandela's authority demonstrates, Mandela's domestic or private life cannot easily be separated or compartmentalised from his political or public career. For Mandela, the commitments and obligations that arise from kinship and community often intersect with his politics, despite his occasional efforts to resist them and notwithstanding his own self-acknowledged shortcomings as a husband and a father. Indeed he may have experienced such commitments as all the more morally compelling and the more emotionally comforting because of the disrupted history of his domestic affairs. The social connections provided by kinship networks remained important to Mandela even after his arrival in Johannesburg. Initially, of course, they supplied him with important sources of support and solidarity. Throughout his political career Mandela maintained at least a qualified sense of obligation to his aristocratic kinsfolk, despite the disapproval that this aroused among his more Jacobean comrades. His attachment to the values associated with family and clan remain evident today in his quite genuine delight on encountering children, but these values shape his politics in a much more profound way. For in Mandela's thinking there is a tension between two sets of ideas about democracy.

In many of his most formal expositions about his civic beliefs—his prepared speeches and addresses—he uses the vocabulary associated with the conventional institutions of liberal government, the 'ordinary democracy' as Mandela has called it that organises and regulates difference, and in doing so maintains adversaries as competitors. Such professions by Mandela of his belief in liberal institutions are quite sincere. But in the same discourses there appear references to a quite different consensual model of decision-making. Here Mandela finds his inspiration in idealised recollections of pre-colonial African practice in which rulers encourage unity through presiding over discursive or deliberative practices. In this model, agreement is facilitated through a set of principles linked to ideas about obligation, to family, to friends, and to clan and nation. Mandela's extraordinary loyalty to a political movement is partly an expression of this patrimonial association of concepts of family, community, citizenship, and democracy.

This conflation of these concepts is sometimes, although not always, evident in his political thinking and practice.

In a very general sense, preoccupations about social obligations, about manners, about how people should behave, and about what is proper constitute the key concerns in Nelson Mandela's politics. His willingness to acknowledge goodness where he finds it is a capacity that is nurtured by caring 'about the little things in life', to quote the words of Graca Machel, his third wife. Over and over again in this book's narrative, Mandela draws moral and political sustenance from encounters in which everyday courtesy, consideration, and even generosity soften conflict. The lessons that Mandela learned as a child about the importance of defeating one's opponents without humiliating them were deeply engrained. They shaped a politics of grace and honour that, notwithstanding its conservatism, was probably the only politics that could have enabled South Africa's relatively peaceful transition to democracy, a transition that more than a decade later appears to have resulted in a stable constitutional order.

In this book I have been able to exploit a rich range of biographical and autobiographical writing about Mandela and his contemporaries. Aside from the intellectual debts that I owe to the authors of these works, I am also grateful for other more personal kinds of help that I have received during my research and writing. For help in locating archival materials I am very grateful to: Michele Pickover, Carol Archibald, and Kate Abbott of the Historical Papers Section, Cullen Library, University of the Witwatersrand; Marcelle Graham and Diana Madden of the Brenthurst Library, Johannesburg; Verne Harris of the Nelson Mandela Foundation; and Gerrit Wagener, Zahira Adams, and Natalie Skomolo at the National Archives of South Africa, Pretoria. Robert Edgar drew my attention to Mandela's first published article as well as a file of early correspondence between Mandela and the Bantu Welfare Trust. Luli Callinicos allowed me access to the transcript of her interview with Mandela, enabling me to obtain fresh insights about his legal practice and his friendship with Oliver Tambo; Barbara Harmel's and Philip Bonner's interviews with Umkhonto veterans conducted on behalf of the Albert Einstein Institute's South African Civil Society Project also constituted a major resource in the research for this book. Roger Southall arranged for an early despatch of his and Kristina Bentley's incisive study of Mandela's contribution to the Burundi peace process. I have benefited from attentive readers and sympathetic listeners, and providers of other kinds of support at the University of the Witwatersrand Institute for Social and Economic Research, among my former colleagues in the School of Social of Social Science also at Wits, the Department of History at the University of Stellenbosch, and the Department of History at Emory University, Atlanta; in particular my thanks are due to Michelle Browne, Philip Frankel, Magda Gale, Clive Glaser, Darryl Glaser, Shireen Hassim, Peter Hudson, Ivan Karp, Corinne Kratz, Stephen Louw, Sheila Meintjes, Trish Milliken, David Monyae, Noor Nieftagodien, Noam Pines, Julie-Kate Seirlis, John Stremlau, Raymond Suttner, Rupert Taylor, and Eddie Webster. The final shaping of the manuscript owes much to discerning commentary from my editor, Luciana O'Flaherty, at Oxford University Press. This volume is dedicated to my family: Carla, Kim, Guy, and Lewis.

Tom Lodge

Johannesburg and Limerick, 2005

LIST OF PLATES

LIST OF ABBREVIATIONS

AAM	Anti-Apartheid Movement
ANC	African National Congress
ANCYL	African National Congress Youth League
ANCWL	African National Congress Women's League
ALN	Armée de Liberation Nationale
ARM	African Resistance Movement
BCM	Black Consciousness Movement
CODESA	Congress for a Democratic South Africa
COSATU	Congress of South African Trades' Unions
CPSA	Communist Party of South Africa
CYL	(African National) Congress Youth League
FLN	Front de Liberation Nationale
FRELIMO	Frente de Libertaçao de Moçambique
IFP	Inkatha Freedom Party
IRC	International Red Cross
ITN	Independent Television News
MK	Umkhonto we Sizwe
NEC	(African National Congress) National Executive Committee
NWC	(African National Congress) Working Committee
OAU	Organization of African Unity
PAFMECSA	Pan African Freedom Movement of East, Central and West Africa
PAC	Pan-Africanist Congress
SACP	South African Communist Party
SAIC	South African Indian Congress
SRC	Student Representative Council
SWAPO	South West Africa People's Organization
TAC	Treatment Action Campaign
TANC	Transvaal African National Congress
TIC	Transvaal Indian Congress
TRC	Truth and Reconciliation Commission
UDF	United Democratic Front
WFDY	World Federation of Democratic Youth
YCL	Young Communist League

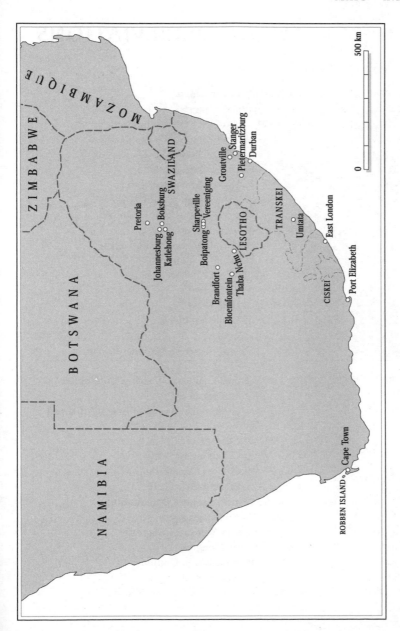

Map of South Africa

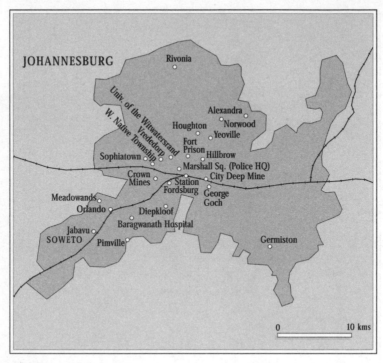

Map of Johannesburg

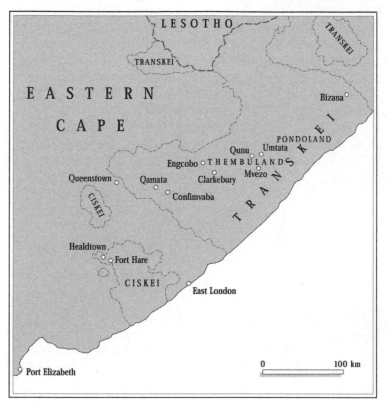

Map of Eastern Cape

CHILDHOOD AND UPBRINGING

In the world into which Nelson Mandela was born in 1918, children were best seen, not heard. 'We were meant to learn through imitation and emulation, not through asking questions', Mandela tells us in his autobiography.[1] 'Education we received by simply sitting silently when our elders talked,' he explained to Fatima Meer.[2] Despite his early upbringing in a village community composed mainly of women and children, from infancy his social relationships were regulated by strict conventions and precise rules of etiquette. In this vein, much of the emphasis in most accounts of Nelson Mandela's childhood has fallen on what he was told and what he presumably learned rather than on what he felt or perceived.

Lineage enjoys pride of place in Mandela's testimonies about his childhood. When Meer wrote her 'authorised' biography in 1988, Mandela himself, then still in prison, compiled a family tree and supportive notes for a genealogy passing through ten generations. This indicated his line of descent in the Thembu chieftaincy as a member of its 'left-hand house' of King Ngubencuka, who presided over a united Thembu community in the 1830s. The Thembu were one of twelve isiXhosa-speaking chieftaincies that inhabited the Transkei, the largest of South Africa's African peasant reserves situated on South Africa's eastern seaboard. The Thembu left-hand house, descendants of Ngubencuka's third wife, by convention served as counsellors or advisers to the royal household, the sons of Ngubencuka's 'Great House'. In this capacity, Mandela suggests, his father Henry Gadla Mpakhanyiswa can be thought of as the Thembu paramount's 'prime minister', though more prosaically he was accorded the post of village headman at Mvezo near Umtata by the administration of the Transkeien territories, a secular authority of white magistrates and other officials. Henry Gadla and his family belonged to the Madiba clan, named after an eighteenth-century Thembu chief: Mandela today prefers to be called Madiba by his friends and associates.

Much is made of Mandela's aristocratic or even princely status in the various narratives of his life. In these Mandela's genealogy is an important source of his charismatic power. 'Since he was a small boy in the Transkei, Mandela was treated as someone special', notes Richard Stengel, Mandela's collaborator on his autobiography. 'His political confidence' was substantially derived from 'the security and simplicity of his rural upbringing'. Mandela himself maintains that much of his childhood was a form of apprenticeship shaped by know-ledge of his 'destiny', in which he would ascend to office as the key counsellor to the Tembu chiefdom. Popular accounts of his birth and upbringing, including those prepared by the African National Con-gress (ANC) in the early 1960s, accentuate his social status and his royal connections.[3]

Nelson Mandela's father, Henry Gadla, was a relatively wealthy man in 1918, rich enough to maintain four wives and thirteen children. Mandela, incidentally, was the most junior of Gadla's four sons and he has never explained why he was cast in the role of future counsellor to the Thembu paramount. His mother, Nonqaphi Nosekeni, may have been his father's favourite wife; such considerations could influence inherited precedence among sons.

In the 1920s, the Transkei could still support a peasant economy although most young men migrated elsewhere to work: Mandela remembers that in his mother's household 'milk was always plenti-ful'.[4] Mandela was named at birth Rolihlahla, 'to pull the branch of a tree', or less literally 'troublemaker', the first son of his third wife. Henry was the leader of a predominantly 'red' or pagan community, though Mandela's illiterate mother had converted to Methodism at the instigation of Henry's friend Ben Mbekela, an educated Mfengu. The Mfengu were the first of the Xhosa sub-groups to convert to Christianity, allies of white settlers in the frontier war of 1877–8; given the resulting historical animosities Henry's friendship with Mbekela was quite unusual. Henry lost both wealth and position after his dismissal from his post as village headman, a dismissal prompted by a dispute over the extent of his jurisdiction with the local magistrate. Rolihlahla, his mother and his sisters went to live near kinsfolk in Qunu, 30 miles from Mvezo. Henry visited, once a month, as custom dictated, until his death from TB in 1928. Mandela was present when his father died, apparently,[5] although he does not mention this in his autobiography. Mandela started attending school in Qunu and was given an English name, Nelson, by his teacher, Mrs Mdingane.[6]

According to his surviving relatives, Mandela's learning began well before he started attending mission school. Apparently, as 'a solemn boy among the many descendants of the great Xhosa chief, Ngubengcuka' he would listen by the fireside to his great uncles' accounts of the Xhosa frontier wars with the British[7] as well as more recent conflicts: 'Bulhoek and Bondelswarts were names that lodged painfully in his memory just as they loomed vividly in African consciousness.'[8] His awareness of an African proto-nationalist tradition was reinforced, Mandela tells us, by the lessons that he absorbed at the Great Place of Jongintaba Dalindyebo, the Regent of the Thembu, who accepted Mandela as his ward and companion to his own son, Justice, a move requested by Henry Gadla shortly before his death, another indication of a special regard for his son that Mandela leaves unexplained, as was the legacy of a revolver that Henry left him. Mandela's first 'authorised' biographer, Fatima Meer, records that the pre-teenage Mandela especially sought out instruction from his elders and that 'the young Nelson, tutored at Tatu Joyi's feet, was fired to regain that *ubuntu* for all South Africans'.[9] Meer, however, was writing during the late 1980s when ANC elders were confronted with a generational revolt, and she may have had her own reasons for stressing Mandela's respect for patriarchal authority. Mandela himself concedes that, although the 'real history of our country' was unavailable in the standard British textbooks, he was to discover quite soon that Chief Joyi's lessons 'were not always so accurate',[10] a gentle signal in his narrative of an opening of an intellectual and emotional distance between himself and the world of his childhood.

Standard British textbooks were to play their role in shaping Mandela intellectually through primary school and later through his

high school education at the two elite Methodist institutions of
Clarkebury and Healdtown. Mandela told Nadine Gordimer in 1962
that he was 'bitterly disappointed' by his first history lessons at
Clarkebury because his textbooks and teachers 'recognized only
white leaders . . . Africans [were] described in them as savages and
thieves'.[11] In fact, both schools employed black as well as white
teachers and, among the former, Weaver Newana enlivened history
classes with his own versions of the oral narratives that Mandela had
heard at his father's fireside and Jongintaba's Great Place. Healdtown
also hosted a visit by Samuel Mqhayi, *mbongi* and historian, who spoke
to the assembled students and staff on 'the brutal clash between what
is indigenous and good, and what is foreign and bad' before reciting
the stirring call to arms that he had written on the occasion of the
Prince of Wales's visit, a performance that Mandela remembers as
leaving him both 'galvanized and confused'. On the whole, however,
the values, ideas, and principles instilled in the curriculum were
'English', Mandela recalls,[12] and, indeed, the majority of staff were
British ex-patriates, not South Africans.[13] Not that the English ideas
instilled in Healdtown pupils necessarily required a reversal of the
principles around which *imbongis* constructed heroic narrative.
During the early 1960s, mission-educated political prisoners on
Robben Island would recite Macauley's lines on Horatius to honour
their fallen comrades: 'And how can man die better/Than facing
fearful odds/For the Ashes of his fathers/And the temples of his
Gods?'[14]

Relationships between black and white staff were at least formally
collegial, as is indicated in contemporary school photographs, and
Mandela was deeply impressed by one incident in which the house-
master, Reverend Seth Mokitimi, in front of the boys 'stood up' to
the authority of the principal, demonstrating 'that a black man did
not have to defer automatically to a white, however senior he was'.[15]
The left-wing journalist, Phyllis Ntantala, however, who attended the
girl's section shortly before Mandela's arrival, complains about the
racism that she believed characterised relationships between black
and white teachers at Healdtown, noting that they ate separately and
played tennis in different groups. She compares the atmosphere to the

more convivial regime at Lovedale College, where 'there was some semblance of inter-racial living among the staff members'.[16]

At Clarkebury and Healdtown, Mandela may have consciously resisted becoming a 'black Englishman'[17] but both institutions as well as his earlier Methodist schooling influenced him profoundly all the same. In Umtata in 1994, in a speech at a Methodist conference, Mandela acknowledged 'the role' that the Church had played in his life, including its spiritual values.[18] Though this tribute should be interpreted in the context of the occasion on which it was rendered, the organisation, culture, and etiquette of the communities that he joined as a youth left enduring imprints. In the 1950s, as an ANC leader, Mandela was credited with the conception of a plan for a street-based organisation: much of the vocabulary that described the officials and the structures in this scheme derived from Methodist church nomenclature.[19] The controlled daily regime of boarding school may have helped to instil self-restraint and a degree of personal austerity. Boxing and athletics supplanted the childhood games of stick fighting and other contests in which he had learned 'to defeat opponents without dishonouring them'. On this point, Mandela's memory is corroborated by one of his Qunu contemporaries, Dalibungu Joyi, who in 1990 told journalists not just about Mandela's prowess as a stick fighter but also about his magnanimity, 'even in his childhood'.[20] His participation in sport at school and college remained important to him retrospectively: in 1979 he wrote to one of his daughters asking her to track down the whereabouts of a Athletics Union photograph that should have been kept at Fort Hare University College from 1940.[21]

School also augmented his respect for order, discipline, structure, and authority: as a prefect at Healdtown, classmates remember an exemplary (if uncharacteristically self-righteous) occasion when Mandela 'leapt onto the dining room table and exhorted his fellow students to take more responsibility for their behaviour'.[22] He did not appear to have especially impressed his teachers, however. Enid Cook, who taught him English, remembered 'Mandela as being rather average in the class room; his interests were more sporting than academic'.[23] She may have under-estimated her own success as a mentor.

On the eve of his departure on a visit to Britain in 1993, Mandela told journalists that 'he had not discarded the influence which Britain and British influence and culture exercised on us'.[24] In his autobiography Mandela confesses 'to being something of an anglophile. . . . In so many ways, the very model of a gentleman for me was an Englishman. . . . While I abhorred the notion of British imperialism, I never rejected the trappings of British style and manners.' Mandela's first encounter with British manners was at the dining room table at the rectory near Jongintaba's palace, to which he had been invited by one of the daughters of the manse, Winnie Matyolo. Notwithstanding hearthside history lessons, Jongintaba's household was Christian and anglophile: Jongintaba's wife was named NoEngland (Mother of England). Jongintaba himself drove Mandela to Clarkebury in his Ford V8, introducing him to the Reverend Cecil Harris whom he told his ward was an 'Xhosa at heart'. By his own account, Mandela developed an 'intimacy' with the Harrises about which he reminded their daughter, Mavis, 50 years later in a letter from prison.[25]

From Mandela's recollections of Xhosa oral traditions recounted during his childhood and from his own membership of a patrician dynasty, South African nationalist historians readily identify connections among pre-colonial institutions, primary resistance to colonial rule, and the ANC's struggle for modern rights. Both in the 1960s and more recently, the efforts of the ANC's leadership to secure the support of 'traditional' rural notables have supplied a strategic motivation to highlight such connections. Mandela himself was to suggest in his trial speeches that 'the seeds of revolutionary democracy' were present in the consensual procedures that he observed at Jongintaba's court. Mandela claims that his own notions of leadership were substantially shaped by what he observed as a child at the Great Place.

But the world in which Mandela grew up was complicated by the presence of competing institutional sources of power, culture, and moral authority, which, moreover in their local contexts, influenced each other. Thembuland had been subjected to a colonial administration since the 1880s and, alongside a bureaucratic administration incorporating chiefs and headmen, an elected system of representation was introduced in stages from 1895 in which a mission-educated elite, again composed largely of headmen and chiefs, assumed leading positions.[26] By 1938, the anthropologist Isaac Schapera, was writing about 'a specifically South African culture, shared in by black and white' within which, 'the missionary, administrator, trader and labour recruiter must be regarded as factors in tribal life, in the same way as the chief and the magician'.[27]

By the time of Mandela's schooling, a printed Xhosa literature existed, initially a product of publishing by the Glasgow Missionary Society from 1821. During Mandela's youth, Samuel Mqhayi, to whom he had listened at Healdtown, was the most influential Xhosa writer. Mqhayi's writing was itself an example of the cultural synthesis between English and Xhosa represented by the literary standardisation of Xhosa in its adaptation of the traditional genre of *isibongi* (praise poetry) to the formal conventions of Victorian English verse.[28] This was a literary culture actively promoted at Healdtown which in 1938 awarded Mandela its annual prize for the best Xhosa essay. Mandela himself began to be a favoured subject of *imbongis* as early as 1954 when David Yali-Manisi wrote his homage to 'the one with strength, the strong iron rod, the black one of Mandela'.[29]

The Methodist church itself, in the Transkei, was substantially African, its members, like Mandela himself, moving backwards and forwards between what they later described as 'British' and 'ancestral' frameworks of cultural reference. The social order at Jongintaba's Great Place was syncretic. Before dispatching his ward to the missionaries' boarding school, the Regent arranged for his passage into manhood through the customary procedures of circumcision and initiation. Mandela's narrative concerning this experience is extremely detailed: in his autobiography it is the most vivid and introspective recollection that he has of his childhood. Mandela recorded his autobiography, partly through oral testimony, in the 1990s. By this time his initiation had become a key episode in his life history, an 'extended narrative' into which he condensed important social and cultural commentary.[30] By then he had told the story many times. Accounts of initiation are not uncommon in the life histories that anthropologists collect in different parts of Africa: with their focus on a rite of personal development they lend themselves to metaphorical references to wider explorations of change and they deserve careful reading. What Mandela's story records is not a tradition inherited pristine and intact, but rather a set of rituals which by the early 1930s were already losing some of their force and meaning.

The lodge was constituted to accompany Justice, Jongintaba's son, through the ceremony. It assembled itself near the 'traditional place' for the circumcision of Thembu kings. Custom required the performance before the ceremony of an act of valour: the cohort settled for stealing, butchering, and roasting an elderly pig. Mandela remembers a moment of shame for having 'been disabled, however briefly, by the pain' of the crude surgery of the circumcision itself. Each initiate received a new name; Mandela's was 'Dalibunga' which can be translated as 'maker of parliaments'. The initiates were permitted to forego the tradition of sleeping with a woman at the end of their seclusion and Mandela violated customary protocol by returning to the burning lodge to 'mourn for my own youth'. For him, the mood of triumph and achievement that should have marked the occasion had in any case been disrupted by the words of Chief Meligqili, summoned to deliver the expected congratulatory homily. Instead Meligqili had told the initiates that the 'ritual that promises them manhood' was 'an empty illusory promise':

> For we Xhosas, and all black South Africans, are a conquered people. We are slaves in our own country. We are tenants on our own soil. We have no strength, no power, no control over our own destiny in the land of our birth. They [the initiates] will go to the cities where they will live in shacks and drink cheap alcohol, all because we have no land. . . . They will cough their lungs out deep in the bowels of the white man's mines, destroying their health, so that the white man can live a life of unequalled prosperity . . . the children of Ngubencuka, the flower of the Xhosa nation, are dying.[31]

The earliest full-length biography of Mandela, by Mary Benson and based on hurried interviews conducted in the early 1960s, does not mention his circumcision; with age its retrospective significance to him may have increased. However, in 1962 he told Nadine Gordimer about his 'impressive . . . entry into man's estate'. Through the course of the Treason Trial in the late 1950s, during the daily car journeys to Pretoria, he entertained his fellow triallist, the leader of the women's Federation, Helen Joseph. with reminiscences 'about his childhood in the Transkei, the traditions, and even the initiation rituals'.[32] Initiation rites were once a matter of secrecy: among some South African communities the procedures of initiation schools were 'forbidden information' for non-initiates.[33] That Mandela could speak about his participation in the lodge with white women suggests that, by the 1950s, he had distanced himself considerably, emotionally and intellectually, from this rite of passage, as well as suggesting the extent to which he could feel relaxed in their company. Among the political activists and urbane professionals who constituted Mandela's social circle in the 1950s, however, experience of circumcision would have been by no means universal. Biographies of Mandela's contemporaries suggest that, outside the Transkei, Christian converts tended to eschew initiation and that in the countryside Christians and non-Christians constituted separate communities.[34] Within the Transkei and eastern Cape towns, though, Xhosa Methodist congregants commonly sent their sons to circumcision schools because to live as an uncircumcised adult was considered dishonourable and unclean among unconverted 'Red' and Christian 'school' alike.[35]

For a privileged few, however, manhood could be postponed for some years after initiation, so they could become, in the words of one of Mandela's clansmen, people 'of great books and important papers'.[36] After taking his school certificate exams one year early, in 1939 Nelson Mandela proceeded to Fort Hare University, wearing his first suit, one of an annual intake of around 50 black southern Africans. He was photographed on the occasion, the earliest photograph of him that was ever taken. His ambition at that stage was to acquire the qualifications that would enable him to become a court interpreter: to that end he registered for courses in English, anthropology, politics, native administration, and Roman Dutch Law. Benson suggests that Mandela developed an ambition to become a lawyer in his early teens after observing litigation at Jongintaba's Great Place, although most biographers date Mandela's decision to train as a lawyer to after his arrival in Johannesburg in 1941. Mandela notes that despite advice to study law he decided on court interpretation, because this would give him a career in the rural civil service, then a 'glittering prize'.[37] Court interpreters were indispensable officials in the South African legal system, in a context in which many African accused would have been unable to follow court proceedings in English or Afrikaans. Mandela's recollections of Fort Hare are cryptic about the content of the academic programme that he followed, although we know from Robert Sobukwe's later experience that Lord Hailey's authoritative (and liberal) work on British colonial policy was a key text in his native administration course, taught at that time by Z.K. Matthews, Fort Hare's first black lecturer.[38] Mandela's strongest friendship at Fort Hare was with his kinsman, Kaiser Matanzima. Matanzima, later the ruler of an independent Transkei and, as a Bantustan leader, a fierce opponent of the ANC, shared his allowance with Mandela, found a place for him in the Wesley residence, and introduced him to playing soccer. Mandela joined the Student Christian Association and helped conduct Sunday school classes in neighbouring villages with Oliver Tambo, later to become a close friend and his predecessor as president of the ANC, although at that stage no more than an acquaintance. He became involved in the drama society, playing a role as Abraham Lincoln's assassin.

In contrast to people who attended Fort Hare both a few years earlier and later, Mandela's fellow students seem to have been relatively unaffected by the wider world of politics. Govan Mbeki, who graduated in 1937, attended an institution at which students were animated by the Italian invasion of Ethiopia. Mbeki himself was introduced to the volumes of the Little Lenin Library by the visiting African–American left-wing sociologist, Max Yergan. Sobukwe, who joined Fort Hare in 1947, spent nights with his friends reading aloud Eddie Roux's *Time Longer than Rope*, a popular history of black South African political protest, as well as subscribing to Nnamdi Azikiwe's *West African Pilot*. In 1953 an ANC-affiliated journal, *Fighting Talk*,[39] reported that Mandela had joined the Congress while at Fort Hare and his conversations with Benson suggested to her that his 'burgeoning nationalism was stimulated' there, partly as a consequence of his 'close' friendship with Tambo.[40]

Mandela himself, however, indicates that his commitment to African nationalist politics was much more hesitant. With other students he cheered prime minister General Smuts' support (opposed by ANC militants) for the war on Germany and joined discussion sessions at Wesley Hall after BBC radio broadcasts. One student, Nyathi Khongisa, took the line that the British deserved no support: like the Boers they were oppressors; he was reputed to belong to the ANC and so most students perceived his views as 'dangerously radical'.[41] A holiday encounter in the streets of Umtata, in the company of fellow student Paul Mahabane, the son of the ANC's Chaplain General, in which Mahabane refused to run an errand for a magistrate, represented behaviour that made Mandela 'extremely uncomfortable': he was then 'not ready to do the same himself'.[42] Mandela's few contacts with whites had been limited to people who had treated him with consideration and even, in the case of the Harris household at Clarkebury, affection. This is one of the most obvious contrasts between Mandela's testimony about his childhood and the memoirs of many of his contemporaries, especially those who grew up in cities or on white-owned farms.[43] The point is worth stressing because public memory of African childhood usually depicts a racially polarised world. In a dramatised version of Mandela's life published in the 1990s, the author attributes to Mandela the memory of visiting his uncle 'on a farm, somewhere in the Transkei'. In this wholly fictional episode, Mandela witnesses 'elderly men and women being driven just like little children in the hands of that young white boy'.[44] Mandela did not grow up in this kind of setting; his kinsfolk were still relatively independent peasants not farm labourers and they would have migrated to Johannesburg to work on the gold mines if they could not make a livelihood from their land holdings.

Mandela's participation in a student protest that resulted in his expulsion from Fort Hare is often perceived as a crucial point in his progress to political militancy. Several accounts confuse or conflate two separate events: a boycott of the Student Representative Council (SRC) elections that occurred in 1940, prompted by complaints about the quality of food served in the dining hall, and a more serious eruption the following year when students went on strike after a teacher had slapped a canteen worker. Mandela was involved in the SRC electoral boycott because he had been nominated before the elections and in fact was elected by the very small minority who chose to vote. Prompted by 'a sense of obligation to the students', as well as Matanzima's urgings, Mandela alone among the six who now constituted the SRC refused to take up his position, despite an injunction from the principal, Alexander Kerr, to do so or undergo expulsion. His own unusually strong sense of dignity would have been one consideration in influencing his behaviour: Tambo recalled his memory of Mandela during this period as a sensitive propensity 'to retaliate against insult or patronage'.[45] The more politically coloured accounts of Mandela's departure from Fort Hare locate him as the main instigator, with Tambo, of a protracted student strike, but in fact there was no evidence of any collective solidarity evoked by Mandela's lonely protest. Kerr's memoir of Fort Hare does not refer to the 1940 incident;[46] this is not surprising: SRC protests over food-related issues were commonplace and dated from Fort Hare's foundation—the food was notoriously dreadful, partly as a consequence of economy but also as a result of 'the incredibly inaccurate European notion of what Africans were content to eat'.[47]

Whether Mandela would have withstood Jongintaba's exhortations to make his peace with Kerr and return to Fort Hare in the weeks that followed is a question that Mandela self-deprecatorily leaves unresolved in his autobiography, because another issue was to prove a more decisive turning point. Shortly after his return to the Great Place, he and Justice were told by Jongintaba that he had arranged marriages for them. Both resolved to defy the regent through flight to Johannesburg. Accounts of this journey vary: to one researcher Matanzima claimed that he offered the pair assistance and slaughtered a sheep in their honour; in another they hired a car.[48] Mandela himself admits that they sold two of Jongintaba's oxen to obtain the money for a train ticket to Queenstown and thereafter managed to secure a lift. Justice had already arranged a job in Johannesburg, as a clerk at Crown Mines: Mandela's status as the companion of the Regent's son ensured that he too could find prized employment above ground at the mine, as a compound policeman. His career on the gold mines was short-lived, however: a furious telegram from Jongintaba ensured his dismissal. At this point, Mandela went to stay with his cousin, Garlick Mbekeni, in George Goch township and, on informing Mbekeni that he wanted to become a lawyer, Mbekeni took him to the office of Walter Sisulu, an estate agent with useful connections.

Even these early stages of Mandela's life are the subject of conflicting interpretations by biographers. Mandela's first biographer, Mary Benson, treated his childhood perfunctorily: the important developments in her narrative begin after Mandela's arrival in Johannesburg. And, as we have seen, in the impression that she developed from her conversations with Mandela, well before leaving the eastern Cape, he had become a disciple of a modern political movement. At this point, she believed, Mandela had put his rural upbringing firmly behind him. For example, his rejection of his guardian's plans for his marriage reflected a deeper political compulsion: 'By this time he realized he was being prepared for the chieftainship and he made up his mind never to rule over an oppressed people.' 'My guardian was no democrat', Nelson Mandela told Benson many years earlier when she interviewed him; 'he did not feel it worthwhile to consult me about a wife'. In any case, 'he found the strict traditional life at the royal kraal dull'.[49]

This view of Mandela as estranged from tradition from an early age was widely shared. Benson herself was secretary of the Treason Trial Defence Fund in the 1950s and was close to many of the events that she describes: her views were likely to have reflected the perceptions of the ANC's white liberal supporters, inside and outside South Africa. Much later, in 1988, *New Nation*, a weekly paper edited in Johannesburg by ANC sympathisers, referred to Mandela as 'by birth a Xhosa chief who at a young age resisted all tribal ties'.[50] By then, however, the issue of what constituted authentic 'African' identity was sharply contested within the broad movement that the ANC headed. Winnie Mandela, at odds with the leadership of the United Democratic Front, the dominant pro-ANC group inside South Africa at that time, collaborated closely with Meer in the research for

Higher than Hope, the first 'authorised' Mandela life history, a book that she insisted in her supportive preface was 'the real family biography'.

And, indeed, Meer's book has, as its central theme, family, with its emphasis on the preoccupations of its protagonist as a father and head of a 'large household of dependants'. It is also a volume about family in the sense of lineage, succession, dynasty, and inherited greatness. *Higher than Hope* is the chronicle of a royal leader, the descendant of kings who 'ruled all the Aba Tembu at a time when the land belonged to them and they were free'. It is about a man who learned his patrimonial history in 'silent veneration' at the feet of his elders and who was inspired thence with a lifelong mission to recapture for all South Africans 'the *ubuntu* of the African kings'. Mandela told Meer that, without a father from the age of ten, he was brought by 'a member of our clan' from whom, 'according to custom I was his child and his responsibility'. In the same vein, Meer notes that Mandela's second marriage was to another representative of aristocratic lineage, to the daughter of a line of marauding chieftains. Winnie's upbringing owed much to the influence of her grandmother, a reluctant convert to Christianity. From her she learnt 'things that my mother had taken care to see I'd never learn':

> She took me into the ways of our ancestors, she put the skins and the beads that had once been hers when she was a young girl on me and taught me to sing and dance. I learnt to milk cows and ride horses and cook mealie porridge, mealie with meat, mealie with vegetables, and I learnt to make *umphokoqo* the way Makhulu made it.[51]

In Meer's book, which is strongly influenced by Winnie Mandela's perceptions, it is this world that defines the Mandelas' moral centre. Because, although Nelson learns to 'manage' and 'integrate' Johannesburg, 'from the standpoint of Orlando [his neighbourhood in Soweto], the city was never home, he remained "intensely rural" . . . it was the first half of his life that really mattered when it came to roots'. Notwithstanding his wider political and social loyalties, 'there were deep rooted historical identities that could not be denied . . . the first experience of human solidarity . . . in the family, in the clan, in the tribe . . . [these] constituted the real identities, the nurseries for larger solidarities'.[52]

Is this true? One view of Mandela's politics suggests that his evocations of the tribal democracy that he had witnessed at Jongintaba's Great Place deserve serious consideration as representing the 'hidden consistency in his political thought'.[53] In Mandela's 'tribal model', democracy is essentially discursive: everyone should be free to express their views 'without interruption', despite any 'hierarchy of importance' among the speakers. Meetings would end in 'unanimity' or consensus or not at all. 'Majority rule was a foreign notion.' Only at the end of such meetings would the Regent speak. 'His purpose was to sum up what had been said and form some consensus among the diverse opinions.' In this model of democracy, 'the question of leadership [is] settled beforehand, and kept quite separate from the question of how the popular will is to be interpreted'.[54] Mandela's references to such procedures in his autobiography were written in the early 1990s, at a time when South African leaders, as never before—Mandela included—were preoccupied by the idea of consensus. Mandela's willingness to draw inspiration from his childhood in which social harmony is achieved 'not through negation of differences, but through the development of moral codes for overcoming them'[55] was rather more exceptional in 1962 when he spoke at his trial about *kgotla* or *imbizo* proceedings as the incubators of 'seeds of revolutionary democracy', although this argument was shortly to become quite a serious proposition within the South African left.

Other observers have noted Mandela's 'patriarchal' voice[56] and patrician manner, relating these to his lineage and upbringing, but Mandela's relationship with the pre-colonial institutions that he describes in the opening chapters of *Long Walk to Freedom* is by no means straightforward. Consensual decision-making may exemplify a particular kind of democracy but it is at odds with the 'ordinary democracy' of majority rule that Mandela declared as a preference during South Africa's constitutional negotiations and Mandela himself admits that 'there are times when a leader must move ahead of his flock'. But, at a deeper level, the values and obligations that are associated with family and kinship, values that constitute the moral centre of a patrimonial system, in Mandela's autobiography assume a much less confident position in his own story. As he conceded in old age, 'every man has twin obligations' and in serving his people Mandela was prevented from fulfilling his roles as a 'son, a brother, a father and a husband'.

For Mandela grew up in a setting in which fathers were absent and in which sons sought out surrogate parents to replace the dead and the distant. Mandela suggests that when Henry Gadla died he felt 'not so much grief as cut adrift'. There is a recurring image in his book of a child putting on the clothes of his absent father: young Rolihlahla wears his father's cut-down trousers when he first attends school and Nelson's son dresses up in his father's clothes after Nelson's divorce— the image becomes a poignant metaphor for loss and loneliness. And if Mandela is 'cut adrift' by Henry's death, how much more so by his separation from his mother and the world of women in which he had lived so far and by his move to the Great Place of men and chiefs. Separated from his family Mandela learned early to repress outward shows of emotion. One of the more obvious lessons he learned in this area, to control pain and its accompaniment, fear, was one of the defining qualities of manhood that he learned as a child. But men if they are to be whole must have private lives as well as public responsibilities and, in his later life, the pain that Mandela spoke about most frequently was his anguish at his inability to act as a good father. After her father's death, Gillian Slovo was told by Mandela about:

> . . . how one day he had gone to hug his daughter and she had flinched away from him, and burst out, 'You are the father to all our people, but you have never had time to be a father to me'.[57]

As a child Mandela was 'cut adrift' from ordinary family intimacies from the age of nine and subsequently occupied a position of privilege in the communal life of Jongintaba's court. As we have seen, Mandela's own account of his upbringing emphasises his experiences rather than his feelings. His emotional detachment from the community in which he grew up would certainly have been reinforced by the closed institutional culture of boarding school and university, although the prevalent religious ethos of these institutions as well as the Anglocentric moral values that they endorsed, buttressed rather than subverted Transkeien authority.

There are clues, however, that suggest an unusually self-contained child whose status may have accentuated the remote self-sufficiency generated by growing up alone. Such clues are present in his account of his initiation into manhood. They are present in his relationship with the Thembu regent. Jongintaba was more than simply a dutiful guardian, allowing his ward unusual liberties such as riding his horse, driving him home to his mother for occasional visits, and supporting him through high school and university. Yet, in the concluding episode of his upbringing, Mandela betrayed his guardian by stealing his oxen, an action that for many years he had difficulty in describing accurately. Some of the boys who were his companions at the Great Place survived to speak to journalists in the 1990s and they supply a rather different impression to the air of piety that infuses 'Africanist' narratives of Mandela's life. Rather than sitting in silent veneration at the feet of his elders, Chief Joyi recalled Mandela 'at the meeting of the elderly people, headed by the King . . . as a young man who knew how to express his views'. Chief Mtirara, also a Mandela kinsman, remembered Mandela as a 'cunning' practical joker who would swap his bedclothes with other sleeping boys after wetting his blankets: Mtirara presented the story as evidence of Mandela's precocity and independence though the anecdote could also be cited to suggest vulnerability and distress.[58] In Mandela's first draft of his autobiography, written in prison in the 1970s, he referred to various male friendships that he made at school: in the published version these companions have disappeared although Mandela does describe in some detail his first early romantic encounters with women, a reflection perhaps of his ability in later life to feel at ease in women's company, romantic or otherwise, in a way that he could not with men.[59]

To read into all this a susceptibility to political or generational rebellion would, however, be an overstatement: by the age of 20 the patriarchal world of the Madibas was Mandela's world and, contrary to the implication of his own later professions of retaining the outlook of 'a simple country boy', it was a complicated world with its own high culture. When he left for Johannesburg, Mandela was not consciously seeking an alternative to the future that Jongintaba had mapped out for him, but, even so, in comparison to his clansmen he was especially susceptible to new sources of inspiration. As early as the age of nine on his arrival at Jongintaba's court, Mandela 'felt many of his established beliefs and loyalties ebb away';[60] they left an emotional and moral space that, although inhabited by the organised and institutionalised domains of his older childhood, stayed vacant. The new friendships that Mandela would make in Johannesburg would help to fill this space—in particular, on walking into the shabby downtown office of Walter Sisulu, Mandela finally left the world of his childhood and lineage.

2

BECOMING A NOTABLE

Nelson Mandela's first encounter with Walter Sisulu represented the beginning of his most enduring friendship. Sisulu was six years older than Mandela, also born in Thembuland, in the village of Qutubeni as a member of the Gcina clan. He was the son of Alice Sisulu, born out of wedlock, and his father was Victor Dickinson, a white government official. Dickinson acknowledged paternity of Walter and contributed financially to his early upbringing but he did not live with Alice and after a few years he moved away and lost touch with his African family. Sisulu spent his childhood in his aunt's house at Cofimvaba, dropping out of school in Standard V and leaving home to work at the mines in Johannesburg in 1928. Just 18 he was deemed to be too young for underground duties and he was released from his contract; for the next few years he found employment in a variety of unskilled jobs before his dismissal after leading a strike at a biscuit factory. He then began a career as a small businessman, selling advertising for *Bantu World*, the main African newspaper, published weekly, identifying potential African account holders for the Union Bank before, in 1939, opening Sitha Investments, an estate agency that bought and sold property in the two Johannesburg neighbourhoods where Africans could buy land, Alexandra and Sophiatown. By this stage Sisulu had become a well-known personality around Orlando, the township to which he had moved in 1934. He led the Orlando Music Corporation, a successful choir, as well as joining a Xhosa cultural association, the Orlando Brotherly Association. The Association held meetings at which its members would read aloud and then discuss Xhosa epic poetry. He also began to engage himself in politics: throughout the 1940s he chaired a local branch of the African National Congress (ANC), then a body with only a few thousand members concentrated chiefly in Johannesburg, Durban, and Port Elizabeth.

Sisulu was 'one of our best people in Johannesburg' and moreover, 'our homeboy', Garlick Mbekweni told Mandela.[1] After his introduction, Mandela explained why he had been suspended from Fort Hare University and spoke about his commitment to completing his degree through correspondence with the University of South Africa. His ambition was to become a lawyer. Could Sisulu assist? In this capacity, Sisulu was unusually well connected. His agency conducted much of its business through the legal partnership of Witken, Sidelsky & Eidelman. Lazar Sidelsky was one of a handful of attorneys in Johannesburg who took African clients and charged them fair prices as well as helping them to obtain mortgages. Sisulu found Mandela immediately impressive, apparently marking him 'at once as a man with great qualities' as he told Anthony Sampson nearly 60 years later.[2] Sisulu's consciousness of his own Thembu identity might have made him especially appreciative of Mandela's patrician background. Perhaps, however, the initial impression Mandela made on Sisulu was not quite so portentous: Sisulu told another biographer that at his first meeting 'I saw a bright young man with high ideals'.[3] He helped other people, especially 'homeboys', in comparable ways through the decade, including Oliver Tambo, later Mandela's legal partner. Shortly after joining the ANC Sisulu had become friendly with Dr A.B. Xuma, the organisation's president, and Xuma had told him about his concern that 'the youth' should play a busier role in the ANC. Sisulu had undertaken to make an especial effort to recruit talented youngsters into the Congress.[4]

Even so the initial faith that he placed in Mandela was remarkable: he promised to speak to Sidelsky about an articled clerkship—a very special favour that would have required him to capitalise on some of the goodwill that he had accumulated with Sidelsky, because firms even as liberal as Sidelsky's very rarely offered articles to Africans— and he also committed himself to paying for Mandela's tuition fees at the University of South Africa, through which Mandela would complete his BA degree by correspondence. In addition, Sisulu ignored a message from Xuma, who had heard through his contacts at the

Chamber of Mines about Mandela's flight from the Great Place: on no account, Xuma urged, should Sisulu help Mandela or Justice. At that stage, ANC leaders were anxious to remain on good terms with chiefs and rural notables. But Sisulu was as good as his word to Mandela, persuading Sidelsky to take on his young protégé and, moreover, to waive the premium that attorneys normally charged for accommodating articled clerkships. In fact Mandela would have to wait before serving articles: he needed to obtain his BA first although Witken, Sideslky & Eidelman employed him in various office duties, paying him £2 a month, until his graduation nearly two years later in December 1942. Then he would begin earning a fully articled clerk's salary—just over £8 10s. a month—about the same as an African factory worker. Sidelsky also lent him £50 to help with essential expenses and to lessen these gave him an old suit of his own that Mandela was to wear, much repaired and patched, for five years until he could afford to buy his own. More than just a benign employer, according to Mandela, Sidelsky 'practically became an elder brother to me'[5] and they remained on warm terms with each other through Mandela's legal career. In the 1990s Sidelsky's son recalled for journalists an affectionately avuncular Mandela visiting his father at home in the early 1950s.[6]

Sisulu may have been acting in the role of a 'big man' at his first meeting with Mandela, but friendship blossomed between the two men very swiftly, deepening because, during his first months in Johannesburg, Mandela stayed for periods with Sisulu at his home in Orlando. Mandela was attracted by the older man's evident authority as a cultural broker, both 'homeboy' (that is, someone who grew up nearby) and man about town, in what was for him an intimidating if exhilarating new environment. But Sisulu, although outwardly phlegmatic and bluntly down to earth, could also project warmth, affection, and trust. The friendship between Mandela and Sisulu seemed to stem from intuitive understanding of each other's personalities, a relationship often expressed in comfortable silences rather than lively conversations. More of an elder brother or mentor than a patron, Sisulu rapidly became a key influence in Mandela's life.

While Mandela learned his new duties—for the first two years they were chiefly clerical, filing papers, and so forth, although later he learned how to draw up contracts for the firm's African clients—at work he made new friends. Witken, Sidelsky & Eidelman already employed another African as an interpreter and a messenger, Gaur Radebe, with whom Mandela would share an office. Radebe was a helpful and lively companion. Notwithstanding his modest status in the office and his lack of formal education, he was an influential citizen, serving on the Western Native Township Advisory Board as well as playing an important role in both the ANC and the Communist Party. Mandela later believed that Radebe deliberately gave up the chance of obtaining articles by resigning from the firm, telling Mandela that 'it is important to the future of our struggle in this country for you to become a lawyer'.[7] In another version of this anecdote, Sidelsky was reluctant to article Mandela until Radebe forced his hand. He told Mandela, 'these fellows are not going to article you whilst I am here' and resigned to make his co-worker more indispensable to the firm.[8] It was through another Communist Party of South Africa (CPSA) member who worked at Sideslky's, Nat Bregman, that Mandela himself first started attending Communist Party meetings as well as multiracial social gatherings.

Meanwhile Mandela managed to achieve reconciliation with Jongintaba, meeting him during the Regent's visit to Johannesburg. Jongintaba restored his allowance, although this financial relief was brief because the Regent died the following year. Mandela later tried to persuade Justice to return to the Transkei, pointing out that, as a chief's son 'he had a different destiny from that of myself', not advice that Justice welcomed at the time, though later, in the 1960s, Justice would become a Transkeien politician. Both men travelled to Jongintaba's funeral, arriving too late for the interment. Mandela stayed on for a week, 'a time of retrospection' as well as 'rediscovery' of the lessons that he had learned from an enlightened and tolerant ruler who 'listened to and respected different opinions'.[9] In a later trip to the Transkei, to mark his graduation at Fort Hare (for which Sisulu lent him money so that he could buy a new suit), he spent a weekend with Kaiser Matanzima at the Chief's place in Qamata. His nephew urged him to return to the Transkei—he, Matanzima, would shortly open a law practice in Umtata, but Mandela demurred; his place was in Johannesburg.

For his first year or so in Johannesburg, Mandela stayed mainly in Alexandra, a square mile of tightly congested African freehold, six miles north of the business district, dubbed 'dark city' because it had no street lights. He first lodged with a family friend, Reverend Mabutho, but after a week or two his new landlord, on discovering that his new lodger had absconded from the Great Place, told Mandela that he must leave, a telling instance of the reach of Jongintaba's influence. The Reverend, however, found him new lodgings close by, a backyard cement-block room with the Xhima family, a tiny space large enough for a door, a window, and an iron bedstead, where Mandela shared facilities with five other tenants. One of these tenants was Schreiner Baduza, an important local political activist in the Communist Party, whom Mandela described in one of his prison letters as 'among his best friends of those days'.[10]

Overcrowding and general squalor notwithstanding, Nelson Mandela enjoyed living in Alexandra; it was for him 'a home where I did not have a house' as he noted later in his autobiography.[11] Significantly some of his most vivid and anecdotal memories about people and friendships are from this period of his life, a time during which, in his recollections, he discovered inner resources: self-confidence and self-reliance. He courted Ellen Nkabinde, a classmate from Heald-town, taking her for walks and picnics on the waste-ground around the township—there were few secluded places within Alexandra. Ellen represented rather an adventure because she was Swazi and Mandela 'felt daring in having a relationship with a woman who was not Xhosa', despite the disapproval that this match incurred from the redoubtable Mrs Mabutho, the minister's wife, who well after his exile from her household still invited him to Sunday lunch.[12] Ellen provided romantic partnership and, at least as importantly, for this newcomer to the city, a motherly role as well. After a few months, Ellen moved away and was replaced in Mandela's affections by Didi, his landlord's daughter, who occasionally brought him food from her mother's kitchen over weekends. Mandela believed at the time that his interest in the lovely Didi was unreciprocated: she had a 'flashy, well to do' boyfriend who owned a car and 'who would stand outside in the yard and put his hands in his waistcoat and look altogether superior'. Mandela's efforts to delay Didi when she brought him his food were to no avail; he offered her unsolicited advice about her (neglected) studies, because, 'awkward and hesitant around girls . . . I did not now what else to talk to her about'.[13] Perhaps, however, he made a deeper impression than he thought. Today near Mandela's yard there is a *shebeen* (tavern). Its proprietor claims that she is the granddaughter of 'a woman Mandela almost married' who once lived next door to him.[14]

In 1942 Mandela ended his stay in Alexandra by accepting an offer from a clansman to move into the *induna*'s (headman's) quarters at the Witwatersrand Native Labour Compound, saving on rent and transport. Through this lodging he met the Queen Regent of Lesotho. She interrogated him about his prospects and ambitions and teased him about his clumsy Sesotho: what sort of leader cannot speak to his people in their own language, she asked. He remained at the compound for several months and then more or less moved in with Sisulu in Orlando, staying there for weeks at a time, when other temporary living arrangements in Alexandra failed him. Sisulu was now engaged and his future wife, Albertina, already presided over a busy hospitable household. There in late 1943 Mandela met Sisulu's first cousin, Evelyn Mase, the daughter of a mineworker from Engcobo in the Transkei, who had quite recently arrived in Johannesburg and, at the time of her meeting with Mandela, was training as a nurse. Mandela was ready to fall in love again and this time, with the encouragement of Sisulu, Mandela's advances were reciprocated by the 'quiet pretty girl from the countryside who did not seem overawed by the comings and goings at the Sisulus'.[15]

Married to Mandela for 14 years and mother to four of his children, Evelyn Mase remained until her death in 2002 a very private person. Late in life she spoke about a marriage that despite or perhaps because of a 'whirlwind courtship' was premature, and she claimed, for most of its duration, unhappy.[16] For Mandela the warm domesticity of the Sisulu household arrangements was a compelling attraction in getting married, and the Sisulus' approval of his engagement to Evelyn helped to strengthen his resolve. As she recalled, 'everyone we knew said we were a very good couple'.[17] Mandela's reminiscences of Evelyn and his life with her are guardedly respectful—hers of him more censorious although she concedes that he could be a tender father. However, with Mandela's encouragement Evelyn became active in a nurses' trade union; she did not share her new husband's public concerns—in fact her increasing engagement in Jehovah's Witness evangelism, if anything, pulled her away from public life. Mandela's commitment of time to work and politics intruded early in their life together: married in a civil ceremony, 'Nelson was too busy' to take her down to Qunu to meet his mother, she told researchers 40 years later. In any case there was the more compelling task of finding somewhere to live together. This could not be achieved immediately. For two years, the Mandelas stayed with Evelyn's sister and her husband, a clerk at the City Deep mine. In January 1946 they moved into their own home in Orlando, moving up the Council's list of prospective tenants because of Evelyn's pregnancy. Normally there was a ten-year waiting list and the council's considerate treatment of the Mandelas was unusual—apparently Mandela had a professional acquaintance with the township superintendent, a senior (white) official.[18]

Orlando is located in the heart of today's Soweto, an official acronym for south-west townships, where construction of a few municipal houses for African tenants began in Pimville, in 1904. Orlando, named after a city mayor, began to be built in 1932. By the time of Mandela's arrival in 1946 there were more than 12,000 houses, arranged in densely packed plots on the east and west slopes of the Klip river valley. The township was 11 miles from Johannesburg's centre, connected to it by two railway lines, the only public transport available. Most of the houses were red brick, with two or three rooms, including a kitchen and one public tap to every 12 dwellings. Waterborne sewage began to be installed in 1949; before then and well afterwards, residents used bucket toilets in the corner of every yard, emptied twice a week. During the war many householders took in sub-tenants to help pay the rent, assembling shacks for them in their backyards, a practice tolerated by the municipality because of the housing shortage and Johannesburg's new demand for industrial labour. The buildings were very simple when tenants moved in, with earth floors, unpainted walls and no ceilings, and internal walls that did not meet the zinc roofs. Later, in the 1950s, tenants could purchase the houses on leasehold, although it was impossible for them to obtain any ownership rights on the land; these would be conceded only three decades later. The security provided by leases encouraged the better off to make improvements. At 8115 Orlando West, the Mandelas would later erect an outbuilding with two more rooms as well as a garage. By the mid-1950s the house would have indoor plumbing, although no electricity.

To any outsider, Orlando would have represented a bleak land-scape: 'row upon row of red brick houses relentlessly continuing, with no focal point on which the eye could rest'.[19] The few public build-ings supplied occasional interruptions to the grid of tiny brick and concrete cubes: a secondary school (later the incubator of the student rebellion of 1976), a recreation centre, police station, the Lad's Hostel, a clinic, a child welfare refuge, a crèche, the Mtutezele Home for Unmarried Mothers, the Animal Welfare Trust, a few churches, and a couple of dozen trading stores, mainly small groceries. For its own inhabitants its topography was differentiated by less obvious but more diverting neighbourhood attractions: the hookers near the Number Three Shelters in Orlando West 'wearing figure belts, bobby socks, brown and white golf shoes and gabardine skirts', who saucily accosted those pedestrian commuters who could not afford the shilling taxi ride to take them home from the station; the lanes high up the hillside in Orlando East where there were no electric lights, the home of the *gumbagumba* (gumboot) dancers, the fearsome Otto Town gang, and the Nice Time Sweepers football club who played Wednesday fixtures with the Orlando Police.[20] In 1949, this setting accommodated around 100,000 people, slightly more men than women, about a quarter of Johannesburg's African population.

Twenty-five per cent of the working population were factory workers and another fifth worked as domestic servants or washer-women. Professionals and white-collar workers were a tiny minority, about 2 per cent,[21] and of these most would have been clerks. Even so Orlando would develop a reputation as 'the Africans' "snob sub-urb" '.[22] However, in the 1940s and 1950s, in townships such as Orlando, class and status distinctions did not separate people geo-graphically. Obligations of hospitality to kinsfolk made for large households. The normal Orlando dwelling sheltered around ten people who might work in a range of occupations, teachers sharing living space with labourers and servants. Individual attributes—sartorial style, personal possessions, especially automobiles, decorous etiquette, and education—were much more significant markers of status than the places where people lived. Although people of high social status were conscious of their distinction they did not live in social isolation from the poorer and less educated.

At the time of their marriage the Mandelas would have been representative of the better-off section of the community: their joint income of about £25 a month would have left a reasonable sum after deductions for rent (17s. 6d.) and transport (£2) for clothes and food though soon Mandela was paying high school fees for his sister, Leabie, and he regularly sent money home to his mother. Even so, for a while, Mandela felt that he could afford smart suits: 'I shop only at Markhams' he grandly informed his fellow student Ismail Meer, naming one of the smartest outfitters when invited by the latter to join a group who were planning a visit to a clothing sale in Vrede-dorp, down the road from Wits.[23] Mandela's stylish dressing was not simply a matter of vanity because, both within and especially outside Orlando, wearing a suit and dressing formally was of particular importance in a wider social setting that withheld recognition of status and distinction to middle-class Africans. But Mandela's main-tenance of the 'indices of class'[24] could and would impose sacrifices. Six months after his marriage, with Mandela's completion of his articles and his commitment to full-time study at Wits, Evelyn, with her monthly salary of £17, became the sole breadwinner. There were university fees to pay, which a study loan from the liberal charity, the South African Institute of Race Relations (SAIRR), only partly covered. Predictably, Sisulu acted as the main guarantor for the loan. Through Mandela's studies, the SAIRR loans accumulated; by the time he qualified in 1952 they totalled £352. Mandela began repaying the debt in 1954 but other financial pressures prevented him from maintaining his instalments: as late as 1958 he still owed the SAIRR's evidently quite indulgent Bantu Welfare Trustees £337.[25]

Even so, despite his precarious domestic finances, Nelson Mandela remained a member of a tiny elite. If the size of genteel African society could be reduced to census statistics, about 51,000 people and their dependants belonged to it in 1951—the professionals and clerical workers counted that year.[26] The 1946 census enumerated just 18 African lawyers and only 13 articled clerks. The most common middle-class occupation for Africans in 1946 was teaching (7,505), followed by clerical work (3,687) and shop assisting (3,628). The church (2,697 ordained African priests) represented the other main career option. Evelyn Mase would have been one of 190 African nurses, nationally.[27] Within this elite, lawyers enjoyed especial public esteem and would continue to do so for decades. Lawyers in South Africa, as in many colonial or semi-colonial settings, were over-represented in the leadership of political parties, a consequence of a vocational predisposition 'to see themselves as the embodiment of public interest'.[28] Ten years after Mandela completed his articles the sociologist Leo Kuper was told by a member of the African legal fraternity that:

> People take it for granted that I am a leader. They engage me in the street and invite me into their homes for advice . . . doctors and lawyers are at the top of the hierarchy. Lawyers have a very high prestige and you will find that at weddings people are always anxious to please them. They will be given special positions, they are always introduced as 'Mr So-and-So, the lawyer'.[29]

Within his home neighbourhood this was the kind of public reception that Mandela could expect quite quickly—of becoming Mr So-and-So, the lawyer, of being a 'somebody', certainly by the time he had fully qualified as a lawyer in 1952 but probably well before then. A striking memoir of a visit to his home in Orlando, written by an Indian friend, Adelaide Joseph, confirms his stature as a notable within this community:

> The impression of the Mandela family in the township was unbelievable. One Sunday Nelson took us around in the car. What an experience! He

wanted to show us Orlando. . . . Every road and street we turned into, people were shouting 'Mandela, Mandela'. They knew that car and they knew that man. . . . There wasn't a man, women or child that spotted him, that didn't signal, greet him or shout his name. . . .[30]

Of course Adelaide Joseph was writing about the time period when Mandela had achieved national political prominence, but even quite early on Mandela and Evelyn were visibly members of an exalted social set, combining professional status with aristocratic connections. Adelaide Tambo's first encounter with Mandela was in 1949, 'at a wedding reception at the Bantu Men's Social Centre'. He was accompanied by Evelyn. Adelaide Tambo asked 'people who he was, and they said he was a prominent leader. I think he was practicing law then . . . he was outstanding. He seemed to be dominating the place. He was tall and elegantly dressed, and his wife was also elegant'.[31]

Despite smart outward appearances, at home the Mandelas lived modestly, although they kept an open house for the main visitors, especially kinsfolk who would stay for weeks and even months. Mandela rose early every morning to run a few miles before breakfast, a habit maintained from the discipline of boarding school. He joined a boxing club and worked at the Community Centre several times a week: boxing had become a major recreation for young men in African townships in the 1940s, but Mandela maintained his commitment to the sport until well past middle age. Fifty years later visitors to his official residence would find one of his favourite pictures on the wall: himself as a young man in boxing shorts sparring with Jerry Moloi, the South African middle-weight champion of the early 1950s. In the first few years of his marriage he undertook a significant share of household tasks. He liked shopping especially because he was fussy about his food, insisting on buying expensive fresh fruit and vegetables. He could cook, evening meals as well as breakfast, and when his children were born, Thembi in 1946, the short-lived Makaziwe in 1948, Makgatho in 1950, and the youngest, Maki, named after her elder sister, in 1953, he made a point of bathing them and putting them to bed in the evening. Makaziwe fell ill at the age of nine months: Mandela was present when she died in hospital: 'I have never

known whether or not I was fortunate to witness that painful scene.'
It was an experience that 'haunted' him for a long period and about
which 20 years later he wrote that it 'still provokes painful memories'.[32] In general, his recollections of his young household are happy.
Mandela tells us that he 'enjoyed domesticity' and this is probably
true; his older children remember a father who told them stories and
took them out on excursions. Evelyn maintained a highly structured
domestic routine with the help of Mandela's mother who arrived to
stay with them in 1949, initially to obtain medical treatment and then
to help out with the household; she and Evelyn got on well. Joe
Matthews, one of a sequence of house guests, believes that Makhulu,
Mandela's mother, was genuinely fond of Evelyn, recognising in her
the same qualities of strength and stability that she herself possessed.[33]
Matthews suggests that traditional restraints would have inhibited
intimate conversations with her son of the kind that she could have
quite easily with her daughter-in-law; even so during the decade or
so that she spent at the Mandela home on Orlando, she helped Mandela compile a family history that was later confiscated by the police.

Evelyn's reminiscences suggest a household often filled with kinsfolk. Aside from Matthews, Matanzima was a frequent guest in the
late 1940s and early 1950s. There were other more exotic guests,
however. In 1946 the Mandelas accommodated Reverend Michael
Scott, a British Anglican clergyman who had become involved
with the nearby 'Tobruk' squatters' movement, a community of ex-
servicemen, before falling foul of its leadership. Scott arrived with a
companion, another priest, Reverend Dlamini, who annoyed Evelyn
by criticising her cooking; to restore domestic peace Mandela took it
upon himself to persuade the Tobruk squatters to accept Scott and
Dlamini back into their ranks.

The friendships that Mandela recalls from this period are not ones
that he shared with Evelyn; they developed mainly through the connections that arose from work and university, connections that
quickly drew him into the political currents that were beginning to
animate Johannesburg's African community. Deeply impressed by
the street-smart Radebe—'my superior in every sphere of knowledge'—Mandela began attending ANC meetings. For most of its

history since its formation in 1912, up to the 1940s, the ANC had been a rather sedate body, meeting in conference every year and otherwise undertaking very little activity but, with the accession of Dr Xuma to its presidency in 1940, a branch structure was instituted and members of the Communist Party began to work through the ANC in their efforts to establish a following among a now rapidly expanding African urban workforce. Together with veteran communist J.B. Marks, Radebe had helped to establish an African Mineworkers' Union in 1946, using the ANC's good offices to appoint organisers in the rural locations where labourers were recruited. In 1943, Radebe persuaded Mandela to participate in the Alexandra bus boycott, accompanying him on the long walk to town, 12 miles there and back, with thousands of other residents in a successful nine-day protest against a rise in fares, an experience that Mandela found exhilarating and impressive.

Meanwhile, his other workmate, Nat Bregman, introduced him to fellow Communists, including Michael Harmel, one of the Party's key thinkers. Harmel, the son of an Irish pharmacist, combined infectious charm as well as a bohemian lifestyle with doctrinaire rigour on issues of political principle. He made a living out of journalism, editing, and teaching, but his true vocation was political. Three years older than Mandela, by the late 1940s Harmel was becoming the Party's main advocate of the 'internal colonialism' thesis. Here the argument was that in South Africa, despite its relatively advanced economic status, the oppression of black workers was 'colonial' or racial in character and hence did not generate the kind of class consciousness that might be expected in an industrial society. In this sort of setting and in the absence of a popular black working class movement, socialists should align themselves with African nationalist movements seeking to influence them rather than rejecting them as inherently reactionary. Revolution would occur in stages and the immediate goal for communists should be the establishment of a 'people's democracy'.[34]

Harmel's unassuming manner belied his intellectual authority: at Mandela's first meeting with him he was dressed—as ever—shabbily and wore no tie; it took some time for Mandela to discover that this 'simple and soft-spoken man' was 'a live wire loaded with current'. Harmel himself was too self-effacing ever to describe their relationship anecdotally; in his historical writing about the period he refers to Mandela by his initials, refraining from using his first name. Mandela quickly grew to admire his new friend's modesty, 'his freedom from the chains of convention that make the average intellectual behave like a marionette'. In the mid-1940s he spent a considerable amount of time in Harmel's company: a letter of condolence that he wrote in 1974 to Barbara, Harmel's daughter, refers to 'a long line of recollections' including his experiences of Harmel's teaching at the Party night school in Fox Street, protest meetings on the City Hall steps, a lift club run by the Harmels, and evenings at the home he shared with his wife Ray, a Lithuanian-born garment worker and trade unionist.[35]

From 1943, Mandela's university classes brought him into contact with a number of other communists among the white and Indian student community. One of his lecturers, Bram Fischer, was an important as well as a socially distinguished member of the Party. Fischer provided legal help when Mandela was charged with boarding a tram in the company of Ismail Meer, another new friend, whose flat in Fordsburg Mandela made his base during his time at Wits, staying overnight if the evening classes extended beyond the last train to Orlando. Early in his friendship with Meer, Mandela was intrigued to discover that they shared a common experience—circumcision.[36] Meer at that time was living with Ruth First, another leading figure in the younger generation of communists who would commit the Party to a nationalist liberation struggle.

Important as these new friendships were—and their impact upon Mandela will be explored in Chapter 3—at this early stage the main contribution to his political formation was from people closer to home, especially among the group whom he encountered in his visits to the Sisulu household. In particular there were Anton Lembede and Oliver Tambo. Lembede was born in 1914, the son of a Free State farm labourer, educated at Catholic mission schools, and training as a teacher at Adams College in Natal; he first worked as a teacher in the Free State where he was impressed by the organised gathering strength of Afrikaner nationalism evident in the small country towns where he lived. He took three correspondence degrees including an MA in philosophy as well as an LLB before serving articles in Johannesburg between 1943 and 1946 with Pixley ka Seme, one of the very few black South African legal partnerships in Johannesburg. By the time of his meeting with Mandela, in 1943, Lembede had already worked out a philosophical base for a new creed of racially assertive African nationalism.

Lembede's ideas were based on his conviction that each nation had its own peculiar character and that national communities were subject to Darwin's eternal law of variations.[37] In such a social universe, no nation could find common philosophical ground with another. Africans, continentally, formed a single nation, reflecting a uniform cultural predisposition derived from a spirit of the environment—in other words, a social consciousness formed by adaptation to the geography of a particular region. Such adaptations, in the case of the coloured races, endowed their members with physical superiority. Africans on the whole shared a view of the universe:

> . . . as one composite whole; as an organic entity, progressively driving towards greater harmony and unity whose individual parts exist merely as interdependent aspects of one while realizing their fullest life in the corporate life where communal contentment is the absolute measure of values. His philosophy of life strives towards unity and aggregation; towards greater social responsibility.[38]

For Lembede one of the implications of this viewpoint was that black South Africans were participants in an anti-colonial national struggle that was indivisible from other struggles on the continent, despite South Africa not being, in the strictest sense, a colony. Accordingly, they should avoid engagement with 'foreign ideologies' such as communism and they should acknowledge the political imperatives of racial solidarity as opposed to those arising from class oppression. Uncompromising ideological emphasis on African racial identity represented for Lembede the most effective antidote to a pathology of inferiority, a state of mind perpetuated by dependence on liberal or Marxist allies. Africans had no need for such external sources of inspiration; in their ultimate state of self-realisation Africans would be naturally socialist and democratic because of egalitarian predispositions that Lembede believed they had inherited from pre-colonial society. Such a future social order would be inhospitable to white South Africans, although Lembede's followers disagreed about what the likely future of whites would be in an Africanist democracy. Lembede, on the whole, thought whites could not become Africans.

For Mandela this was heady stuff—such ideas immediately 'struck a chord' with him. Lembede was not just intellectually formidable; he proved to be an engaging companion. He lived near Sisulu in Orlando and Mandela often travelled home with him from work. On one occasion Mandela decided to visit a former teacher of his, now married to a nurse and living in Orlando East. He was taken aback to find the 'house shut and a terrible smell emanating from within, of herbs and medicines'. It was clear that 'a professional herbalist was doing his job', an inference that was confirmed when Mandela's former teacher's wife emerged and told him her husband had become ill while studying law, accusing Mandela of bewitching him. Mandela was deeply troubled by this episode and 'went straight to Anton Lembede and told of this experience'.[39] Lembede only laughed; despite his belief that Africans should take pride in indigenous cultural practices, Africanism for him was a modernist movement; it did not require the revival of every pre-colonial institution or belief. Mandela introduced Lembede to Meer, his fellow law student: Meer escorted Lembede around the Wits campus, visiting the law library. Here, Meer recounted, Lembede 'saw the law books in the original Dutch and said, "This is what the bastards have kept away from me" '.[40]

In the course of 1943 Mandela began attending a gathering of 'young intellectuals' dubbed 'the graduates', a group brought together by Xuma, in his efforts to cultivate a new leadership generation of distinguished young men, emblematic of African claims to have achieved 'the status of full manhood'.[41] They included Sisulu. Among the others was Tambo, destined to become with Sisulu Mandela's closest associate, colleague, comrade, and friend. Tambo had recently arrived from Fort Hare, teaching science at St Peters, an elite boarding school run in southern Johannesburg for African secondary students by the Community of the Resurrection. Tambo had boarded there in the 1930s, winning a scholarship from his mission school in Mpondoland. One year older than Mandela he came from a more common or non-aristocratic household, but Mandela was in fact somewhat in awe of his former Fort Hare classmate, admiring his 'diamond edged' intellect.[42] Tambo was quiet and reserved, serious, and even austere, he disliked public attention, and he was a careful listener. A devout Christian, he held back from casual friendships with men and women but in Mandela's case he made an early commitment of loyalty and affection. As Mandela and Tambo became associated with each other politically and professionally, their friends perceived in them qualities that were complementary: 'Mandela was generally seen as "show boy" while Tambo was considered to be the brainpower, the engine-house.'[43]

Among Dr Alfred Xuma's 'graduates', as well as the other ambitious young men who encountered each other at Sisulu's house, Lembede's ideas had an electrifying effect. Several of them were members of the ANC and, towards the end of 1943, one of these, Wits medical student Lionel Majombozi, proposed forming an ANC Youth League that would develop a political programme around Lembede's Africanist project. Before holding their first meeting, the group decided to seek Xuma's approval for the constitution that they had drafted. There are different versions of the ANC president's reception of their proposals; in his autobiography Mandela maintains that Xuma objected strongly to their plans—he wanted a more loosely constituted body than the proposed League. Madie, Xuma's American wife, took it upon herself to lecture the delegation about the need for Africans to adopt Booker T. Washington's ethos of economic self-help as a preliminary to any struggle for political rights. Mandela is cited in an earlier source, however, as characterising the meeting with Xuma as 'genial'.[44] Whatever the tone of the discussion, in the end Xuma gave the proposal his blessing as did the ANC at its annual conference in December 1943. The foundation meeting of the Congress Youth League (CYL) was held in April 1944 and Mandela was elected to it as a member of its executive.

The Youth League opened its ranks to all Africans between the ages of 12 and 40, as well as those other people who 'lived like and with Africans'. CYL adherents attained automatic membership of the parent body, the ANC, on their seventeenth birthday. The CYL's manifesto began by declaring that no nation could free an oppressed group other than that group itself. The manifesto then subjected the ANC to sharp criticism: it was organised weakly and tended to represent only the more privileged Africans; its leadership lacked 'national feeling' and tended to behave reactively rather than assertively. The CYL's purpose would be to infuse the national liberation movement with 'the spirit of African nationalism'. It would serve as a 'brain trust'. In its 'creed', the CYL rejected 'foreign leadership', insisted that leaders should represent popular aspirations, and maintained that there existed an essential unity among all Africans 'from the Mediterranean to the Indian and Atlantic Oceans'. Africa was 'a black man's country', Youth Leaguers exhorted, and if Africans collaborated with other groups they should do so as 'an organized self conscious unit'. The CYL should be wary of any associations with the Left—there had in fact been substantial overlap between membership of the ANC and the Communist Party from the late 1920s—not just because communist ideology sometimes merely cloaked white paternalism but also because it was more profoundly misleading and divisive: Africans did not experience varying kinds of class oppression—they all shared a common oppression 'as a group—a nation'.[45]

In the various popular protests that had become such a striking feature of wartime Johannesburg and other big cities, in activities such as bus boycotts, land occupations by squatters, and the riots that occasionally accompanied such eruptions, the Youth Leaguers discerned public 'manifestations of the new spirit—the spirit of nationalism'. It was their duty as leaders, 'to go down to the masses'.[46] Youth Leaguers should acknowledge only one leader—the people—and the League should take its tactical cues from spontaneous popular militancy.[47]

Although Mandela was a founding member of the League, at this stage he was an enthusiastic disciple rather than an original exponent of these ideas and arguments, deferring to their authors' intellectual authority. On being asked to write an article about law for the

Bulletin of the Transvaal African Students' Association, a body in which the Youth Leaguers predominated, Mandela 'felt less inclined to comply with [the] request, for, my knowledge of the subject is, at best, very limited'.[48] He contributed a brief commentary on the difficulties that African law students confronted in securing positions as articled clerks; his own good fortune was most unusual. Even so, despite his law studies and his work at Sidelsky's he became increasingly immersed in political activity: by 1948, Evelyn claimed, he was often away from home for days at a time, engaged in League-related errands and meetings. Much of the League's energies were directed at opposing various joint programmes with the Communist Party and the Indian Congresses agreed to by senior ANC leaders.

In 1948 Mandela, as secretary of the League, actually called for the expulsion of communists from the parent body, a motion that was defeated at the League's conference. The same gathering proposed an extension of the League's membership with the establishment of branches nationwide. Mandela helped to set up one of the largest branches, at Fort Hare University. One year earlier, the League found itself at odds with the ANC over its plans to boycott a Royal Visit: Mandela himself had mixed feelings because he rather approved of royalty, even the British variety, but in any case the government made no arrangements for formal encounters between Congress leaders and the British visitors. At the end of 1947 Mandela was elected on to the Transvaal Provincial ANC (TANC) executive—his first important office—and in this capacity led the League's opposition to a joint CPSA/Indian Congress/ANC 'Votes for all' campaign. Apparently Mandela originally supported the initiative—he presided over a launching banquet as a master of ceremonies but was then persuaded by Tambo to withdraw his backing. The TANC then withdrew from the undertaking (which itself did not elicit much popular enthusiasm) and fell out with the TANC President, Constantine Ramahanoe, who maintained his own endorsement of 'Votes for all' in defiance of his executive. Ramahanoe lost his position to be replaced by the Communist leader, J.B. Marks, with whom Mandela had developed a warm relationship. Mandela had liked Ramahanoe—who for a while had adopted Mandela as a protégé—as well but voted against him all the same: 'loyalty to an organization takes precedence to loyalty to an individual', he noted.[49]

By this stage the League ideas had shifted slightly: Lembede's sudden death in July 1947 created room for advocates of a slightly more flexible approach on the question of whether other races could become citizens in a free South Africa. Lembede himself could in practice be pragmatic, co-operative, and even affable in his personal dealings with African Communists and their allies, especially after his election to the ANC leadership in 1946. Leaguers admired Communists' activist commitment. In this vein, during the 1946 mineworkers' strike, Mandela accompanied Marks on his visits to the Witwatersrand compounds, introducing Marks to several of his kinsfolk among the *isibondas*, the elected room heads who played such a crucial role in the local leadership of the strike. The Johannesburg District Committee of the CPSA was deeply involved in the leadership of the strike—many of its members were put on trial thereafter.

Communists were more wary of direct involvement in other less disciplined sorts of popular insurgency; they held back from actively supporting the squatter movement led by James Mpanza, a convicted murderer and the self-proclaimed 'King of Orlando' who led 20,000 sub-tenants out of the township to build their shacks on vacant land, organising the community on the basis of a political party, the *Sofazonke* ('we will die together'), and building a fortune from the rents that he collected. The Youth Leaguers were less fastidious and collaborated quite closely with the mercurial Mpanza. Lembede and Mandela offered Mpanza legal services. Lembede and Sisulu also mediated between the squatters and the police, persuading a police brigadier not to attack a crowd that had besieged municipal constables who had demolished some shelters. Later Mandela and the other Youth Leaguers, together with Mpanza, devised an ingenious legal strategy to force the Council to take responsibility for the squatters and provide land for them. Mandela moved a motion at a meeting of the Orlando Residents' Association, formalising the eviction of the sub-tenants from the township (their presence there had in any case been technically illegal). A thousand householders then marched through the streets, and a subsequent Council meeting adopted a proposal by the sole Communist Party representative for Hillbrow, Hilda Bernstein, that it should make a vacant plot in nearby Jabavu township available for Mpanza's followers.

As his involvement with Mpanza's movement suggests, by the late 1940s Mandela had become a significant public figure, beginning to occupy key positions in the main African political movement of the era. What made him so special in the perceptions of his contemporaries? Almost from the time of his arrival in Johannesburg, he was the beneficiary of generous material assistance and moral support but even so the rapidity of his ascent to a leadership position was remarkable and deserves explanation. Patrician lineage and extensive kinship connections, an important theme in this chapter's narrative, were of course helpful although the expectations of people of higher rank then Mandela were modest enough: Jongintaba's son Justice, by virtue of his status, obtained a clerical job in a mining compound, not an exalted professional position. Even so, given intellectual aptitude and professional accomplishments, patrician genealogy would certainly help to qualify someone for a leadership position in urban African society in the 1940s, particularly in a context in which modern politicians tended to be commoners—as in the case of Lembede, Tambo, or Sisulu. Within the ANC in the 1940s, a leadership discourse that employed metaphors of virile masculinity to project a programme of national revival accorded a privileged status to young men who were no longer expected to defer to the authority of elders. Mandela was a particular beneficiary of a quite startling reversal of generational authority, perhaps especially amenable to assuming a 'youth' cohort identity because of his rural upbringing as a member of a privileged age set.

Inherited or ascribed social status could have taken Mandela only so far. It would not have made much impression on Sidelsky, for example, somebody who was decisively helpful in enabling Mandela's access to an elite profession with all the prestige that it conferred among black South Africans on even its quite junior members. One important factor was the immediate physical impression that Mandela made upon those who met him for the first time. Women especially commented upon his height and 'magnificent' or 'splendid physique'.[50] Standing at six foot four inches he was, in the context of the 1940s, quite literally a giant, a 'towering imposing man, actually quite awesome'.[51] Charm was another crucial attribute, especially in his capability for developing friendships across racial and other social divisions. Here it was not just affability or good manners or his physical presence that impressed people but a genuine capacity for empathy, for interesting himself in the circumstances of other people with very different social backgrounds to his own, possibly an effect of the occasional relatively egalitarian social relationships with white people that he had experienced as a teenager. He assumed authority easily and early, probably a consequence of the institutional regimes that had governed a childhood lived largely outside family. Though capable of strong emotional commitment to friendships he learned quite quickly the ability to compartmentalise the obligations that arose from them, separating political loyalties from personal affinities, a crucial attribute in the assumption of what some historians term 'the mask of command'. Most importantly, though, was an extraordinary self-assurance that affected the way others behaved to him. This characteristic may have been a consequence of noble status or alternatively, as has been suggested, the 'consequence of a discrepancy between noble origin and his experience of being cast adrift in the city'.[52] More likely, however, its origins are earlier, to do with having been born in a patrimonial society as the favoured son of a favoured wife of a strong man, the son chosen for preferment, the inheritor of his father's estate.

While Mandela was establishing himself in black Johannesburg's high society, the wider political environment was changing swiftly. Acute social tensions that arose from industrialisation during the Second World War prompted two different sets of political challenges to General Jan Smuts' administration, in office since the declaration of war in 1939. African nationalist and Communist political leadership began to seek an organised following among black workers. After 1936 the few thousand African voters who had remained in the Cape Province lost their positions on the common roll, entitled instead to vote for white parliamentary 'native representatives' and a Native Representative Council. Within the almost exclusively white domain of electoral politics, the government's position was weakening. The ruling United Party itself was the outcome of 'fusion' in 1933 between General Hertzog and other Afrikaner leaders in the National Party and the pro-imperial South African Party. 'Fusion' was an effort to build white political consensus before South Africa's departure from the gold standard, a move that followed British devaluation, increasing the price of gold and enabling fresh investment in manufacturing. In reaction to the compromise with British imperialism represented by General Hertzog's decision to take the National Party into government through 'fusion', a group led by Daniel Malan formed the 'Purified' National Party in 1934. Meanwhile, more generally, Afrikaner Nationalism constituted itself as a mass movement under the direction of a secret and elitist *Broederbond*. This body sponsored a range of functional organisations, including savings banks, trade unions, boy scouts (*voortrekkers*), and cultural bodies.

During the early 1940s, Afrikaner nationalism began to develop an ideology and programme around the idea of apartheid (apartness), emphasising a more rigid and codified racial separation in reaction to the acceleration of African urbanisation that accompanied industrialisation and the government's slight loosening of racial restrictions during the war, developments that were perceived as threatening the material interests of semi-skilled white workers. Apartheid policies, including a halt to permanent African urbanisation as well as various restrictions on Indians and coloureds, appealed to white workers fearful of African competition for their jobs, and to Afrikaner shopkeepers eager to exclude Indians from main street commerce. The National Party also drew support from farmers who in an era of rapid industrialisation found it increasingly difficult to recruit labour.

With votes from white workers, farmers, and shopkeepers, the National Party won a narrow electoral victory in May 1948. It was to remain in power for the next 46 years. New racist legislation followed the Nationalist victory, seeking to tighten up urban segregation and attempting to restrict African migration into cities, bringing African schools under state control, banning inter-racial sex and marriage, prohibiting mixed race residential and business districts, ending altogether the already very limited African voting rights, and, from the late 1950s, extending the embrace of 'influx control' to African women. For the first time African women would be compelled to carry passes indicating their right to live in towns. Implementation of this programme was hesitant, piecemeal, and uneven, however, partly because of conflicting interests among white South Africans.[53] Despite the government's rhetorical commitment to apartheid, during the 1950s the African urban population expanded and became more politically assertive.

3

VOLUNTEER-IN-CHIEF

Nelson Mandela's reaction to the National Party victory was one of consternation: he was 'stunned and dismayed', he recollected 50 years later.[1] Other African National Congress (ANC) leaders were more indifferent and Oliver Tambo actually welcomed the change, telling Mandela that 'now we will know exactly who our enemies are'.[2] For the Youth Leaguers, during the first couple of years of the apartheid era, however, hostility to any political co-operation with communists or Indians remained a major preoccupation. In January 1949, for example, Mandela, as an officeholder in the Transvaal ANC, rejected an appeal from Ahmed Kathrada that he should sign a joint statement with Indian Congress leaders on the recent Indian/African riots in Durban, arguing that the ANC should condemn such hostilities on its own. During 1949, the Youth Leaguers were engaged chiefly in drafting and redrafting a 'programme of action' which would commit the ANC to militant tactics—strikes, boycotts, and civil disobedience. In November, Mandela accompanied Peter Mda and Walter Sisulu in visiting Dr A.B. Xuma to argue that the ANC should take its inspiration from Gandhi and Nehru's Indian campaign against British imperialism and adopt the League's programme. Invoking Gandhi's authority, notwithstanding their own antipathy to collaboration with the organisations that Gandhi had helped to establish in South Africa, may have been a shrewdly calculated ploy by the Youth Leaguers, given Xuma's own record of rhetorical co-operation with South African Indian Congress leaders. Xuma demurred, however; the movement's supporters were not ready for such action and the ANC would be inviting its own suppression by the government, he maintained. His visitors told him that if he did not endorse the programme they would vote against a renewal of his presidency at the forthcoming conference. Xuma erupted: he would not be dictated to by a clique of arrogant youngsters and what did they know of Gandhi and Nehru?[3]

As things turned out, Mandela would not vote against Xuma: he had just obtained a clerical position with a lawyers' firm and could not take leave to travel to attend the ANC's conference in Bloemfontein. In his absence, his fellow Youth Leaguers triumphed, deposing Xuma and installing their own nominee, James Moroka, a Free State medical practitioner, as well as gaining seats on the ANC's National Executive. Sisulu was elected secretary-general, in theory a full-time paid position in which he would join a clerk and a typist at the ANC's office at New Court Chambers, in Johannesburg's Commissioner Street. In fact the modest and irregularly collected annual membership subscriptions and occasional donations from Indian businessmen and African professionals barely paid for the office expenses, let alone a regular salary for the secretary-general. At Sisulu's suggestion, in February 1950, Mandela was co-opted onto the National Executive to fill the position created by Xuma's resignation after the conference.

In subsequent months both Mandela and Tambo took the lead in various efforts to curtail Communist influence in the ANC. Threatened with legal prohibition, the Communist Party of South Africa (CPSA) mobilised support from trade unions and its allies in the Transvaal ANC to summon a 'Defend Free Speech Convention', reportedly attended by 10,000 people. At this and subsequent meetings that called for a worker 'stay-away' strike on 1 May in protest against the impending Suppression of Communism Act, Mandela emerged 'with calm authority' as 'heckler and disrupter in chief',[4] helping, for example, to break up a Communist Party meeting in Newtown, pulling Yusuf Cachalia off the stage. On another occasion, he interrupted veteran communist J.B. Marks mid-oration and demanded that he address the crowd. 'There are two bulls in this kraal', he told his audience, '. . . a black bull and a white bull. J.B. Marks says that the white bull must rule this kraal. I say the black bull must rule? What do you say?' 'The black bull, the black bull', onlookers responded.[5] Despite such opposition, the Communist

Party organisation generated considerable support for the strike, an achievement that impressed the Leaguers. On the evening of 1 May Mandela and Sisulu were present when police baton charged a gathering in Orlando West: elsewhere that day police opened fire on the CPSA's 'Freedom Day' meetings, killing 18 people.

In the following weeks, the Youth League principals dropped their antipathy to collaboration with the Communists, 'an insignificant party with no substantial following', as Mandela loftily noted in *African Lodestar*, the Congress Youth League's (CYL's) cyclostyled newsletter. Sisulu had been moving in this direction for some time and indeed on one occasion in April Mandela accused him of having 'sold out to Indians'.[6] 'Joint Action' with the Indian Congresses— that is, a second stay away on 26 June—was agreed upon at a National Executive meeting in Thaba Nchu on 21 May, which once again Mandela could not attend, although subsequently he put in time most days at the ANC headquarters. Mandela remained convinced that calls for political co-operation with 'Indian shopkeepers and merchants' would engender opposition among most Africans whom, he believed, viewed the Asian community as exploitative. Several sources record a heated argument over this issue which he had at this time with the YCL's Kathrada, at whose apartment in the city centre Mandela occasionally stayed after evening classes at Wits university. Twelve years Mandela's junior, Kathrada brashly challenged him to a public debate in Soweto. The incident rankled Mandela sufficiently for him to raise Kathrada's 'disrespectful' behaviour at a joint Congress meeting.[7]

His attitude to Communists was softening, however. On a drive to Natal in the company of younger Youth Leaguers Diliza Mji and Joe Matthews, he praised the Communists' willingness to make common cause with Africans. He was, during this period, apparently, meeting with Moses Kotane, the CPSA general secretary, at his home every night and, encouraged by Kotane and Michael Harmel, had undertaken a reading programme of Marxist classics. The 'Joint Action' of 26 June was referred to as a 'Day of Mourning' not a strike or stay at home, a deliberate downplaying of the working class political orientation evoked by the 1 May protest and it elicited only weak support around Johannesburg. ANC followers were probably apprehensive about police reactions and Mandela and his comrades could not rely on the structured kinds of organisation that had been available to the Communist Party; no trade unionists were appointed to the co-ordinating committee that prepared the event. Mandela's ambivalence about 'Joint Action' with Indian organisations continued and he was still ready to argue that the ANC should campaign against apartheid laws on a racially exclusive basis until the end of 1951.

The ANC's national leadership's commitment to mass campaigning against 'unjust laws' in conjunction with the Indian Congresses dated from an agreement concluded in July 1951. Mandela's early biographies suggest that he and Sisulu were the progenitors of the Defiance Campaign,[8] the ANC's most impressive foray into civil disobedience during the 1950s. Mandela himself, writing in prison in the mid-1970s, maintains that Sisulu 'broached the idea of a civil disobedience campaign' and that 'the idea immediately appealed to me and I readily accepted'.[9] This may have been the case but the ANC executive meeting on 17 June, which took the decision to invite other 'national movements' to discuss joint protests, was probably also independently inspired by calls for 'political strikes' for 'votes for all' and against oppressive laws by the Franchise Action Group, a body established in Cape Town in February 1951 to oppose the removal of coloured voters from the common roll. Certainly, for the Port Elizabeth ANC leader, Raymond Mhlaba, the chairman of the organisation's strongest branch, the strike call by the Franchise Action Group was the decisive prompt.[10]

The strategic planning for the Defiance Campaign was undertaken by a four-person planning council in which Marks and Sisulu represented the ANC, and it conducted its work against a background of continuing Youth League dissent. Mandela arrived at the ANC's annual conference in December, still resolved to oppose interracial co-operation. As he explained later, 'I feared that joint campaigns where Africans had few literate and trained men, and where they lacked economic resources and influential contacts, could give to minorities enjoying these advantages an influence out of all proportion to their numbers'.[11] Mandela was dissuaded from his objections by the mood of the delegates: when he canvassed his arguments he received a 'lukewarm reception'.[12] His speech as president of the Youth League of the ANC (ANCYL), a position to which he had been elected the previous year, included a very qualified endorsement of the 'Senior Congress's' call for participation by other national organisations, 'bearing in mind . . . the political theses that the mind of the masses must be directed towards the fight against [prime minister] Malan and must not be diverted from this for any reason'. The corollary of African claims to leadership in South Africa was that 'Congress should take initiative in calling *all the people* in South Africa to join its struggle' [my emphasis].[13] In the following months, though, Mandela would assume as 'Volunteer-in-chief' the most public position at the helm of the preparations for the Defiance Campaign, a role that would bring him a national public following unmatched by any other African politician.

Mandela explains the changes in his position as the consequence of Kotane's influence as well as insights offered by 'the scientific underpinnings of dialectical materialism'.[14] There is contemporary evidence to support these explanations. His 1951 speech as Youth League president opens with a Leninist depiction of 'the most dangerous enemy' of Africans: 'the heads of trusts and cartels' who 'sustain (colonial rule) with loans, capital and arms'. The speech then proceeds with a depiction of a South African 'situation' that was developing 'in the direction of an openly fascist state', a view that reflected contemporary Communist Party analysis, a scenario in 'which the possibility of a liberal capitalist democracy [is] extremely nil'. Poised against the 'dying world' of 'monopoly capitalism gone mad' was 'the labour power of the African people'.[15] Taking their cue from earlier Marxist explanations of European right-wing totalitarian regimes in the 1930s, South African Communists during the 1950s viewed what they took to be South African fascism as an expression of capitalism in a final crises-ridden degenerate phase.

Textual authority on dialectical materialism of one sort or another was readily available to Mandela from a range of his closer associates. By 1951, Kathrada had restored his friendship with Mandela. From late 1951 to May 1952, Kathrada worked at the Budapest headquarters of the World Federation of Democratic Youth (WFDY). From Hungary, 'he sent a great deal of Communist literature to Nelson Mandela, who was a voracious reader'.[16] Kathrada's WDFY's connections were later to prove important in securing invitations and travel arrangements that enabled a succession of ANC personalities to visit eastern Europe and the Soviet Union. More generally, within the ANC, Marxist ideas became widely diffused during the early 1950s, as is evident from educational materials provided for the rank-and-file membership, including a lecture series, 'The world we live in', that Mandela himself used.[17]

Quite aside from the intellectual appeal of the Communist Party's world view, Mandela's conversion to the multiracial politics of what was projected at the time as a united front against fascism was also prompted by his friendships and by the social confidence engendered by his professional life. Part-time law studies at the University of the Witwatersrand between 1943 and 1949 brought him into contact with white radicals, especially after the appearance on campus of ex-servicemen in 1946. Some members of the Communist Party also took the initiative in making contact with Youth Leaguers: Ruth First, for example, would visit Sisulu every week in his estate agent's office during the late 1940s and through such 'exchanges' it was easy enough to discover 'common interests'.[18] Some of Mandela's more 'Africanist' or racially separatist contemporaries viewed such engagements as his own political arguments with Joe Slovo and First as the cause of 'a watering down of his affiliation to African nationalism and of becoming more amenable to the influence of the Communists'.[19] Ismail Meer, a fellow law student with whom Mandela developed a lasting friendship, wrote later that 'Indianness . . . at a group level' was more of a problem for Mandela than communism.[20] Even so, Mandela's professions of 'exclusivist' Africanist sentiment appear a bit laboured. Increasingly the narrow solidarities of the more doctrinaire Youth League ideologues were emotionally at odds with his own personal experience, however intellectually appealing he may have found them initially. Many Youth Leaguers were ready to 'condemn any relationship with Indians or whites',[21] but interestingly the friendships that Mandela recalls most vividly and affectionately in old age from this period are with Indians. Amina Cachalia whose husband, Yusuf's, speech Mandela disrupted in 1950 remembers her first meeting in 1949 at which 'he was very nice and very warm and friendly . . . with us it clicked and we liked each other a good deal',[22] Ben Turok, a young member of the Communist Party when it reconstituted itself in 1953, in his encounters with Mandela on Congress committees, found in him an unusual combination of 'natural charisma' and kindly 'approachability'.[23]

By contrast, African contemporaries from this period, even friends or close associates, in their recollections often emphasise those qualities in Mandela that set him apart, attributes of social distinction. Adelaide Tambo remembers her husband's best friend as 'being too much of an English gentleman, whatever that meant'. He stood out, she recalled by 'the way he carried himself'. Moreover, Mandela came from the Transkei and as a consequence expected people to defer to him: 'they are very disciplined people and young men have to respect older people.'[24] Ellen Kuzwayo, a schoolteacher in Pimville who joined the Youth League in the mid-1940s, includes this striking passage in her autobiography:

> I remember the glamorous Nelson Mandela of those years. The beautiful white silk scarf he wore stands out in my mind to this day. Walter Max Sisulu, on the other hand, was a hardy down to earth man with practical clothing—typically a heavy coat and stout boots. Looking back the third member of their trio, Oliver Tambo, acted as something of a balance, with his middle-of-the-road clothes![25]

Matthews who first 'sighted' Mandela at the Fort Hare campus where his father was a professor, and who was also a distant kinsman through his mother, told one interviewer how 'Mandela's clothes always looked as if they had been picked . . . he was different'. The difference was not simply a question of sartorial style but also of manner. 'People who grew up in these royal houses', Matthews explained, tend 'to assume that they are going to rule people, or govern people and so on'.[26] Matthews also believed that Mandela 'had very few friends in which he could confide'. It is possible that with whites and Indians, especially with women, the conventions of his patriarchal status among Africans became for Mandela less important and less inhibiting. What is striking was his ability to shift from one kind of social etiquette to another, an ability that indicates an unusual imaginative capacity for empathy.

Meanwhile his professional work, even in relatively liberal firms, required a series of compromises about a different and more ambiguous sort of professional status, as he explained in 1964:

> To Mr Sidelsky, I will always be indebted. Two of the experiences I had in the firm are worth recording. On my first day at the office the White senior typist said, 'Look Nelson, we have no colour bar here. When the tea-boy brings the tea, come and get yours from the tray. We have brought two new cups for you and Gaur Radebe, another African employee. . . . When the tea arrived Gaur boycotted the new cups and picked up one of the old ones. I had no desire to quarrel with him or the senior typist, so for months I did not drink the tea. Some months later a new typist, also White, was in the habit of asking me for work when she had nothing to do. One day I was dictating to her when a White client came in. She was obviously embarrassed and, to demonstrate that I was not her employer, she took 6d from her purse and said, 'Nelson, please go and get me some hair shampoo from the chemist'.[27]

Mandela had the assurance and poise to cope with such situations. As noted above, though, the anecdotes suggest something else. They indicate a depth of perception and flexibility as well as a capacity for negotiating social relationships and crossing social boundaries. In these anecdotes there are conciliatory predispositions that contrast sharply with the strained and absolutist language in his formal addresses recorded from this period. As Mandela began to *live* his politics from day to day as an activist, the distinctions between his responses to daily routine experiences and his formal political repertoire lessened.

Mandela's first contribution to the Defiance Campaign was helping to draft a letter to Prime Minister Malan demanding the repeal of unjust laws and driving to Bloemfontein to collect Dr Moroka's signature. Moroka signed the document willingly enough; apparently he 'never himself expected to suffer, having so many Afrikaner friends' (several local farmers were among his patients).[28] Mandela had acquired a driving licence six months previously and had consequently become 'a one man taxi service' for the ANC which had few qualified drivers even in its leadership.[29]

Ostensibly, the Defiance Campaign's purpose was to achieve the repeal of the Bantu Authorities Act, the Group Areas Act, the Voters Representation Act, the Suppression of Communism Act, pass laws, stock limitation controls, and various 'petty apartheid' regulations. ANC leaders hoped that the campaign would build activist membership for their organisation and to signal its new militancy: hence the choice of the word 'Defiance', in preference to the less combative phrase 'pass resistance'. The choice of the laws targeted was prompted by hopes of arousing support across racial divisions as well as in the countryside: as things turned out curfew regulations (a feature of the pass laws) and minor apartheid regulations were the laws that resisters defied most frequently.

Ten thousand volunteers were to be prepared by 26 June for disciplined civil disobedience in readiness for the first stage of the campaign and a 'Million Shilling Drive' was to be instituted. In fact most of the money needed for organisation and supporting volunteers' families during their prison sentences was raised in larger sums, donated chiefly by Indian businessmen, well in excess of a million shillings.[30] ANC dependence on Indian financial contributions remained a sensitive issue among Africanist Youth Leaguers, although donations from Christian Action, a British charity headed by Canon John Collins, were also important, 'directly keeping the campaign alive' in its latter stages according to the British High Commissioner.[31] The organisers envisaged two stages in the campaign: initially small bands of trained volunteers would break laws in the main cities; later the campaign would become more generalised with larger-scale and more dispersed participation accompanied by strikes or stay at homes. Even the Indian planners of the campaign were generally not doctrinaire Gandhists who sought the moral conversion of authority. Indeed, Mohandas Gandhi's son Manilal was an early critic of the ANC's plans; in his view Africans had insufficient commitment to key *Satyagraha* ('truth-firmness') principles such as non-violence.[32] In Mandela's own strategic understanding of the final stage 'the government would not be able to administer certain laws'.[33] In a speech in Durban, 'bowled over' by the turn-out of 10,000 people, about half of them Indians,[34] he went even further, suggesting that if the Defiance became generalised the government might feel compelled to remove discrimination and concede mass suffrage, or if it did not white voters might 'vote it out of power'.[35] Disappointingly, in Durban subsequent participation in the Campaign was slight, less than 200, as the inter-communal rioting of 1949 local ANC leaders had remained nervous about joint campaigning with Indian political leaders. Throughout the 1950s well-attended mass meetings would not always generate the sustained activism that the ANC was hoping to achieve.

Sampson suggests that the 'national organisation' of the campaign was 'Mandela's achievement' and it is certainly true that during the months preceding the campaign and during it, between June and September, he travelled extensively, often by train, sometimes walking long distances from small-town stations to meet organisers. How much the organisation of the campaign depended on national co-ordination is debatable, however. The National Volunteers Co-ordinating Council that Mandela headed never met.[36] In the region in which the Campaign would enjoy most impact, the eastern Cape, 'highly individualistic' branches generally acted on their own initiative[37] and the suggestion by his biographers that Mandela was engaged in 'house to house' level mobilisation is misleading. In any case, each of the provinces had their own 'volunteers in chiefs'. In the Transvaal, the provincial chief volunteer, Marupeng Seperepere, wore a military-style khaki drill uniform with gold epaulettes at public meetings, even though he like other leaders insisted that the campaign should remain non-violent. As Govan Mbeki noted much later, non-violence notwithstanding, the 'highly disciplined volunteer corps' had a definite paramilitary dimension, and they were drilled 'along military lines'. They 'had to be reminded at every meeting that we were non-violent'.[38] Explaining the aims of the campaign to middle echelon leaders and resolving misunderstandings between them were probably the more important functions that Mandela performed rather than the grass roots activities such as recruiting and branch building emphasised by his biographers.

Whatever the significance of his administrative contribution to the campaign, Mandela's real importance was as a public personality who animated popular enthusiasm. Significantly, the Defiance Campaign was the first black South African political event to attract significant media attention and its launch coincided with the appearance of *Drum* magazine, the first photo-journalism directed at black readers. Through *Drum*'s columns Mandela became a visually public personality. According to one of its editors, *Drum* deliberately fostered a 'photographic calling to the whole black nation', and generally Mandela welcomed the attention paid to him by its reporters, though on one occasion he had to plead with the editor not to publish an 'endearing though certainly comical' photograph of him in gym shorts pulled over track trousers, worn to help him sweat off weight.[39] Other ANC principals were more wary of the limelight. As the media-shy Tambo admitted to a colleague at the time: 'I am going with the current; and the current is carrying me with Nelson Mandela'.[40]

Quite aside from his public engagements, Mandela was kept very busy. Sisulu confirmed that Mandela was in the ANC's national office every day[41] despite his recent qualification as an attorney (solicitor) and subsequent employment by Hyman Basner. Basner, a former 'native senator' and until 1939 a member of the Communist Party, was heavily critical of what he took to be the Gandhist inspiration of the Defiance Campaign.[42] In August he opened up his own practice in rooms in Chancellor House, the building that accommodated the ANC and Indian Congress offices; Tambo would join him as a partner in December.

Civil disobedience began on 26 June, as planned, although Mandela's own arrest that day was accidental; he was detained by the police in central Johannesburg along with Yusuf Cachalia while observing a group of curfew breakers, and held for that evening and the next before his release on bail. He and Cachalia were later acquitted. While under arrest he managed to persuade a junior officer to breach regulations and allow him to share a cell with Cachalia.[43] Volunteers were expected normally not to apply for bail, but Mandela and other key leaders needed to remain at liberty so that they could continue to direct operations. In the end, Mandela did not undertake his own act of defiance. In mid-August, after a cabinet meeting had discussed the campaign, Mandela was arrested a second time and charged under the Suppression of Communism Act. He was put on trial with 20 other ANC officials in November. Among the witnesses called by the prosecutor was a messenger employed in the ANC office, who turned out to be a special branch police inspector.[44] All the accused received 20-month prison sentences suspended for nine months, a sentence that Mandela retrospectively viewed as 'fair-minded and reasonable', given the judge's acceptance that the ANC leaders had diligently enjoined the volunteers 'to follow a peaceful course of action'.[45] Despite Mandela's attempts to dissuade him, Dr Moroka obtained separate legal representation and in his defence he emphasised his hostility to communism and his social connections with Afrikaners in the Free State, a defection that lost him the ANC presidency. In December Mandela was among 52 ANC leaders who were 'banned' for six months—that is, restricted from leaving Johannesburg without permission or meeting with more than one person at a time. In October he was elected as president of the Transvaal Provincial ANC in October (to replace Marks, a 'listed' Communist and hence legally prohibited) and at the ANC's annual conference he became deputy president to serve under Chief Albert Luthuli, an elected chief on a mission reserve in Groutville in Natal, a member of the ANC since 1945, and its Natal provincial president from 1951. The authorities withdrew their recognition of Luthuli's chiefly status in November 1952 because of his refusal to end his ANC membership.

Luthuli's membership of the ANC was quite recent: he joined only in 1945. He was born in 1898 in Rhodesia, the son of a Seventh Day Adventist preacher but was brought up by his uncle, Martin Luthuli, from whom he took over as chief of the Abasemakholweni Christian mission community. Albert Luthuli taught at the elite Adams College for ten years before assuming the chieftaincy. In the next two decades he administered local government and justice and led the Zululand Bantu Cane Growers Association. At the time Luthuli joined the Natal ANC, the provincial body was divided: his social distinction and newness to Congress politics motivated Youth

Leaguer support for his candidature for the provincial presidency against an old guard who had predominated since the 1920s. For most of his subsequent political career in the 1950s, Luthuli would be restricted by banning orders of increasing severity. Confined to his home district, Luthuli was unable to play an assertive role in planning or leading ANC campaigns. His influence lay in his widely acknowledged moral integrity, his social prominence as a Christian notable, and his courageous embrace of the ANC's militancy—'sacrificial service' he called it—in which 'the road to freedom' would be 'via the cross'.[46] Less socially aloof than any of his patrician predecessors, Luthuli was a figure who commanded respect and loyalty across a wide social and political spectrum,

Just over 8,000 volunteers were convicted during the campaign. Defiance acts peaked in September, when 2,345 volunteers were charged, an upsurge in protest prompted by the arrest of national leadership. In October activity was proliferating, spreading to smaller towns in the eastern Cape and workers began striking in support of volunteers who after their prison sentences were refused re-employment. Riots in the two main centres of the campaigning, in East London on 9 November and in Port Elizabeth on 18 November, checked the impetus of protest—ANC followers were demoralised by both the violence of the rioters and the subsequent police reactions. Protest was also inhibited by the passage of a Criminal Law Amendment Act that imposed harsh penalties for politically motivated law breaking. Rank-and-file membership in the eastern Cape favoured the continuation of the campaign into its final stage with the emphasis on strike action, but civil disobedience dwindled sharply and ended altogether in March 1953. In Mandela's view the ANC had erred in not calling off the campaign sooner—an unpopular view in which he had been influenced by a conversation with Xuma, the former ANC president. Sisulu, though, had to visit Port Elizabeth to persuade ANC leaders there to end an 'indefinite' strike against a local curfew that had been imposed during the campaign.[47] By December most of the leaders were immobilised by bannings, and the 'unjust laws' remained in place although the ANC's evaluation of its efforts was positive: its following had swollen to 100,000, its organisational capacity had expanded, and 8,000 of its activists, in Mandela's words, 'had braved the police, the courts and the jails'. Most of the protest had occurred in Port Elizabeth and East London. Mandela told researchers in 1953 that this was the effect of a deliberate choice; the ANC wished to demonstrate its independence from Indian political influence and so decided to emphasise organisation in areas where Indian activists had no presence. The reasons for the western Cape's prominence in the Campaign were more complicated, but Mandela's perceptions, as recorded in an interview,[48] are interesting; they suggest that his movement from Africanist sectionalism took rather longer than he himself suggests in his later autobiographical writing.

For the remainder of the decade, ANC campaigning only occasionally evoked the same intensity of popular commitment that was evident in at least the eastern Cape during the Defiance Campaign. From mid-1953 until early 1955 national leaders were strongly committed to attempts to mobilise resistance to the first removals of families from Sophiatown, an inner city district in Johannesburg, in which Africans had retained freehold landownership and which the government was determined to expropriate because of its symbolic significance as a centre of cosmopolitan African urbanity. Towards the end of 1954 the ANC also began planning for protests against the implementation of the Bantu Education Act, which would begin in 1955 with official assumption of control over mission schools and the institution of an intellectually impoverished syllabus for African primary schoolchildren. At the same time the movement was engaged in preparations for a Congress of the People. This event was held in June 1955 outside Johannesburg, an assembly of 3,000 delegates drawn mainly from ANC branches that approved a 'Freedom Charter' which the ANC itself adopted the following year. A multiracial Federation of South African Women, to which the ANC's Women's League was affiliated, began organising protests against the extension of pass laws to African women in 1956. At the end of that year 156 ANC leaders were charged with treason and the preliminary hearings of a trial that would last until March 1961 began in January 1957. That year, the ANC's trade union affiliate, SACTU (South African

Congress of Trade Unions), led an 80 per cent effective (among African workers) 'stay away' in Johannesburg and Port Elizabeth, in support of its call for a 'One Pound a Day' minimum wage; encouraged by this success the following year the ANC leadership called for a similar three-day protest to coincide with parliamentary elections in April: generally low rates of absenteeism persuaded the ANC's Johannesburg-based National Working Committee to end the protest on the evening of its first day, 14 April. On 26 June 1959, the ANC announced 'a second phase' of the anti-pass campaign, which up to then had confined itself to opposing the issue of passes to women: a series of nationwide protests and demonstrations intended to reach a climax on 26 June 1960.

Mandela's biographers and several more general standard histories place him in a central directing role in these events. Certainly, Mandela himself at the time was highly conscious of his authority; apparently both Sisulu and his wife Albertina were concerned that he could be rather too domineering, although as Albertina conceded much later: 'it didn't matter because the people liked to look up to a leader who was regal and maybe a bit distant'.[49] Matthews remembers him disconcerting a gathering of ANC notables in Port Elizabeth in April 1952, mainly his elders, by informing them in the middle of his after-dinner speech that he was 'looking forward to becoming the first president of a free republic of South Africa'.[50] Anthony Sampson's 'authorised' biography reflects the ANC's preferred projection of the younger Mandela at the time it was written, in the early 1990s, as a pioneering militant, one of the more radical ANC leaders, a 'maverick', increasingly impatient with non-violent methods.[51]

In this vein, Mandela is credited with an early effort to restructure the ANC in anticipation of working in a more clandestine insurgent fashion. Sampson suggests that, in his public addresses at this time, 'Mandela the revolutionary was now openly competing with Mandela the lawyer'.[52] Mandela is generally perceived to have been the architect of the ANC's new organisational scheme, in which the base units of the ANC would be 'cells', one for every township street, themselves divided into 'blocks' of seven households each. Seven cells would constitute a zone, four zones would embody a ward headed by 'prime stewards', who when they met together would embody a branch secretariat. Although the ANC announced these plans publicly, Mandela and other leaders understood this structure as more suited to the 'new methods in our struggle' which he described to a Soweto audience that included plain clothes policemen on 13 December 1953—methods that would require activity 'done behind the scenes, even underground', a phrase that has suggested to some commentators that he and other ANC leaders were anticipating the organisation's legal suppression.[53] The new structure would enable the ANC, as Mandela noted in his presidential address to the Transvaal provincial congress that year, to undertake activities that would 'find expression in wide-scale work among the masses, work that will enable them to make the greatest possible contact with working people'. From now on, he urged, 'the activity of the Congresses must not be confined to speeches and resolutions'.[54]

The M Plan's origins were, in fact in the eastern Cape. As Mhlaba recalled in an interview 40 years later, 'Headquarters chose to call it the Mandela Plan . . . [but] the plan was actually mooted from this area',[55] though in his published autobiography he reverted to the more standard attribution of the plan's authorship to Mandela.[56] Wilton Mkwayi, another Port Elizabeth leader, confirms that the subdivision of branches into street-based units 'became Mandela's plan because after discussing this, we told him that we see this as a better way of organizing and therefore as volunteer in chief, he has to go out and tell other areas'.[57] Mkwayi's explanation is an indication of the national popular stature that Mandela had acquired during the campaign, as well as the way in which his comrades deliberately nurtured his charismatic appeal. The M Plan remained mostly confined to the eastern Cape notwithstanding Mandela's personal commitment to 'grass roots level organization of the ANC',[58] lecturing 'study groups' in Orlando despite his banning. Generally, in the branches in and around Johannesburg, street structures remained undeveloped, although the Sophiatown Youth League branch, constituted in 1953, appointed cell stewards who were put in charge of street groups of activist *amavoluntiya*.[59]

Although in his platform rhetoric Mandela would cast himself and his colleagues in a vanguard role, 'professional revolutionaries', who must 'never be against the mass movement of the people',[60] he was at least as frequently during this decade among those ANC principals who advocated caution and restraint. During the Defiance Campaign, the organisers' insistence on selective recruitment of volunteers and their careful training and tight discipline may have discouraged more widespread participation. Naboth Mokgatle, then a Pretoria-based trade unionist, records that 'hundreds and thousands were turned away by Congressmen' and 'new groups were not sent to defy until others had been released from prison'. During a visit Mandela made to Pretoria, Mokgatle succeeded in speaking to him and the local leadership. Mokgatle argued that the campaign planners' incremental approach could be likened to 'throwing things in a machine [and] then allowing the owners to dismantle it, clean it, sharpen it and put it together again before throwing in another thing'. His advice, though, was 'in vain'.[61]

Between mid-1953 and February 1955, Mandela was closely involved in the leadership of opposition to the removal of Sophiatown's inhabitants to Soweto, first announced by the Minister of Native Affairs in 1951. Houses for this project began to be built in Meadowlands in 1954 and in mid-January 152 families received notices to quit their Sophiatown homes by 12 February. The provincial ANC began organising weekly meetings to discuss resistance to the impending move from mid-1953; in April 1954 the ANC's National Executive decided to make the opposition a national anti-apartheid campaign. Mandela was a conspicuous figure at many of the anti-removal meetings and worked closely with Robert Resha, a dedicated and popular Youth League leader, responsible for organising the Sophiatown branch along the lines prescribed by the M Plan. One speech made by Mandela in June 1953 achieved later notoriety as a court exhibit:

> As I spoke, I grew more and more indignant. . . . As I condemned the government for its ruthlessness and lawlessness, I overstepped the line: I said the time for passive resistance had ended, that non-violence was a useless strategy and could never overturn a white minority regime bent on retaining its power at any cost. At the end of the day, I said,

violence was the only weapon that would destroy apartheid and we must be prepared, in the near future, to use that weapon. . . . At that point I began to sing a freedom song, the lyrics of which say, 'These are our enemies, let us take our weapons and attack them' . . . when it was finished. I pointed to the police and said, 'There, there are our enemies'. . . .[62]

Of course to an extent Mandela on this occasion may have been responding to the mood of an angry crowd but, as he noted in his autobiography, his words 'that night did not come out of nowhere' but reflected a developing strand in his political thinking. At about this time Sisulu was preparing for a journey to China; Mandela asked him to discover whether the Chinese would supply the ANC with weaponry (the Chinese advised against any premature turn to guerrilla warfare). Mandela's contemporaries from this time stress his relative 'self discipline'[63]—not a description that would fit a personality momentarily swayed by public sentiment. However, in a much reported incident shortly after this speech, Mandela was present at a meeting held in the Odin cinema when there was a very real possibility that those in attendance would attack the police after the latter had marched in and arrested one of the speakers. Mandela jumped on to the stage and distracted the audience by singing a freedom song while Father Trevor Huddleston persuaded the police to withdraw.

Subsequent preparations for resisting the removals included the recruitment of 500 volunteers led by Joe Modise, a tough local truck driver. At no stage did the ANC decide on the precise form that resistance would assume nor did they anticipate what kind of force they might have to oppose. On 8 February 1955, the Western Areas Resettlement Board announced that the first removals would take place the next day, three days earlier than expected. Modise's freedom volunteers wanted to erect barricades and obstruct the entry of officials but instead had to settle for the tamer course of moving a few of the targeted households into temporary accommodation. On behalf of the ANC executive, Mandela persuaded an initially reluctant Modise to tell the volunteers to stand down and not defy the authorities. This was sensible enough counsel because they would have been no match for the 300 armed police who accompanied the Board's lorries on the dawn of removal day. Here, of course, Mandela was speaking on behalf of a collective body but as will become evident below there is a pattern to his leadership during the 1950s that suggests at the very least tactical circumspection.

In 1954, for example, he argued against the ANC calling for an indefinite boycott of the Bantu Education schooling which was due to begin at primary level the following year, an option favoured by many Executive members including Tambo, and adopted at the ANC's December national conference as a national campaign. Mandela favoured rather a more limited protest—a week-long symbolic withdrawal of children from their classes. When the boycott began, after a delay because of weak preparation, its impact was very uneven. In 1955, Mandela visited the Transkei during a brief interval between the bannings that the authorities began imposing upon him in December 1952. Here he had two encounters with Kaiser Matanzima to try to persuade him to challenge the Bunga's (the Transkeien legislative assembly's) recent endorsement of the Bantu Authorities Act, the law that strengthened chiefly powers. His advocacy was unsuccessful but his kinsman's obduracy must have impressed Mandela because on his return he proposed to the ANC's National Working Committee that the ANC should *support* participation in the new structures of Bantu Authority: 'my idea was that our movement should be a great tent that included as many people as possible.'[64]

Two other instances of Mandela finding himself at odds with more militant currents within the ANC will serve to underline the point. First, in 1958 the ANC decided upon a three-day 'stay away' to coincide with the white parliamentary elections (the somewhat quixotic intention was to influence white voters). To the chagrin of some of the better organised ANC branches in Johannesburg, ANC leaders including Mandela decided to abandon the strike on the evening of the first day after receiving disappointing reports about worker turnout. Tambo was given the unenviable task of explaining why to furious branch officials in Sophiatown.[65] During the NEC's post mortem on the strike Mandela became involved in a heated disagreement on the use of picketing, an illegal measure that was quite widely used at bus terminals and the like. Mandela would have none of it, maintaining that 'it is best to rely on the freely given support of the people' although he conceded that coercion against a 'dissident minority' might at times be acceptable.[66] Second, in October the same year, it was Mandela who persuaded ANC Women's League leaders to allow the ANC to apply for bail for arrested protestors (including several wives of executive members). Helen Joseph, one of the key figures in the Federation of South African women that helped co-ordinate the protests, remembered that this decision was imposed by the ANC on the women: Mandela himself records that at his suggestion the prisoners were polled to discover whether they favoured bail—understood at the time as the less militant alternative to staying in prison—and only then did Lilian Ngoyi, the League leader, agree with the Executive.[67]

There were persuasive tactical considerations that may have prompted ANC leaders: one of their fiercest critics suggested at this time that issues of principle were often, within Congress circles, 'discussed not as theoretical questions but as a matter of practical business'.[68] Mandela increasingly shared with Communists in the movement a recognition that before any action 'you have got to have the machinery, you have got to have the organization'[69] and he may have been more aware than most of his fellow ANC Executive members about the shortcomings in ANC's base level organis-ation, given his efforts to re-conceptualise its structure. Moreover, as Mandela himself suggests at times, ANC followers more generally, outside the most politically combative centres such as Sophiatown, may have themselves been morally unready for direct and forceful confrontation with state authority.

Other more critical explanations have been offered, though, for ANC leadership restraint. Within the ANC itself, in exile, during the 1980s a 'Marxist Workers Tendency' suggested that three decades earlier the movement's predominantly 'middle class leaders' sought an 'impossible middle way' by 'reconciling labour and capital—by first supporting and then trying to hold back the struggles of work-ers', that during this period ANC strategic thinking was constrained by 'illusions of reconciliation and compromise'—in other words it stemmed from ideological concerns not just tactical circumspection.[70] The premise of this argument, that the ANC was activated by narrow considerations of class interest, is questionable, although it is the case that among ANC *and* Communist Party principals there was an evident 'lack of enthusiasm for purely worker issues' as Ben Turok, then a member of the CPSA's underground leadership,[71] notes in his autobiography.[72]

ANC leaders, including Mandela, during the 1950s *did* believe in the possibility of racial conciliation. Helping to sustain such beliefs were the occasional courtesies and even empathy that they encountered in the most unexpected quarters. Such experiences, although exceptional rather than routine, are an important theme in Mandela's 1994 autobiography. On his way to Dr Moroka in 1952 he ran out of petrol and obtained fresh supplies from a 'friendly and helpful' farmer, a relation of the Prime Minister, Hans Strydom.[73] Later that year during the Defiance Campaign, Mandela and Yusuf Cachalia arrived in Boksburg a few hours before one of the batches of volunteers was due to warn the magistrate about the impending action, so as to ensure that the police would be present to make the necessary arrests. The magistrate, Mandela recalled in prison:

> . . . invited Yusuf Cachalia and me into his office and warned that undue publicity on matters that ought to be discussed quietly and directly by South Africans alone was undesirable. His office, he said, would always be open to us and we could always bring a problem to him. He felt confident that in this way we could make greater progress in finding proper solutions. I had not expected anything so polished and gentle from a white official and I was monetarily caught off-guard. But I freely appreciated the force of his argument and I expressly commended him, for his sober approach. . . . This impromptu discussion ended on a friendly note. As an attorney I had appeared before the official on several occasions. He was a capable man for whom I had developed a lot of respect. His reaction to the manner in which we advised him of the beginning of acts of defiance in his district was consistent with his fine personality.[74]

In 1954, the Law Society attempted unsuccessfully to remove Mandela from the Attorney's Roll. Before the court hearings, he 'received offers of help even from a number of well known Afrikaner lawyers . . . supporters of the Nationalist Party'. Their response,

Mandela recalled 30 years later, 'suggested to me that even in racist South Africa professional solidarity can sometimes transcend colour'.[75] During the 1956–61 Treason Trial, Mandela and his fellow accused even 'developed a certain affection' for the prosecutor, the former pro-Nazi 'New Order' politician, Oswald Pirow, whose 'habitual polite reference to us as Africans . . . contrasted with his supremacist political leanings'.[76] Mandela was not alone in finding evidence of humanity in the ANC's courtroom adversaries, although he may have been overstating the case with respect to the feelings of his fellow accused about Oswald Pirow. Kathrada remembers the formidable Judge Kennedy's sister, who served as the court clerk, providing home-cooked food for Chief Luthuli during his detention through the 1960 State of Emergency: she also sent a wreath when Elias Moretsele, the ex-TANC (Transvaal Provincial ANC) president, died of a heart attack. Kennedy, himself, initially feared as a 'hanging judge', during the proceedings 'became unexpectedly reasonable, to the point where we actually began to like him'.[77] Away from the courtroom, during his detention under Emergency regulations, Mandela was allowed to visit his office over weekends escorted by a sympathetic Sergeant Kruger, with whom he developed a tacit 'gentleman's code'; remaining in the car and not attempting to escape while Kruger bought snacks to share during the drive.[78] While Mandela's wife Winnie was in prison after her arrest in the 1958 pass disturbances, she befriended two teenage wardresses, both white Afrikaners, who subsequently broke regulations by travelling in a segregated train to visit the Mandela home at Winnie's invitation; they were dismissed from their posts.[79]

Incidents such as these underline the complexity and uncertainty of social—and political—relationships in South Africa during the 1950s. Although Mandela habitually referred to authority in this era as fascist, in his day-to-day interaction with officials he expected—or at least demanded—behaviour bound by the conventions of good manners and mutual respect that he had absorbed from childhood. This ambiguity—the alternation between a rhetorical discourse, a formal language of high politics—which characterised the state as a monolithic tyranny and a more liberal or conversational acknowledgement of human goodness wherever it might be found, finds its reflection in the fluidity and even the irresolution of Mandela's (and other ANC leaders') strategic thinking at this time. What, then, were the ideas that underlay political activism during this era?

The ANC's aims were spelled out in 1955 (and adopted by the organisation in 1956) in considerable detail. Beginning in 1954, a 'National Action Council for the Congress of the People' established by the ANC and allied organisations, including the Congress of Democrats, a mainly white body established just after the Defiance Campaign, presided over a second army of 'Freedom Volunteers' tasked with the collection of 'demands' for inclusion in a 'Freedom Charter'. In April 1955, a group appointed by the Council began sorting out thousands of suggestions for inclusion into the Charter. Seven members of the ANC's National Executive Committee (NEC) reviewed a draft version of the Freedom Charter on the eve of a Congress of the People held on 26–7 June. It had been written very hurriedly by Lionel Bernstein, working by himself from a trunk-load of petitions, only a few days beforehand.[80] Bernstein belonged to the Congress of Democrats, a body of white sympathisers of the ANC established during the Defiance Campaign. Many of its members, including Bernstein, were also members of the now clandestine Communist Party that had discreetly re-established itself in 1953. For the Congress of the People, 3,000 delegates assembled on an open patch of ground owned by an Indian shopkeeper in Kliptown, on the borders of Soweto, to listen to a reading of each clause of the Charter. Although delegates could make speeches from the floor all the draft clauses were approved intact by a show of hands before police bearing automatic weapons brought proceedings to a halt on the second day. The police announced that they believed that treason was being contemplated and confiscated all the documents and noted down everybody's addresses before sending delegates and speakers home. The Charter was adopted by the ANC in 1956 at a special meeting in April, despite objections from a group of 'Africanists', members of the ANC Youth League in Orlando East. Between the Congress of the People and the ANC's adoption of the Charter, Volunteers collected 100,000 names in a 'Million Signature Campaign'.

The Charter contained a list of basic rights and freedoms. It began by reaffirming the multiracial character of South African society ('South Africa belongs to all who live within it, black and white'); it went on to promise equal status for all 'national groups', to argue for the transfer of the mines and monopoly industry to the ownership of 'the people as a whole', to guarantee equal opportunities to all who wished to trade and manufacture, to advocate the re-division of land 'among those that work it', the ending of restrictions on labour and trade unions, as well as proposing a comprehensive range of welfare provisions.

For remaining 'African Nationalists' within the Youth League and elsewhere in Congress, the inclusion of the racial minorities in a broad notion of South African citizenship was unacceptable and the Orlando group would eventually break away from the ANC to form a rival Pan Africanist Congress (PAC) in 1959. In his autobiography Mandela claims that he was among those Youth Leaguers in the 1940s who adopted a racially essentialist notion of African citizenship.[81] Certainly his recorded views up until 1953 suggest that he was sceptical about the merits of multiracial mobilisation but there is no contemporary source that supplies insight into his then ideas about the constituents of a free South Africa. By 1955, however, Mandela's thinking had changed considerably. Mandela participated in the planning of the Congress of the People—he convened a Resolutions Committee that proposed the shape of the campaign preceding the Congress.[82] His banning precluded a public appearance at the Congress although Mandela was present on the first day at the edge of the crowd. He was among the NEC members who approved the draft Charter on 25 June. Squire Makgothi, then a Youth League official who was actively engaged in the preparations for the Congress of the People, claimed later that Mandela 'was one of the prime movers'. Despite Mandela's ban, in the evenings, Makgothi accompanied him on visits 'to the shanty towns and so on to speak to people about it'.[83]

In June 1956 Mandela wrote an exposition of the Charter for a left-wing journal, *Liberation*. Here he explained that the 'Charter is more than a mere list of demands for democratic reform'. It was a revolutionary document, he insisted, because the 'changes it envisaged' could not happen 'without breaking the economic and political setup'. To achieve them would require 'mass struggles on the widest scale' conducted by a 'united front' for which 'opportunities are growing every day'. Such struggles should be based upon 'concrete and immediate demands'. However, he noted, the Charter was 'by no means a blueprint for a socialist state'. It proposed the transfer of power to 'the people', not a single class 'but all people of this country, be they workers, peasants, professional men, or petty bourgeoisie'. To be sure, the Charter's implementation would strike 'a fatal blow at the financial and gold-mining monopolies and farming interests that have for centuries plundered this country'. The breaking up and 'democratization' of such enterprises would 'open fresh fields for the development of a non-European bourgeois class which would for the first time own productive property in its own name. As a consequence "private enterprise" would "flourish as never before" '.[84]

Not everyone agreed with Mandela's interpretation of the Charter. Turok was allowed to strengthen the commitment to public ownership at a preliminary meeting that reviewed the draft Charter (after it was seen by the ANC NEC members)[85] and as a keynote speaker he suggested that after the Charter's enactment, workers' committees would manage the mines and the other big industries.[86] He managed to persuade an initially unenthusiastic Harmel, the CPSA's chief doctrinal authority, that these proposals accorded with the Party's vision of a 'National Democratic Revolution'.

At this time, the South African Communist party (SACP) internally justified its *de facto* alliance with the ANC through references to a common goal of 'national democracy', a transitional stage on the road to communism which, Soviet theorists maintained during the 1950s, the 'national bourgeoisie' in colonial or semi-colonial territories could work in conjunction with other groups in a struggle against imperialism that would take a 'non-capitalist road to socialism'. During such a phase capitalists would exist but would not predominate politically or economically.[87] This does not mean that the Charter was consciously written with these preoccupations in mind, but it may help us to understand the way that it was understood by left wingers in Congress (and right wingers too who objected to what they perceived as the document's socialist content). Much of Mandela's writing at the time indicates the extent to which his political thinking was influenced by the Communist Party within Congress (which Sisulu joined in 1953 at the time of its clandestine reconstruction and to which many of Mandela's other closest associates belonged). This is evident in his frequent references to the 'openly fascist' character of the South African state, which he characterised as the political expression of 'finance capital' in its monopoly stage as well as his interpretation of African 'mass struggles' as essentially anti-imperialist, not merely anti-colonial, characteristic phraseology in CPSA analyses of that time.[88]

Not all of Mandela's thinking was so obviously derived from the Party's world view. In fact his anticipation of the Charter's opportunities for the non-European businessman probably reflected a rather more benign view of private enterprise than his associates in the Party might have expressed. Indeed later, in exile, the ANC itself would embrace a rather more radical projection on South Africa's destiny and, when the movement reprinted Mandela's essay, it appeared without the phrase about the private sector.[89] On trial in 1963, however, Mandela maintained his insistence that the Freedom Charter implied 'nationalisation' that 'would take place in an economy *based* on private enterprise' [my emphasis] and repeated his contention that the Charter's realisation would open up fresh opportunities for the African middle class. He also stressed his 'respect for British political institutions', including the British parliament, 'the most democratic institution in the world' as well as the impartiality of the British judiciary,[90] opinions that he acknowledged the Communist Party would perceive as reactionary. Of course such contentions might have been influenced by the context in which they were expressed, but it is unlikely that Mandela would have misrepresented his political convictions in a trial in which he offered few other concessions to expediency. Approval of British institutions did not imply abandonment of African heritage: as Mandela observed in the same courtroom deposition, he retained 'admiration of the structure and organization of early African society' in which all land 'belonged to the tribe' and 'there was no exploitation'. The kind of leadership

Mandela himself exercised within the ANC, as 'a chairman who would wait until all views had been heard before he decided on his own position',[91] might have been consciously modelled on the consensual authority that Mandela himself believed characterised pre-colonial African kingship.

Quoting Nehru, Mandela noted in 1953 that 'there is no easy walk to freedom anywhere and many of us will have to pass through the shadow of death before we reach the mountain tops of our desires'.[92] For Mandela and many of his comrades the route that their walk to freedom might take remained uncertain for the rest of the decade and even beyond. Kathrada has suggested that Mandela viewed the issue of whether the ANC should form alliances with other organisations through a 'strategic schism'[93] and although he resolved this particular question early on he remained influenced by competing ideas about politics. On the one hand, Mandela found the moral absolutism of the 'professional revolutionary' compelling and persuasive: throughout the 1950s he kept pictures of Lenin and Stalin on the wall above his desk in his Orlando home. In the vision that he projected in his 1953 speech to the TANC of a Manichean struggle in which 'the labour power of the African people' would be ranged against 'an openly fascist state', there appeared little room for compromise.[94] Yet, as we have noted Mandela's leadership of the ANC's 'struggle politics' often appeared to be based on the premise that significant numbers of white South Africans might be open to democratic persuasion notwithstanding his angry denunciation of white liberal 'vacillations'[95] as well as his impatience with those ANC leaders such as Chief Luthuli who made a point of seeking advice from such figures as the novelist and Liberal Party leader, Alan Paton.[96] It is true that Mandela began at least considering the prospect of violent insurgent politics in 1953 and, two years later, a car journey along the Cape's 'Garden Route' prompted a playful appreciation of 'opportunities for guerrilla hide-outs'.[97] It is also the case that ANC's leaders' choice of peaceful forms of civil disobedience in the 1950s was exploratory rather than premised on any strategic conviction. Tambo's statement at a 1955 ANC conference was illustrative:

We shall not have to wait long for the day when only one method will be left to the oppressed people of this country—precisely what that method will be it is impossible to say, but it will certainly be the only method, and when that has been employed and followed up to its logical conclusion, there will be no more struggle, because one or the other of the conflicting forces—democracy or fascism—will have been crushed.[98]

Despite such uncertainties, Mandela continued to profess in public his belief that 'nation-wide campaigns of agitation'[99] could win significant victories. In his testimony at the Treason Trial, in August 1960, Mandela could even in the wake of the Sharpeville massacre envisage a very different *denouement* to the conflict from the one anticipated by Tambo in 1955. 'Suppose, as a result of pressure', the prosecutor asked Mandela during his cross-examination, 'the ruling class were to agree next month to a qualified franchise for the Africans . . . and next year, as a result of further pressure, a more important concession is made, a further concession in 1962, and so on . . . do you think that the people's democracy could be achieved?'

Mandela: 'Well this how I approach the question. I must explain at the outset that Congress as far as I know, has never sat down to discuss the question. . . . We demand universal adult franchise, and we are prepared to exert economic pressure to attain our demands, and we will launch defiance campaigns, stay-at-homes, either singly or together until the government should say, "Gentleman, we cannot have this state of affairs, laws being defied, and this whole situation created by stay-at-homes. Let's talk". In my own view I would say, yes let's talk, and the government would say, "we think that the Europeans at present are not ready for a type of government where there might be domination by non-Europeans. We think we should give you sixty seats. The African population to elect sixty Africans to represent them in Parliament. We will leave the matter over five years and we will review it at the end of five years". In my view, that would be a victory, my lords; we would have taken a significant step towards the attainment of universal adult suffrage for Africans, and we would then for the five years, say we will suspend civil disobedience; we won't have any stay-at-homes, and we will devote the intervening period for the purpose of educating the country, the Europeans . . . I'd say we should accept it, but of course, I would not abandon the demands for the extension of the franchise . . .'[100]

Mandela went on to suggest that the emergence of parliamentary parties, the Progressive Party and the Liberal Party that were now willing to put forward the demand to extend the franchise, was itself a demonstration of the recent impact of ANC pressure. Such views may have been a reflection of tactical legal imperatives but subsequently the movement to which Mandela belonged was going to make one last effort to mobilise its following in a campaign for a constitutional convention. Mandela would also have been highly conscious of the presence in the courtroom of Chief Albert Luthuli whose commitment to gentler kinds of conciliatory politics was probably much stronger than his own. Even so, the relaxed tone of the exchange, and the readiness of Mandela's response to the prosecutor's question, are striking: it does suggest that the kind of situation proposed by Advocate Hoexter represented an option that Mandela had already considered quite seriously.

Mandela's testimony also tells us how much at ease he was in the courtroom with its polite conventions and reasoned dialogue, one of the few arenas in which black South Africans could claim rights and status as citizens, 'the only place in South Africa where an African could possibly receive a fair hearing and where the rule of law might still apply', he believed.[101] Harold Wolpe, a legal colleague of Mandela as well as a left-wing political associate, once observed that Mandela was a better lawyer inside the courtroom than out of it.[102] Others have made more ambitious claims. During the 1980s, the French philosopher, Jacques Derrida, offered a perceptive deconstruction of Mandela's courtroom addresses to discern 'a man of the law by vocation' whose objections to the injustice of apartheid laws does not prevent him within the courtroom from maintaining 'a respectful admiration for those who exercise a function exemplary in his eyes and for the dignity of the tribunal'.[103] Even outside such tribunals, Mandela's professional discipline could influence his behaviour in other less formal settings; one of his house guests, Robert Matji, remembered his host 'cross examining' his son Thembi about Thembi's possession of another boy's textbook 'as if he was standing trial in the Supreme Court . . . he even started quoting from various laws'.[104] Mandela's attitude to the law was morally complex not merely instrumental. For him trials and courtrooms were not simply platforms for political expediency and his testimony within them should not be disregarded lightly. During the 1950s, Mandela's world was complicated by a diversity of loyalties, political, professional, and private, and the latter two now deserve consideration.

Mandela's career as a lawyer lasted ten years, from his first case after qualification in 1952 to his own self-defence in a Pretoria magistrate's court before his imprisonment a decade later. He struggled to qualify and was refused permission to retake exams that he had failed at Wits University in 1949 despite an appeal that he wrote to the University authorities detailing the 'very difficult and trying conditions' under which he combined his part-time studies (for which he paid £500 a year) while maintaining a livelihood. Quite aside from the material concerns of a part-time student, Mandela had to contend with a Dean of Law, Professor H.R. Hahlo, who made a habit of informing African students that they would be better off in a different faculty because their minds were unsuited to the study of law.[105] Mandela finally passed his exams through the professional body, encouraged by a sequence of liberal employers themselves keen to employ Africans to meet the needs of their own black clients. Mandela turned out to be a self-confident lawyer, not averse to playing to the gallery. In his own favourite anecdote he defends a domestic servant accused of stealing her employer's laundry. Walking over to the table of evidence, Mandela studied the items of clothing and with the tip of his pencil picked up a pair of knickers. Turning to the witness box and brandishing the underwear he asked the accused's employer 'Madam are these yours?' The woman was too embarrassed to assent and the magistrate subsequently dismissed the case. At times, however, he needed all the assurance that he could muster as on the occasion when a magistrate refused to acknowledge his status as the defending attorney without Mandela showing him his certificate, not a normal requirement. The transcript of the exchange survives with Mandela insisting on his right to continue defending his client before finally picking up his files and walking out, warning the magistrate that he would be back. After a Supreme

Court petition the magistrate was reprimanded and told to recuse himself.[106]

In its early years, his partnership with Tambo was a commercial success, with the office often receiving a dozen clients a day, and employing a succession of articled clerks and secretaries, many of these later to become ANC luminaries. Mendi Msimang, today the ANC's treasurer-general following a spell as the South African High Commissioner in London, started his career serving articles in the office of Mandela and Tambo. The practice expanded with the scope of apartheid regulations with the client base, including peasant farmers who had refused to obey government land-use regulations, group area offenders who had fallen foul of residential and business segregation, chiefs who refused to sanction cattle culling, and of course the men and women who lacked the passes and permits that increasingly officials required from Africans to maintain a normal livelihood in South African cities. Keeping such cases out of the courts was the first imperative for any successful effort to protect people threatened with 'endorsement' out of town under the pass laws. 'The average official wanted to be bribed', Mandela recalled, but 'we in politics could never do that'. Fortunately:

I had a couple of senior officials who were very friendly to me and I was able to help a lot of people by just going to them and to say look I can't go to court on this question, I have no right, but these are the circumstances. This man has worked here for so many years and he has got children there at school and he is going to have to lose his house and son. And some of the officials, you know, listened to me.[107]

The grotesque protocols of racial population classification brought another stream of clients to Mandela and Tambo, especially coloured people who had been 'reclassified' as Africans, losing relatively better-paid jobs and certain civil rights as a consequence. Mandela defended one ex-servicemen who had joined a 'coloured' regiment only to be classified as an African upon demobilisation. Mandela organised a hearing of the Classification Board and produced his client's light-skinned sister, a very pretty girl who had won prizes in beauty competitions, together with all the relevant birth certificates and identity documents. He had a solid case but for the sake of form the officials on the Board asked Mandela's client to turn around and stand with his back to them:

> And they looked and they started nodding to each other and they said, 'No, Mr Mandela you're quite right, he is a coloured'. I don't know what they saw in his back but they saw something to tell them that he was coloured.[108]

Official interference in ordinary daily life could intrude itself into the most routine and innocent activities. Maggie, Robert Resha's wife, had to summon Mandela's assistance one evening in 1958 when the police arrived shortly after she and Robert had been entertaining friends, black and white. Maggie was clearing glasses and was carrying these on a tray with a bottle and a corkscrew. A police officer seized the tray and informed her that she would be arrested for selling European liquor. She was held most of the night at the police station until Mandela arrived to pay her bail. Later, however, the case was dismissed after the police failed to attend the court hearing: apparently this happened quite frequently in minor cases in which Mandela was involved—police disliked being cross-examined by him.[109] Until the 1980s, most black South Africans were prohibited from buying or keeping any alcohol other than traditional beer. Genteel townsfolk could obtain exemption from such restrictions and Mandela maintained a liquor cabinet in his home, for guests, because he remained teetotal himself. As with the Reshas, Mandela's social circle was multiracial, his encounters with white South Africans extended well beyond politics to embrace concerns with ordinary domestic preoccupations. He knew Helen Joseph well enough, for example, to commiserate with her later from prison after she had reported to him the death of one of her pets. He was familiar enough with the Fischer household to admire relationships that existed between Bram Fischer and his domestic servants: 'the woman who worked for him . . . she regarded Bram as a brother, and she would be involved in his parties not just as a waiter but as a colleague'.[110]

Mandela and Tambo also maintained an extensive civil law practice and as the only African-owned law firm increasingly looked after the affairs of Johannesburg's tightly knit middle-class elite—to which of course they themselves belonged; Richard Maponya, later Soweto's most prominent businessman, was a close friend as well as a client, and linked to Mandela by kinship: Marina Maponya, his wife, was Mandela's cousin. Mandela joined with other members of this group of Soweto notables as a patron of the Jan Hofmeyr School of Social Work and he also played an active role in the affairs of the Donaldson Orlando Community Centre, where he worked out in the gym most evenings. Prosperity and professional success brought with it social standing—'a name on letterheads' as his second wife put it[111]—and modest luxuries—an Oldsmobile saloon and suits from Kahns, bespoke outfitter to the white elite professionals who frequented the nearby Rand Club, and business lunches at Kapitans, a Mauritian-owned Indian restaurant in Diagonal street that welcomed African customers. In 1956, Mandela travelled to Umtata to buy himself a plot of land, an acknowledgement of patrimonial obligation, for, as he explained, 'a man should own land near his birthplace'.[112]

From 1957, with both its partners attending daily hearings of the Treason Trial, the practice became harder to sustain and by 1958 Mandela was in financial difficulties: he could not afford to pay the balance of the sum owing on his Umtata land holding. He had no savings and apparently never kept a bank account. By now he had fresh obligations of family and kinship. Mandela's first marriage had been failing since 1952 when Evelyn attended a six-month midwifery course in Durban, an absence that fuelled salacious gossip about her husband,[113] gossip that was confirmed on Evelyn's return when she was confronted by a strange woman who 'started coming home, coming into our bedroom'. On confronting her husband, he was 'cold and distant', she recalled 40 years later.[114] Mandela himself attributes the breakdown of his marriage to Evelyn's conversion to being a Jehovah's Witness and her increasing indifference to his political commitments. Evelyn finally moved out her children and her furniture from the Orlando family home in January 1957.

Several months later Mandela began courting Nomzamo Winifred Madikizela, a recently qualified social worker attached to Soweto's Baragwanath Hospital. She was the sixth of eleven children. Winnie was the daughter of Columbus Madikizela, a headmaster who had become a prosperous businessman, running several trading stores and a fleet of buses from Bizana in the Transkei. Her great grandfather was Madikizela, an important nineteenth-century chief in the Mpondo kingdom, a distinguished lineage of which Winnie would always be intensely conscious. She was born in 1934, 16 years later than her future husband. Her mother, Gertrude, was descended from a union between an Mpondo woman and a white trader, 'coloured' in South African terminology, and as a *Mhlungu* was to suffer through the early years of her marriage from racial abuse by her mother-in-law, treatment that made a sharp impression on Winnie and her siblings. A further element of domestic conflict was her father's renunciation of his ancestral culture in favour of a strict and puritanical Methodism: Winnie's grandmother favoured traditional customs, commanding her grandchildren's participation in her homage to the spirits. Winnie loved her grandmother and perhaps as a result of her influence grew up as an assertive and sometimes aggressive child, behaviour for which she was severely beaten by her father—notwithstanding the social norms of a community in which children were normally punished gently. But her father combined harsh discipline with paternal consideration and his daughters attended his school. Gertrude died when Winnie turned ten and in her teens she grew closer to her father, taking over from her mother the tasks of looking after him, laundering and cooking. He reciprocated her affection by encouraging her to read through his library, and later sending her to secondary school and securing a place for her at the Jan Hofmeyr School of Social Work, where she enrolled in 1953.

Two years later she began work at Baragwanath: here in 1955 she encountered Adelaide Tshukudu, then engaged to Tambo and the two women became friendly while sharing a room at the Helping Hand hostel. Her first meeting with Mandela was two years later, however, and during this interval she was wooed by Mandela's nephew, Matanzima, paramount chief of the Emigrant Thembu. She was introduced to Mandela by Tambo during the course of a chance encounter in a delicatessen; out of small change, Tambo asked his partner to buy a snack for his wife and her friend. Mandela thought

Winnie was Adelaide Tambo's relative because both women came from Bizana but Tambo corrected him: 'Don't you know Winnie. She is always dancing up and down in the newspapers.' Black female professionals as well qualified as Winnie Madikizela were then quite unusual and her picture had already appeared in the *Golden City Post*, a weekly tabloid.[115] Mandela had already glimpsed Winnie once by the roadside while driving home some weeks before and remembered her from this occasion: Winnie was strikingly pretty. He telephoned her hostel and invited her for lunch the next Sunday.

Mandela's courtship was abrupt. It started on an oddly impersonal note: on their first day out a friend collected her for the drive to Mandela's office. A lunch at Kapitan's preceded a walk and a discussion about fundraising for the ANC, if we are to accept Winnie's version of the encounter. 'Politicians are not lovers' she explained many years later.[116] Initially reluctant to express his feelings, Mandela fell in love with her quickly, the age between them accentuating the emotions that he felt. On their first afternoon together, after Winnie broke a shoe strap and was walking with difficulty, he 'held my hand as my father would hold a little girl's hand'.[117] Less than a year later, Mandela took the lead in arranging the wedding (which had to wait until his divorce proceedings were over), hardly consulting her, ordering a wedding dress, and placing an engagement notice in the *Golden City Post*. The wedding itself was held at Columbus Madikizela's village in Mpondoland on 14 June 1958, a combination of Methodist and older rituals, 'both a traditional marriage and to some extent a western ceremony',[118] Winnie noted, in which Mandela paid *lobola* (brideprice) as well as arranging an ante nuptial contract, in those days a comparatively unusual precaution, especially among black South Africans.[119]

Winnie's candid memoir of their early marriage describes a 'life with him' that was a 'life without him',[120] a union that had to be shared with a range of older members of a 'well educated highly active multi-racial group in which Mandela had been a central figure for five years'.[121] She made enduring friendships among them, however, notably with Helen Joseph, and immersed herself in public commitments, leading a local branch of the Women's League and, despite her pregnancy, undergoing arrest and imprisonment during the anti-pass protests. She added two fresh rooms to the house, because there were always people to stay, including out-of-towners among the Treason Trial accused, as well as kinsfolk, her own and Mandela's. And though she may have initially been rather in awe of his public reputation, as he drew her into his social circle she became a 'colleague and a comrade', while in their private life Winnie was an equal partner, learning to drive (with difficulty—Mandela was an impatient teacher), finding Anglican boarding schools in Swaziland for his sons, and upbraiding him from his feckless attitude to money—and his willingness to give it away. They were obviously very happy—and though their private time together may have been restricted, within it 'he could be very affectionate', she observed.[122] A rare vignette from their life together is supplied by Maggie Resha, who recounts an occasion when the Mandelas arrived to visit the Reshas in their new home in Soweto. Winnie was driving and managed to park the car in muddy ground. Winnie joined Maggie in the kitchen and both women entertained themselves, looking out of the window in amusement as Mandela struggled furiously in the yard, wrestling with the steering wheel of the Oldsmobile while the tyres gyrated in the mud.[123]

Later, in prison, Mandela would reconstruct their life together in a series of vivid letters. Below is a brief quotation from one of these, written in April 1976. With its mixture of tenderness and remorse it is eloquent testimony to the complicated passions that would animate Mandela's domestic world:

> What you perhaps don't know is how often I think and actually picture in mind all that makes you up physically and spiritually—the loving remarks which come daily and the blind eye you've always turned against those numerous irritations that would have frustrated another woman. Sometimes it's a wonderful experience to . . . think back about the precious moments spent with you darling. I even remember a day when you were bulging with Zindzi, struggling to cut your nails. I now recall those incidents with a sense of shame. I could have done it for you. Whether or not I was conscious of it, my attitude was: I've done my duty, a second brat is on the way, the difficulties you are now facing as a result of your physical

condition are all yours. My only consolation is the knowledge that then I led a life where I'd hardly enough time to even think. . . .[124]

Early biographical treatments of Mandela paid very little attention to his personal affairs. Mary Benson's books, for example, only make perfunctory references to Evelyn Mandela. Nor is there room in the 'modernist' representations of the 'professional revolutionary' Mandela for the complicated loyalties that were a consequence of Mandela's kinship and lineage, loyalties that would be reinforced by his second marriage, this time into another important rural Transkeien dynasty. Retrospectively, Winnie may have overstated Mandela's and her own commitment to ancestral customs. Fifty years later, she contested a court action to deprive her of legal title to the Orlando house and referred to the burial in the garden of her first daughter's umbilical cord, as Mpondo tradition demanded. In fact she and Nelson acknowledged such obligations selectively. Whatever the fate of Zenani's umbilical cord, Winnie vigorously resisted her mother-in-law's attempt to arrange an *inyanga's* traditional herbal bath for the infant.[125] As we have seen, in any case, the 'traditions' that influenced the upbringing of the children of Xhosa notables were culturally syncretic. One convention, however, that Mandela was keen to maintain was the fulfilment of obligations of hospitality and service towards his extended family. Indeed, the performance of such duties may have helped to compensate for the absence of closer relationships during the failure of his first marriage. From the time of setting up his household Mandela maintained an open home, because, as he notes in his autobiography, 'in my culture, all the members of one's family have a claim'.[126] The household would often include Mandela's sister Leabie, and for lengthy periods his mother as well, not to mention any other houseguests invited to stay in the three rooms of the family home at no. 8115, Orlando West.

Shared family concerns could override political disagreements. Mandela was increasingly at odds in his public life with his nephew Matanzima. Notwithstanding Mandela's reservations about the ANC directly confronting the chieftaincy, he was sharply critical of the 'reversion to tribal rule' that he perceived to be represented in the

Bantu Authorities Act.[127] The Act enhanced chiefs' legal authority but detracted from their legitimacy by making the local governments that they commanded responsible for enforcing widely hated anti-soil erosion measures. Autocratic behaviour by Mandela's relatives prompted a succession of delegations of 'Transkeien tribesmen' to seek Mandela's counsel in Orlando.[128] Even so, the two kinsmen nevertheless maintained an active and benign engagement in each other's family affairs. For example, Matanzima joined Sisulu in forlorn efforts to mediate between Mandela and Evelyn. Later Nobandla, Matanzima's senior wife, cared for Makgatho, Mandela's elder son, when he fell sick at school. Many years later, Mandela would write from his cell on Robben Island to ask the British politician, Denis Healey, to help him secure a scholarship for Matanzima's daughter, Xoliswa, so that she could attend an English university.[129] Looking after such matters was a compulsion of honour as well as affection, in a social setting in which 'all members of one's family have a claim'. And in a powerless and impoverished community in which Mandela represented such an important source of benevolent alternative authority such claims extended well beyond family. As his new wife ruefully observed after their first outing together:

> Leaving the restaurant, going to his car, we took something like half an hour. Nelson couldn't walk from here to there without having consultations. He is that type of person, almost impossible to live with as far as the public is concerned. He belongs to them.[130]

Within two years of Winnie Madidkizela's marriage to Mandela, however, even her very limited 'life with him' would end altogether.

4

MAKING A MESSIAH

Nelson Mandela's career in clandestine insurgent politics was brief.
On 21 March 1960, in Sharpeville, Vereeniging, 30 policemen fired
into a crowd of 5,000 killing at least 69 and wounding nearly 200.
The crowd had been summoned by the Pan Africanist Congress
(PAC), the African National Congress's (ANC's) new rival formed by
'Africanist' dissenters led by Robert Sobukwe. They contended that
the ANC had been deradicalised and deracinated by its co-operation
with Communists, white democrats, and Indian Gandhists. From
January 1960 the PAC had proposed a militant offensive to the pass
laws as an alternative to the ANC's (relatively sedate) anti-pass
campaign, urging its supporters to surrender themselves without
passes outside police stations. Believing that rhetorical emphasis
on race pride was by itself sufficient to evoke a large following, the
PAC undertook little systematic preparation. Its branches were concentrated around the steel-making centre of Vereeniging and in the
African townships of Cape Town. In Sharpeville, high rents, unemployment among school drop-outs, and authoritarian officials
generated angry discontent especially among young people. The
ANC was weak in Sharpeville and PAC activists constructed a strong
network. In Cape Town, the other centre where the PAC enjoyed a
significant following, the new organisation constituted its base among
squatters and migrant workers, the principal targets of fiercely applied
influx control intended by the government to reduce to a minimum
the African presence in the western Cape.

Most of the top ANC leaders, including Mandela, were at the
Treason Trial hearings in Pretoria on the day of the massacre.
Mandela spent the night of 21 March at Joe Slovo's house, together
with Walter Sisulu and other ANC officials, discussing how the

organisation should react to the day's events. They decided that the ANC should call for nationwide pass burnings and a stay at home after consulting Chief Luthuli. Mandela joined a sub-committee, which based itself at the Slovo suburban residence while directing operations. On 28 March Mandela burned his pass in Orlando before an especially invited group of journalists. Two days later, he was arrested, despite an advance warning from a friendly and indiscreet Special Branch officer, with hundreds of others under state of emergency regulations. At the behest of Chief Luthuli, Oliver Tambo left South Africa on 27 April to represent the ANC abroad, in anticipation of the ANC's banning. On 8 April, the ANC and the PAC were legislated prohibited organisations. After five months in prison in Pretoria, Mandela was released with other detainees on 31 August.

Shortly thereafter, a hastily assembled meeting of the ANC's executive decided that the organisation should not disband but rather continue its activities in secret. The Youth and Women's leagues should dissolve, however. A truncated National Working Committee composed of Mandela, Sisulu, Kotane, J.B. Marks, and Duma Nokwe, the ANC secretary-general, were given the responsibility of reorganising along M Plan principles. Mandela was assigned the task of explaining these decisions to the rank and file. This was not always easy and on occasions Mandela needed to be at his most imperious. In Port Elizabeth, for example, members of the old branch executive in Red Location resented being supplanted by a clandestine core leadership. Mandela attended an angry discussion and listened to their views before telling the disaffected branch leaders:

> . . . you have no reason to be angry about this, because the ANC was banned in your absence, and that leadership that was there took action . . . there's no other leader except myself, you see, in the African National Congress. And therefore if you don't like or disagree with the decision taken, the door is open to leave the African National Congress, to go and stay in your house, don't try and make problems. . . . Because I am sure you will never face the anger of the people that would cause you regret for the rest of your life.[1]

In December 36 'African Leaders' including representatives of the PAC and the Liberal Party assembled at a Consultative Conference in

Orlando. This group adopted a resolution calling for a national constitutional convention. The police disrupted the proceedings and
confiscated a quantity of documentation but, undeterred, the Leaders
established a Continuation Committee to organise a larger meeting.
This body quickly fell apart with Liberals and Pan-Africanists accusing the ANC and the South African Communist Party (SACP) of
sidelining them in its proceedings, complaining, with some justification, in the words of former Youth Leaguer and now Liberal Party
member Jordan Ngubane, of 'an invisible hand that moved events
towards its own goal'.[2] In January and February 1961 Mandela visited
various parts of the country preparing for the 'All-in-Africa Conference' planned for 25–6 March in Pietermaritzberg. He also crossed
the Basutoland border with Sisulu for discussions with Ntsu
Mokhehle, the Basotho Congress Party leader. Nearer home he also
had a meeting with Harry Oppenheimer. Oppenheimer refused
Mandela's request for funds to support transport costs for the conference but was nevertheless 'impressed by [Mandela's] sense of power'.[3]
As Oppenheimer sensed in Mandela, ANC leaders were confident
that they had it within their capacity to bring about momentous
political changes.

At the Maritzberg meeting, the expiry of a banning order and an
adjournment in the Treason Trial proceedings enabled Mandela to
make his first public speech since the Sophiatown removals. Addressing 1,400 delegates, as well as foreign journalists, he called for African
unity and a 'fully represented national convention'. Africans should
'refuse to cooperate' with the government if such a convention were
not conceded and 'militant campaigns' would be backed by external
pressure from outside South Africa, he promised.[4] Eye-witness recollections of this event differ. Michael Dingake recalls a speech by
Mandela that 'electrified the conference' with its 'fearlessness and
outspokenness', inspiring those present to raise their 'fists . . . and
arms in piston-like motion' and sing 'the new revolutionary tune:
"*Amandla ngawethu nobungcwalisa nabo bobethu*" [power is ours, so is
justice]'.[5] Contemporary press reports, however, refer only to one
song: 'Spread the gospel of Chief Luthuli'.[6] Benjamin Pogrund, a
reporter for the *Rand Daily Mail*, was also present. In his account,

Mandela, 'not a scintillating speaker . . . on this occasion . . . spoke in solemn terms and did little to arouse the emotions of the audience after the initial excited response to his unexpected and dramatic appearance on the platform'.[7] At the time, in an article he wrote for *Contact*, the Liberal fortnightly, Pogrund did concede that Mandela, 'bearded in the new nationalist fashion' was 'the star of the show'.[8] Pogrund himself told researchers in the mid-1970s that he was convinced 'that the left wing was deliberately embellishing Mandela's image in later descriptions of his appearance at the conference'.[9] Ngubane claimed that throughout the proceedings the absent Luthuli was 'deliberately sidelined' by Communists seeking to enhance Mandela's leadership status.[10] The correspondent from the Communist-edited *New Age* reported no pumping fists but did note that during Mandela's speech 'every sentence was either cheered or greeted with cries of "shame" '.[11] One of Winnie Mandela's biographers was told that Mandela addressed the conference in his bare feet;[12] photographs confirm that he was as ever smartly shod. Retrospectively, Mandela's dramatic public appearance acquired mythological attributes.

In whichever way observers may have interpreted the mood of the delegates, Mandela left the conference convinced that its participants were ready for 'a stubborn and prolonged struggle, involving the masses of the people from town and country'.[13] After his departure the conference resolved in favour of a three-day strike on 29–31 May, to coincide with the Government's proclamation of a Republic. Mandela was appointed the secretary of an otherwise anonymous National Action Council. On 23 March the ANC's National Working Committee had decided that Mandela should 'go underground' to organise the strike surfacing from time to time, 'hoping for a maximum of publicity, to show that the ANC was still working'.[14] On 29 March the presiding judge at the Treason Trial pronounced all the remaining defendants not guilty. After visiting home (in the company of Sisulu, Nokwe, and Joe Modise) to collect a suitcase of clothes and bid his wife goodbye, Mandela disappeared from public view. As Winnie noted later, for her it was a rather impersonal farewell, as she put it, 'there was no chance to sit down and discuss the decision to commit himself totally'; by the time she had packed his bag he had gone and someone else picked it up subsequently. In one representation of this episode, Mandela spoke to her; in another he remains outside and Modise asks her to pack a suitcase.[15] Several days later the police announced a warrant for his arrest.

For the next two months Mandela remained in hiding, mainly staying in Johannesburg although also travelling to Cape Town, Durban, and Port Elizabeth. Members of the Communist Party supplied a series of places to stay. In Durban Mandela attended an ANC executive meeting that debated whether the protest should take the more militant form of a strike (with pickets) or a stay at home: characteristically, in line with his tactical pragmatism of the previous decade, Mandela's preference was for the latter option which would be less likely to expose ANC supporters to police action, and this was the view that prevailed.

As the leading organiser of the strike Mandela was motivated by three principal preoccupations. The first task was to exhort support and commitment within the ANC's networks and trade union networks as well as civil groupings, and to this end he attended a series of discreet night-time meetings 'with Muslims in the Cape, with sugar workers in Natal, with factory workers in Port Elizabeth'. Second, he kept appointments with many of the main English-language newspaper editors to broaden support for the strike beyond Africans as well as generating publicity for its organisers. For this purpose, Mandela cultivated a relationship with Pogrund and used him as the conduit through whom the National Action Council supplied statements to the *Rand Daily Mail*.[16] The third objective of these activities was indeed, as Pogrund had suspected, to extend Mandela's moral and charismatic authority.

ANC and SACP principals had plenty of experience to confirm the importance within their base constituency of messianic self-sacrificial leadership: after all in 1952 the organisation had signed up its volunteers at meetings where crowds sang *Vuka Lutuli* ('Wake up Luthuli') and *Awusoze wale nxa uthunyiwe* ('You will never refuse where you are sent').[17] In Anthony Sampson's opinion, it was Sisulu who recognised that the ANC would soon need a martyr. He told Sampson in 1995 'When we decided he should go underground I knew that he was now stepping into a position of leadership. . . . We had got the leadership outside but we must have a leader inside.'[18] For the SACP's Slovo 'the decision that Mandela should become a fugitive and henceforth live the life of a professional revolutionary' represented a major watershed; in his autobiography the decision, he suggested, was the ANC's exemplary response to popular impatience 'with the discipline of legalism'.[19] Raymond Mhlaba believed that Mandela was 'groomed to take the leadership, even during the time Luthuli . . . [and] in left wing papers, our papers, new prominency was given to Mandela. And he himself, of course, conducted himself to attain that status.'[20]

Not only did left-wing newspapers appreciate the drama of Mandela's challenge to the authorities; the drama was accentuated by a variety of improbable disguises in which Mandela appeared in his fleeting encounters with pressmen and also by the invective directed against him by policemen and cabinet ministers. Editorial comment likened him to Baroness Orczy's aristocratic protagonist, a simile not altogether to Mandela's taste but even so he 'would feed the mythology of the Black Pimpernel' with relish by phoning up journalists from public call boxes and supplying then with copy about his latest exploits.[21] Police questioned Pogrund about the source of his reports on the strike preparations, but otherwise seemed to make very little serious effort to capture Mandela. Locating him would not have been so difficult because all the Special Branch would have needed to do would have been to monitor his wife's movements around town; through his friends Paul and Adelaide Joseph, Mandela arranged several meetings with Winnie at the Josephs' Fordsburg apartment.

Given the expectations generated by this theatrical performance, the strike itself was anti-climatic. Mandela and other Action Council members spent the nights of 28 and 29 May at a 'safe house' in Soweto. Effectively they had cut themselves off from any intelligence that they may have been able to receive from their own organisation—and, more crucially from the ANC-affiliated trade unions that were the main agencies in mobilising participation in the event—because the police established road blocks through the township. Mandela and his colleagues were compelled to rely on the press and radio reports for assessing the progress of the stay aways. Journalists generally reproduced police reports and statements by the Johannesburg Non-European Affairs Department in their estimations of absenteeism. Turnout in Johannesburg was in fact about 50 per cent and participation in the process was even higher in Port Elizabeth, but early press reports suggested much weaker response. On the evening of 29 May Pogrund received two telephone calls from Mandela. In the first of these conversations Mandela told Pogrund that though 'the people did not respond . . . to the extent to which we expected', the ANC leadership was not disheartened. However, the military and police measures used by authorities to discourage the protest raised the question 'of whether we can continue talking peace and non-violence'.

Before the strike, the police had arrested 10,000 people under a new 12-day detention law. Mandela maintained that the stay at home would continue the next day.[22] The following day, however, he and the other Committee members agreed to call the protest off. On 31 May Mandela met television reporters from the British ITN network and repeated to them what he had told Pogrund: 'If the government reaction is to crush by naked force our non-violent demonstrations we will have to reconsider our tactics.'[23] In his subsequent report Mandela announced that 'a full scale campaign of non-cooperation with the Government will be launched immediately'. This would include tax and rent strikes as well as 'various forms of industrial and economic action'.[24] These proposals were still-born: in early June Mandela agreed with Sisulu that he would propose the use of violence to the ANC's National Working Committee.

In Mandela's autobiography the decision to adopt guerrilla tactics follows the disappointment of the May stay away. In fact, discussion of at least the possibility of the ANC embarking on an 'armed struggle' began much earlier. Speaking in London in early May, Tambo observed that, if the South African government crushed the protest with force, 'it would be the last time the ANC would talk of peace'.[25] Members of the SACP, which announced its existence publicly for the first time during the State of Emergency, began discussing the adoption of violence while in detention. Some of them claimed later that a party conference in December 1960 resolved that preparations for a sabotage campaign or even that guerrilla warfare should begin.[26] SACP delegates attending an international conference in Moscow in July 1960 extracted a Chinese promise to provide military training. The next month Michael Harmel circulated a paper that he had written entitled 'What is to be done?', which asked whether the era on non-violent protest was over. In banning the ANC, Harmel contended, the state 'had created an entirely new situation, leading inexorably to the use of violence'.[27] Several members of the party had visited Pondoland in the Transkei in December 1960, the scene of an extensive and on occasions bloody rebellion against Bantu Authorities, and returned deeply impressed: during their visits peasant leaders had asked them whether the ANC could supply them with weapons. From time to time during the 1950s, ANC-led campaigns had featured a violent undertow—for example, in Natal ANC activists opposed to the government's land rehabilitation measures began to set fire to sugar cane fields in 1957 until Sisulu asked them to stop.[28] In Port Elizabeth ANC volunteers threw Molotov cocktails at empty buses on the first morning of the May 1961 stay away to persuade their drivers to return them to the terminals, 'the first time our chaps used petrol bombs', according to Govan Mbeki.[29]

Mandela himself was hardly a successful revolutionary: several commentators have made the point that his career as the leader of an armed insurgency was 'amateurish', particularly with respect to simple security precautions.[30] Such criticisms are not very telling: most guerrillas are amateurs and successful ones are often more lucky than skilful. His and other ANC leaders' decision to adopt violence has also attracted censure but it needs to be understood in its historical context. In 1961, ANC and SACP strategists certainly underestimated the political system's stability and the state's capacity, and, arguably, they overestimated popular propensity for rebellion. The Sharpeville massacre prompted widespread perceptions of a social order in crisis. The shootings were followed by protests in every major town. These included extensive riots in Soweto on the ANC's Day of Protest, a prolonged strike by migrant workers in Durban, and in Cape Town two major demonstrations, on 25 and 30 March, led by the PAC.

The Cape Town protests persuaded the authorities to announce a temporary suspension of the pass laws that endured until 7 April, by which time most of the activist community was in detention under emergency laws. The Emergency prompted a business slump and an exodus of foreign investment: as *The Economist* observed at the time 'Only a madman would buy South African shares'.[31] It was also accompanied by calls for reform from within Prime Minister Verwoerd's cabinet. Foreign investor nervousness proved to be temporary: government success in suppressing the ANC's *Umkhonto we Sizwe* and other insurgent organisations helped to restore business confidence by the mid-1960s. However, emigration from the white minority began on a significant scale in 1960 and remained a constant trend thereafter.

All these developments encouraged African and left-wing leaders in South Africa to perceive the authorities as vulnerable. They were also influenced by their own success in mobilising a popular following in the 1950s—and the occasional outbreaks of violence that accompanied ANC campaigning helped them to believe that there was a substantial popular constituency ready for revolt. From 1960 onwards, this belief sharpened ANC leadership anxiety that, if they did not supply leadership and inspiration to such people, they might be supplanted by more aggressive rivals: *Umkhonto*'s formation was paralleled by other insurgent groups sponsored by the PAC and by a coalition of veteran Trotskyites and disaffected members of the Liberal Party.

Even though several ANC leaders, including Nelson Mandela, had at least speculated about the possibility of an armed offensive against apartheid for several years, they encountered considerable opposition to their proposal to embark on such a course. At the end of June Mandela argued his case at a meeting of the ANC's National Working Committee (NWC). Initially Moses Kotane was hostile. Kotane felt that violence would provoke much greater repression and he felt that there was still scope for the methods that the ANC had used until then—they just needed more imaginative application. Mandela spent nearly a whole day in private discussion with Kotane. In the course of their conversations Mandela reminded Kotane that the Cuban

Communist Party opposed Castro's expedition in Cuba, a decision that its leaders later regretted. At a second session of the NWC, members resolved to canvass the issue at a full NEC meeting. This was held in July in Stanger, north of Durban, at the house of an Indian sugar plantation owner, so that Chief Luthuli could participate. Here Mandela repeated his arguments in front of 60 delegates, and Luthuli was reluctantly persuaded to sanction the establishment of a new military organisation, Umkhonto we Sizwe (MK) (Spear of the Nation), that would function separately from the ANC although ultimately it would be subject to the ANC's authority. There are conflicting accounts about Luthuli's position; in one version it was Kotane who exercised the decisive influence in obtaining the Chief's assent, several months after Umkhonto's formation and after unsuccessful earlier attempts by senior ANC leaders.[32]

Mandela suggested the name for the new organisation: 'we must have an African name', he told the delegates.[33] A second all-night meeting in Stanger explained the case for Umkhonto's formation to the ANC's Indian, coloured, and white allies. Participants remembered Mandela as 'unrelenting in championing the turn to violence', notwithstanding the sentiment among certain of the Indian delegates, including Yusuf Cachalia, that 'non-violence has not failed us: we have failed non violence'.[34] Mandela again emerged as the dominant voice, supported by the younger Indian delegates and, noticeably, white communists. It was agreed that Mandela would form Umkhonto and appoint his own staff. For the time being, it was decided, Umkhonto would engage only in very carefully controlled sabotage operations designed to avoid any casualties. This restraint may have been partly in deference to Luthuli's reservations, but according to Fatima Meer, who spoke to Mandela in 1988 about this period, his instincts then were still 'for talking and negotiating settlements'.[35] Mandela himself believes that all were in agreement that non-lethal sabotage 'offered the best hope of reconciliation afterwards'.[36]

More broadly, in its context, was the ANC's turn to violence the right decision? One line of reasoning is that, in opting for conspiracy and sabotage, the ANC neglected other essential activities. A decade later, Ben Turok, one of its participants, conceded ruefully that 'the sabotage campaign failed on the main count—it did not raise the level of action of the masses themselves'.[37] Mandela himself was to make much the same point. He wrote in prison in the mid-1970s, in establishing Umkhonto 'we had made exactly that mistake, drained the political organizations of their enthusiastic and experienced men, concentrated our attention on the new organization'. The ANC had allowed itself to abandon the work of a political organisation, substituting it with sabotage operations in which most of its followers were reduced to the role of spectators.[38] A rather stronger version of this argument was that through setting up a clandestine militarised elite group the ANC and Umkhonto removed key activists from other organisations where they might otherwise have played a more useful role, in trade unions, for example (which were never altogether prohibited by the government although individual bannings often disrupted their effective leadership).[39] A variation of this point of view is that the options for non-violent mass resistance were not exhausted, as was demonstrated by the relatively strong showing in certain centres during the May 1961 stay away; from this perspective the adoption of violent tactics was premature if not unnecessary.

An important premise of such contentions is that the ANC rank and file were not ready for such a confrontationist course and that the repression that it would invite would simply discourage any kind of mobilisation—in other words, leadership assumptions about popular predispositions for rebellion were inaccurate and merely reflected the extent to which leaders had allowed themselves to become socially and culturally isolated from their following. One of Mandela's friends and contemporaries, the social psychologist Fatima Meer, a few years after Mandela's arrest, suggested that generally black South Africans were politically immobilised as a consequence of the structural characteristics of South Africa's social system: the measure of economic security that it offered (even in the 1950s to an extent the state offered welfare provisions unusual in a semi-colonial setting); the government's willingness to employ police repression against its opponents; and the migratory labour system, which for men created contending focuses of loyalty between town and countryside and deflected their aggression inwards, so that it became 'irrationally dissipated in the neighbourhood and family'.[40] The successes that the ANC achieved in arousing popular protest, as well as the occasional eruptions of spontaneous violence that followed in the wake of political campaigning, should not have been understood as signals of mass militancy, Meer argued. They were 'observed by abstracting the motifs of rebellion scattered through a tapestry, which otherwise speaks of reasonable peace and quiet'. In this setting it is not surprising that, even in ANC rhetoric of the 1950s, one of the most common sentiments is advocacy of redemptive sacrifice in which 'suffering became identified with martyrdom and salvation'. When followers were told by leaders 'won't it be good, my mothers and fathers, when the blood of the youth of the African people is spilling for a good cause', Meer maintained that it 'not only constituted but reached a stage when it became the end in itself'.

Meer's essay is critical, especially of the non-African intellectual influences, liberal, Christian, and Marxist, that influenced the behaviour of African leaders such as Mandela, but her argument can also be read as a vindication of their strategic choices. For the ANC's members and the broader constituency that surrounded them, redemptive heroism supplied inspiration and hope, ingredients in a moral authority that would endure for decades to come.

Essentially, Umkhonto was a joint creation of the ANC and the SACP. Mandela recruited Slovo to serve in his command as Chief of Staff and Slovo understood himself as representing the SACP's Central Committee. Slovo had served in a signals unit in Italy in the final months of the Second World War but he had no combat experience, unlike Jack Hodgson, an engineer recruited onto the Northern Regional Command by Slovo for his explosives expertise. As well as Slovo, Sisulu and Raymond Mhlaba joined the National High Command; as with the subordinate structures of the organisation, Umkhonto were recruited disproportionately from the SACP. Party members were better prepared for clandestine work and they tended to be more disciplined than ANC rank and file.

During these formative stages of Umkhonto, Mandela spent two months staying in Yeoville in a small flat that belonged to Wolfie

Kodesh, a journalist and ex-serviceman who worked for *New Age*, sleeping on a camp-bed, keeping fit with a skipping rope and reading Clausewitz, the nineteenth-century Prussian military theorist. He stayed another month at a different suburban refuge in Norwood before accompanying Harmel to Lilliesleaf Farm in Rivonia on the outskirts of Johannesburg, a spacious house with outbuildings. Lilliesleaf was purchased using Party funds with the initial intention of serving as a refuge for 'people on the run'; it swiftly became Umkhonto's headquarters. Lilliesleaf was bought by Arthur Goldreich, an architect, SACP member, and veteran of the Israeli Irgun. In one interview, Rusty Bernstein recalled Rivonia as a place where there was 'time to read, think and study'.[41] Certainly, Mandela kept himself busy with reflective activities for a large proportion of the time that he spent at Rivonia, consulting whatever and whoever was at hand. As he noted in his autobiography: 'I began in the only way I knew how, by reading and talking to the experts.'[42] Bernstein was the first to help, lending him a book about the Filipino Huq guerrillas, and a tract by Liu Shao Chi, *How to be a Good Communist*. Among the court exhibits preserved from the Rivonia trial are Mandela's handwritten notes, exhaustive summaries of the texts that he consulted at Lilliesleaf. They represent an eclectic mixture of authorities including Harry Miller's *Menace in Malaya*, Eric Rosenthal's biography of General de Wet, Field Marshall Montgomery's memoirs, and, more predictably, Mao's *Strategic Problems of China's Revolutionary War*. In the case of this last text, Mandela's notes ran to 65 pages. He also produced a copious précis of Che Guevara's *Guerrilla Warfare*. Guevara had become an iconic figure within the ANC's left: 'everyone was reading his book', according to Joe Matthews.[43] Mandela's notes on Guevara's writings include the observation that:

> Acts of Sabotage are very important. They are to be distinguished from terrorism, a measure that is generally ineffective and indiscriminate in its results since it often makes victims of innocent people and destroys a large number of lives that are valuable to the revolution.[44]

He also noted that, in Cuba, Batista's army had totalled 12,000 whereas Castro's forces numbered 300. Castro's triumph illustrated the maxim that 'victories in war depend to a minimum on weapons and to a maximum on morale'.[45] Mandela did not spend all his time reading, however. With Slovo and Mhlaba he drew up a constitution for Umkhonto. In a different vein, Winnie was also quite a frequent visitor and on various evenings he would leave Lilliesleaf wearing the overalls and cap that he assumed as Goldreich's chauffeur—in doing so 'enjoying a sense of theatre'.[46] On such trips he would visit Paul and Adelaide Joseph in the Indian neighbourhood of Fordsburg: here on one occasion he recruited Indres Naidoo into Umkhonto; Naidoo was later captured trying to blow up a signal box. To keep appearances up as Goldreich's supposed servant, Mandela tended the garden. One afternoon, Kathrada escorted him to a safe venue to meet a British television journalist who managed to secure an appointment with Mandela through intermediaries after being refused an engagement with Prime Minister Verwoerd. Mandela also met Patrick O'Donovan of the *Observer* who encountered in him 'an inexplicable serenity'.[47] Target practice with an air rifle, the only weapon then kept at the farmhouse, was the closest to any personal preparation that he undertook for any military role that he might play. As his friend Kathrada noted from his stay at Rivonia at the farmhouse, 'there was nothing that could be described as advanced preparations for an uprising . . . [despite] much talk and much shuffling of papers'.[48] This may have been unfair. Ben Turok records a meeting that he had with Mandela and Modise at Lilliesleaf. Modise, the former organiser of the Sophiatown volunteers with whom Mandela had developed quite a close bond since the removals, had invited Turok, trained as a surveyor for a special purpose, 'to look at the logic of South Africa's infrastructure and how it could be disrupted'. Turok had acquired a complete set of cadastral maps for the purpose. Using these he showed Mandela and Modise how 'a small group of highly skilled saboteurs could do a great deal of damage by selecting key targets that were critical in linking the major centres of the country'. On the other hand, Turok concluded, 'there were few areas that offered a safe haven for a group of guerrillas'.[49]

By December, Umkhonto had established four regional commands in Johannesburg, Cape Town, Durban, and Port Elizabeth,

each of which recruited a network of cells as well as setting up training facilities, and hiring isolated properties to train saboteurs. In Port
Elizabeth the cellular structure of the M Plan lent itself to clandestine
military organisation and Umkhonto developed a stronger following
in the eastern Cape than elsewhere. In Durban, Umkhonto drew
heavily on trade-union shop-steward leadership. Mandela toured the
Cape and Natal in October, holding discussions with the regional
commands, and he also stayed for two weeks in Stanger. Meanwhile
Umkhonto manufactured its own weapons, using chemicals and
industrial explosives. Mandela witnessed one of the first experimental
bomb explosions, accompanying Jack Hodgson and Slovo to a dis-
used brick works and using all his charm to dissuade an elderly night
watchman from interfering. In mid-December Umkhonto was ready
for its first operation. On the night of 16 December, a symbolic day
for both Afrikaners and Africans, electric substations and government
buildings in Johannesburg and Port Elizabeth were damaged with
explosives: one of the saboteurs was killed. A leaflet announced the
birth of Umkhonto, a 'new, independent body' that would employ
methods that would 'mark a break with the past'. The leaflet's
authors 'even at this late hour' expressed the hope 'that our first
actions will awaken everyone to a realization of the disastrous situation'. Umhhonto we Sizwe still sought to achieve liberation 'without bloodshed' and that the government and its supporters could be
brought 'to their senses . . . before matters reach the desperate stage of
civil war'.[50]

Mandela was not a direct participator in any of the sabotage. By
December, in Johannesburg, Umkhonto and ANC leaders had agreed
that the ANC should respond to an invitation to attend to the Pan-
African Freedom Movement for East, Central and Southern Africa
(PAFMECSA) conference in Addis Ababa, and prevailed upon an
initially reluctant Mandela to represent them. The final decision to
send Mandela abroad was made by a National Executive meeting on
3 January. The underlying purpose of this journey was for Mandela to
persuade African governments to help with weapons and training
facilities that Umkhonto would need in the event of a move to full-
scale guerrilla operations. This would represent a development that

the ANC had yet to sanction, although four Umkhonto members, including Mhlaba, left South Africa during the course of 1961 to undergo Chinese training programmes negotiated by the SACP.[51] Another reason for Mandela leaving South Africa at this juncture may have been to establish a fuller understanding with the ANC external mission. Apparently, Tambo had been disconcerted by the ANC's qualified embrace of violent tactics in July 1961. In Matthews' recollections, in December Tambo had accompanied Chief Luthuli on his trip to Oslo to receive the Nobel Peace Prize, and 'so to get this news of violent struggle and so on, of course, was totally contradictory to what he had been preaching to everyone abroad'. Tambo had written a letter to the ANC's leadership to express his disquiet.[52] Before his own departure, Mandela once again travelled to Stanger to obtain Chief Luthuli's approval, pausing in Durban to listen to complaints from Regional Command leaders about 'the lack of command and drive on the part of senior leadership in the province'.[53] In his autobiography, Mandela claimed that his meeting with Luthuli was also discouraging. Luthuli was unwell and he could not remember the July meetings that had sanctioned Umkhonto's formation and he reprimanded his deputy. Mandela's contemporary record of the conversation is different, however. Here he records: that he found the ANC president in 'high spirits' and that he approved the trip, although Luthuli 'suggested consultation on the new operation'.[54] Luthuli's attitude to the ANC's decision to participate in the establishment of an armed organisation remained a subject of controversy: the SACP itself produced two opposing perspectives on the Chief's role while General H.J. van den Bergh, head of the security police, later claimed that Luthuli remained opposed to the use of violence. During the 1980s, Chief Mangosuthu Buthelezi, the Chief Minister of the Kwa-Zulu Natal and leader of the Inkatha movement, maintained that he represented Luthuli's principles, not the external ANC leadership, and that Luthuli would have distanced himself from the ANC 'if it were to resort to violence'.[55] Mandela's autobiographical account of the meeting written more than 30 years later may have been influenced by the later disagreements about Luthuli's views. His diary entry, however, is surely the more reliable source, and although it does not indicate whole-hearted endorsement of Mandela's new course it does not suggest disagreement either.

Mandela departed from Johannesburg on 10 January, crossing the Bechuanaland border in the afternoon. Initially his plan was to meet Tambo's old Fort Hare classmate Seretse Khama but his hosts in Lobatse considered that any public programme would be too danger-ous given a strong local presence of the South African Special Branch. Instead he joined Matthews in a specially chartered plane flight and disembarked in Dar es Salaam wearing a conical Basotho hat, a safari suit, and high mosquito boots.

Mandela's pan-African travels, between January and July 1961, represent one of the best-documented periods of his public life because during them he kept a diary. In Dar es Salaam he had a discussion with Julius Nyerere in which he disagreed with the ideal-istic Tanzanian leader about African historical predispositions towards socialism. Nyerere believed that pre-colonial African society was inherently egalitarian and that modern Africans still favoured com-munal economic arrangements. He then visited Sudan before taking a flight from Khartoum to Lagos where he was able to brief Tambo. On 29 January he arrived in Addis Ababa and delivered his speech at the PAFMECSA conference, an address that was co-written and in which Mandela maintained that in South Africa there was still scope for non-violent tactics. At Addis Ababa, Mandela startled several conference delegates with his observation that Arabs could also be Africans. This was a position that was received warmly by north Africans, and it reflected not just Mandela's but also the ANC's increasingly relaxed attitudes concerning racial identity, although it was not a view that was popular among most sub-Saharan delegates. Tactfully, Tambo restrained him from pursuing the point. The west and east Africans were already inclined to be antagonistic because of the ANC's connections with white left-wing and Indian organisa-tions, connections that were derided in PAC propaganda against the ANC at the conference. Mandela himself had a sharp altercation with Zambia's Simon Kapwepwe on the subject of white Communists, a topic that also predominated in his first meeting with Kenneth Kaunda. In Cairo on 12 February, Mandela experienced a frosty reception among officials who had read a hostile commentary on Nasser in *New Age*, a Cape Town weekly edited by SACP members.

Tunisia provided a more hospitable set of engagements including a three-hour meeting on 27 February with President Bourghiba. Bourghiba 'delivered elderly brother advice on methods and tactics and material assistance'[56] including £5,000 for weapons purchases. The king of Morocco was similarly generous. In Morocco Mandela also met a number of leaders from the Algerian Front de Liberation Nationale. Houari Boumedienne gave Mandela advice that he recollected in prison much later—that the objective of most armed liberation movements was rarely the overthrow of regimes but rather to force opponents to the negotiation table.[57] Between 18 and 21 March Mandela stayed at the Armée de Liberation Nationale headquarters at Oujda. Here he was given basic weapons instruction and a series of lectures on the Algerian war. Once again, Mandela kept a diligent record of what he learned:

> . . . the longer the war lasts, the more the massacres increase, and the people get tired.
>
> . . . the relationship between sabotage and operations. Basically sabotage seeks to destroy the enemy's economy whilst guerrilla operations are intended to sap the strength of the enemy . . . sabotage is frequently used for the purpose of preventing the enemy from extending its forces.
>
> Organization is extremely important. There must be a network throughout the country first and foremost. . . . Good organization is absolutely essential. In one Wilaya [district] a year was taken to build proper organization.
>
> A revolution cannot move with two heads.[58]

Mandela was impressed by the Algerian emphasis on the necessity for local organisation as a prerequisite for military operations; it was a point that he would recall in his own later evaluation of the Umkhonto campaign. In a second visit to West Africa through April, May, and early June, Tambo accompanied Mandela through a programme of appointments with mainly unaccommodating officials; Tambo was suffering severely from asthma and on one occasion Mandela had to carry him on his back up a stairway. In Accra, the

'President was busy and would be unable to see us'.[59] In Ghana, hostility to the ANC was mainly the effect of the PAC's success in influencing the views of the various Pan-African bodies head-quartered in Accra. In Senegal the visitors succeeded in meeting President Senghor who informed them about his respect and admiration for Chief Luthuli and promised that Senegal 'would do anything in its power to assist us'.

Despite the warmth of his Senegalese reception and comparable courtesies that he experienced in Guinea, Mandela acknowledged that in African diplomacy the ANC was vulnerable. His own visits to African countries had certainly improved the organisation's contin-ental standing. His encounters with no fewer than 13 African heads of state were important in another way as well. The belief of Umkhonto's leaders that they could exercise a decisive challenge to the state's authority was reinforced by the encouragement that they received from outside South Africa and the stature accorded to their commander by African statesmen even at this early stage.

On arriving in London in the second week in June, he had a tense exchange with Yusuf Dadoo and Vella Pillay, both important people within the SACP's exile community, unsettling them with his emphatic advocacy of the imperative for the ANC to foster a more obviously 'African' profile. In London Mandela's diary refers to 'most cordial' discussions with David Astor, editor of the *Observer*, whose newspaper's coverage of South Africa, in Mandela's view, had hith-erto rather favoured the PAC. Astor secured appointments with Labour and Liberal leaders, including Jo Grimond, Hugh Gaitskill, and Denis Healey. Mandela also met Canon John Collins of St Paul's Cathedral, the founder of Christian Action, and an important fund-raiser for the ANC. As well as his organisation's contribution to the Defiance Campaign, Collins had also managed to secure a large pro-portion of the money needed to pay for the defence in the Treason Trial. Collins and Mandela had first met him in 1954. Collins was still sympathetic but his donors were worried about the possibility that their money might be used to support violence: Mandela felt that he owed 'our close friend' an explanation of the ANC's 'purely defensive action'.[60] Collins' support would continue and indeed the

International Defence and Aid Fund would become the most important source of funding for payment of legal costs—and support for the families of convicted saboteurs and guerrillas. There was time for more relaxed encounters as well, evenings with the Tambos and a dinner with an old friend from Orlando, the writer and pianist, Todd Matshikiza, whose wife Esme remembered feeling that night that Mandela was leaving them 'ready for martyrdom'.[61] Mandela's own thoughts about the future at that time were probably less prescient; he told Colin Legum on the day of his departure from London 'I dread going back and telling Luthuli I am committed to armed struggle'.[62]

His return journey was to be via a second visit to Ethiopia. The original plan was that Mandela would stay in Ethiopia for six months to undergo a full programme of military instruction. On 28 June he began lessons on 'demolitions' with Lieutenant Befakidu. A rigorous routine that comprised 'field-craft drills', sessions at the shooting range, marathon 'fatigue marches', and attendance at demonstrations of more advanced weaponry was brought to an abrupt end after two weeks. In mid-July a telegram arrived calling for his return to South Africa. Mandela's autobiography suggests that 'the internal armed struggle was escalating' and as the Umkhonto commander he was needed.[63] More plausibly, Sisulu was worried that a more prolonged absence would demoralise Umkhonto rank and file, arousing suspicions that Mandela would not be returning.

Mandela arrived back at Lilliesleaf on 24 July still wearing his training uniform, after an all-night drive from Lobatse with Cecil Williams, a member of the Congress of Democrats. As well as his notes and diary he brought with him a suitcase containing cotton prints for Winnie from the African countries that he had visited[64] and a semi-automatic rifle. The weapon was subsequently hidden away, never to be recovered. Winnie and the children arrived at Lilliesleaf the next day, travelling in a Red Cross ambulance with Winnie pretending to be a woman in labour.

That evening Mandela addressed a meeting of the ANC's NWC, emphasising the key lesson that he had learned on his travels, that the ANC should more obviously assume a leading position in its alliances with other organisations and, with respect to public perceptions,

attempt to distance itself from its allies. In his report Mandela noted
the 'wide-spread anti white feeling at the PAFMECSA meeting' and
the 'violent opposition' he encountered 'to anything that smacked of
partnership between black and white' ('partnership' was a term that
had a particularly disreputable connotation for northern Rhodesians
and Malawians). On the topic of the ANC's alliance he told the
Working Committee that, among the delegates with whom he held
conversations, 'there are great reservations about our policy and there
is a widespread feeling that the ANC is a communist dominated
organization'. The ANC 'needed to make adjustments in tactics not
policy'. It must 'regard itself as the vanguard of the pan African
movement in South Africa'. Although it was true 'that our own
situation has its own special features that distinguish us from the rest
of Africa' there were 'serious dangers' if the ANC did not change its
approach. Particular features 'of our work' might 'give the impression
of being dominated'. These include the absence of 'participation at
mass level', in other words the neglect of popular campaigning since
the formation of Umkhonto, and the failure to raise 'the demand for
national independence'. In his report Mandela was also critical of
Luthuli, unusually harshly so, observing that in his recently published
autobiography, 'some of his statements have been extremely
unfortunate and have created the impression of a man who is a stooge
of the whites'.[65] He then proposed to travel to Natal to speak to
Luthuli to counter PAC rumours that while abroad he had become
an 'Africanist', a misrepresentation that may have been an additional
factor in motivating Sisulu's summons to him to return from
Ethiopia.

Despite misgivings about the safety of his proposed trip, Mandela
departed for Natal on 26 July, driving with Williams in his distinctive
new car. Kathrada could not even persuade him to shave off his beard
as a precaution against recognition: the most recent press photographs
showed him bearded Guevara fashion and a clean shave would have
been sensible, but in Kathrada's wry recollection, Mandela 'must have
known how the beard enhanced his looks and personality'.[66] He
spent the next nine days in and around Durban. He had an inconclu-
sive conversation with Luthuli: the Chief felt that the ANC should

not weaken its public commitment to non-racialism merely 'to suit a few foreign leaders'.[67] Mandela responded that what was required were 'essentially cosmetic changes in order to make the ANC more intelligible—and more palatable—to our allies'. He left Luthuli unconvinced; the Chief told Mandela that he needed to consider the matter and 'talk to some of his friends'.[68] On 4 July the Durban regional command assembled for a meeting with Mandela. He told those present that the initial acts of sabotage were the opening shots in what would become a much more extensive guerrilla insurgency 'if the government failed to respond'.[69] Later that evening he attended a party at a journalist's house, still wearing his khaki drill from the Ethiopian training. Here he abandoned any considerations of discretion and explained to the company 'that for the moment Umkhonto was limited to sabotage but if that did not work we would probably move to guerrilla warfare'. The day after, while driving back with Williams to Johannesburg, they were halted by police outside Pietermaritzberg. Mandela had time to hide a gun and notebook between the car seats before submitting to arrest. His active service as a guerrilla commander was over, barely a year after Umkhonto's formation.

5

TRIALS

Mandela's captors treated him with civility. Sergeant Vorster, the officer who halted his car, 'in a very proper way asked me a few questions', he did not bother searching his new charge. At the station in Pietermariztberg, Mandela encountered Warrant Officer Truter, a witness in the Treason Trial who received him 'in a friendly way'. He was allowed to travel to Johannesburg, unhandcuffed, in the back seat of the police car. Fatima Meer brought him food before the journey; he shared it with the two officers who permitted him to take a walk in Volksrust. Mandela made no attempt to escape: he 'did not want to take advantage of the trust they placed in me'.[1] In Johannesburg he was locked up in the police headquarters at Marshall Square, next door to Walter Sisulu, who later applied successfully for bail. The next day both men were charged with incitement of workers to strike and Mandela was also charged with leaving the country illegally, without a passport. Mandela records that he was treated by the magistrate with 'professional courtesy' although his former flatmate, Wolfie Kodesh, remembered Mandela 'transfixing' the magistrate with his stare, 'like a mongoose'.[2] Be that as it may, Mandela, sensing some discomfort among men who knew him as 'Nelson Mandela, attorney at law', discerned what role he should play in court. He decided to represent himself, 'to enhance the symbolism of my role' and 'put the state on trial'.[3]

While awaiting trial, Mandela was held in the Fort prison in Johannesburg, today the location of the Constitutional Court. He was allowed weekly visits from Winnie and officials turned the other way to let him embrace her. Mrs Pillay brought him lunch every day. The British Ambassador sent him history and politics books, explaining to the Foreign Office that 'in the long run we may get some goodwill from Mandela having helped him'.[4] Joe Slovo provided legal counsel and, assisted by Joe Modise, also devised quite a plausible escape plan. One of Modise's childhood friends from Sophiatown had joined the police and was in charge of the courtroom cells in which Mandel would be held during lunch adjournments.[5] Mandela decided against the scheme, handing back to Slovo the document containing the details and asking him to destroy it together with other papers that he had left at Rivonia, a request that went unheeded.

The trial opened on 13 October in Pretoria. Mandela entered the courtroom wearing a leopard skin *kaross* (cloak), the ceremonial costume of Xhosa royalty. Outside the courtroom a praise singer intoned Mandela's family tree. Winnie was present, in beaded headdress and ankle-length Xhosa skirt. The previous week she had been summoned to Mandela's birthplace where the elders commanded her to participate in a ceremony presided over by a *sangoma* (traditional healer), which would protect her husband; she refused, a decision she later regretted. To the accompaniment of shouts of *Amandla! Ngwethu!* ('Power to the people') Mandela entered the courtroom to request a postponement. Officials attempted without success to confiscate the *kaross*. A week later the proceedings resumed. Granted permission to address the court, Mandela, after telling the magistrate that his remarks were not addressed to him in a personal capacity, because he did not doubt his 'sense of fairness and justice', applied for his recusal on the grounds that he did not consider himself 'morally bound to obey laws made by a Parliament in which I had no representation'. 'Why is it', he continued, 'that in this courtroom I am facing a white magistrate, confronted by a white prosecutor, escorted by a white magistrate. Can anyone honestly and seriously suggest that in this type of atmosphere the scales of justice are evenly balanced?'[6] Mandela was subsequently allowed to elaborate his argument at considerable length, despite the magistrate's warnings that he might be 'going beyond the scope of [his] application'. In the end the court agreed with the prosecution that the accused's application had no legal basis. Mandela then pleaded 'not guilty'.[7]

After this preliminary, the prosecution called 60 witnesses including the secretary to the prime minister, Mr Barnard, to whom

Mandela had sent his letter to the premier in 1961 calling for a national convention. Mandela subjected him to a protracted cross-examination, seeking assent to the proposition that Verwoerd's failure to reply to the letter would be 'scandalous' in 'any civilised country', a view that Barnard understandably rejected. The letter remained unanswered because it was aggressive and discourteous, he said. Mandela later acknowledged that 'there may have been something in this'.[8] Mandela again sought the recusal of the magistrate, van Heerden, because he had noticed him departing for lunch with police witnesses; beforehand, however, he wrote to van Heerden warning him and explaining that he bore no personal grudge.[9] Van Heerden refused the application, assuring the court that he had had no communication with the policemen. When the state closed its case, rather to the magistrate's surprise Mandela called no witnesses, informing the magistrate only that he was 'guilty of no crimes'. 'Is that all you have to say?', van Heerden asked incredulously. 'Your Worship, with respect', Mandela replied, 'If I had something to say I would have said it'.[10] The trial was adjourned until 7 November to allow time for Mandela to prepare his plea in mitigation. On 7 November, before the court was called, the prosecutor, P.J. Bosch, requested a meeting with Mandela. In this encounter, Bosch told his adversary how much he regretted having to ask the court for a prison sentence and shook hands, in tears, apparently. In 1964, in Mandela's next trial, there was a similar incident: a member of the prosecution team resigned and before leaving came up to the accused to say goodbye to Mandela.[11] Magistrate Van Heerden, incidentally, addressed Mandela as 'Mr Mandela' throughout the proceedings—an unusual courtesy in its context.

Mandela spoke for a hour in his plea for mitigation. In line with his original intention, his address was hardly a plea, offering instead a political testament. In part this was an indictment of the behaviour of the authorities, unworthy of any 'civilised government . . . when faced with a peaceful, disciplined, sensible and democratic expression of the views of its own population', behaviour 'that set the scene for violence'. He warned that 'already there are indications in this country that people, my people, Africans, are turning to deliberate acts of violence . . . in order to persuade the government, in the only language it understands'. This was a government that itself brought 'law into . . . contempt and disrepute'. He acknowledged and defined his role in leading the 31 May strike movement and told the court why, 'as an attorney who is bound, as part of my code of behaviour, to observe the laws of the country and to respect its customs and traditions', he should 'willingly lend himself to such a campaign'. At this juncture he turned to his background, describing first his childhood and the stories that the elders had told him about a society in which the land belonged to 'the whole tribe' and in which 'all men were free and equal and this was the foundation of government'. In this society there were the 'seeds of revolutionary democracy' that today inspired Mandela and his 'political colleagues'. Its natural justice contrasted sharply with modern life 'in this country' in which 'any thinking African' found himself in continuous conflict 'between his conscience on the one hand and the law on the other'. It was this conflict that compelled Mandela:

> . . . to separate myself from my wife and children, to say goodbye to the good old days when, at the end of a strenuous day at the office, I could look forward to joining my family at the dinner table, and instead take up the life of a man hunted continuously by the police. . . . No man in his right senses would voluntarily choose such a life in preference to one of normal, family, social life which exists in every civilised community.[12]

It was a powerful speech but locally at the time it went mainly unreported: nervous Johannesburg newspaper editors published only a few sentences although the text was reproduced substantially in the international press; as Meredith remarks, his trial performance marked the start of his international reputation.[13] Ten minutes after Mandela finished his oration Magistrate van Heerden pronounced sentence: three years' imprisonment. Mandela turned to the gallery and made a clenched fist salute, establishing the courtroom repertoire for the hundreds of ANC captives who followed him into the dock over the next three decades. He was then taken to Pretoria Local prison. His *kaross* was unceremoniously bundled away, and only when naked in front of the officials did Mandela receive his new clothes, the standard prison uniform, tunic, jersey, and short pants. Mandela protested that he would not wear shorts and he refused his dinner, cold mealie (maize) porridge, as inedible. After an interval, the prison commander, Colonel Jacobs, called Mandela to his office. He could wear long trousers and could be served his own specially prepared food, but while enjoying these privileges he would remain in solitary confinement, locked up in his cell, 23 out of 24 hours with just 30 minutes' exercise. Mandela endured these conditions for a few weeks before asking to be confined with the other prisoners, wearing shorts if he had to.

The other prisoners included the Pan-Africanist Congress's (PAC's) leader, Robert Sobukwe. Mandela sat next to Sobukwe in the prison yard most days, sewing mailbags. The two men enjoyed each other's company, calling each other by their clan names, and debating the respective claims to greatness of Shakespeare and Shaw. Mandela persuaded Sobukwe to sign a joint letter of complaint about their treatment at the prison: Sobukwe was initially reluctant, because he believed that any protest about conditions might be interpreted as an acknowledgement of the state's right to confine them. After seven months, at the end of May 1963, without warning, Mandela was told to gather his few personal possessions. Ten minutes later shackled to three other ANC prisoners he was driven through the night to Cape Town. At the dockside the men were placed in the hold of an old ferry. While they waited there, warders on the quay urinated on them, an incident that Mandela refrained from mentioning in his autobiographies. Their reception at the other end of their sea journey, across the bay to Robben Island, was similarly unwelcoming: 'Dis die Eiland! Hier julle gaan vrek! Haak, haak' (This is the island. Here you will die. Move! Move!). The four men once again undressed, an unvarying ritual that marked entry into any new prison in the South African system. Their clothing was immersed in disinfected water and the men were then commanded to put it on again. An official reprimanded one of Mandela's companions for having his hair too long. Mandela pointed out that all of them had been having their hair cut according to regulations. The officer moved towards Mandela threateningly but Mandela forestalled him with a warning that he would take anyone to court who laid hands on him. At this juncture the Commanding Officer appeared, ending any possibility of further confrontation.

Mandela's first journey to Robben Island was during the most brutal phase of its history but the few weeks he spent there in June–July 1963 were relatively benign. He and the other ANC men were placed in a large and well-lit cell and looked after by coloured warders who were willing to bring them cigarettes and sandwiches. After a few days they began work repairing roads and drainage ditches, sometimes in the company of other political prisoners mainly from the PAC, including Mandela's nephew, Nqabeni Menge. Through such contact Mandela was able to lay to rest a widely believed rumour among the Pan-Africanists that, while abroad, he had joined their organisation.

After six weeks, in mid-July Mandela found himself travelling back to Pretoria. A few days before, the police had raided Rivonia, arresting everyone whom they found there, including Sisulu, Ahmed Kathrada, Govan Mbeki, Raymond Mhlaba, Bob Hepple, Denis Goldberg, and Lionel Bernstein. Hepple and Goldberg were relatively minor figures in Umkhonto, Bernstein was more important, and in the cases of Sisulu, Mbeki, and Mhlaba the police had captured the organisation's key African leadership. Later the police arrested Elias Motsoaledi and Andrew Mlangeni, members of Umkhonto's regional command in Johannesburg The police also discovered a quantity of documents, ten of them in Mandela's handwriting, including the diary that he kept while travelling across Africa. The police held their prisoners under the 90-day detention provision in the new Sabotage Act; during this time, Motsoaledi and Mlangeni were tortured. On 9 October, Mandela joined his comrades, 'disgusted to be still wearing his shorts and sandals',[14] in the Pretoria Supreme Court. The men were charged under the Sabotage and Suppression of Communism Act with responsibility for over 200 acts of sabotage aimed at promoting guerrilla warfare and armed invasion, charges that on conviction could lead to a death sentence.

Mandela's African journal contained evidence to support these charges but the centrepiece of the state's case was a six-page

1. Mandela, photographed at the age of 19, on his way to Fort Hare, wearing his first suit.

2. Walter Sisulu at work in the African National Congress (ANC) office, Johannesburg, mid-1950s.

3. Nelson Mandela sparring with Jerry Moloi. Despite his later affection for this photograph at the time it was taken, Mandela persuaded *Drum's* editor not to use it.

4. Chief Albert Luthuli and Oliver Tambo arriving at Pretoria station, 1959. Luthuli is wearing ANC khaki drill with a 'Nehru' cap, generally favoured by Natal Indian Congress leaders. On his left he is being accompanied by a Freedom Volunteer.

5. Nelson Mandela at his law offices, about 1952. © Jürgen Schadeberg

6. Joe Slovo, Mandela and Ruth First during a recess at the Treason Trial in Pretoria, 1959.

(7)

(8)

(9)

7. Dressed for court. (Photographed for a *Drum* profile, 1958.)

8. Winnie Mandela outside the Palace of Justice, Pretoria, during the Rivonia Trial. Accompanying Winnie is her sister who is wearing Xhosa national dress (Winnie herself was prohibited from doing so after the first day of the trial).

9. Mandela burning his pass in Orlando before an audience of journalists in Soweto, 28 March 1960.

10. Mandela addressing the All-in-Africa Conference, Pietermaritzberg, 25 March, 1961.

11. Mandela during his visit to the FLN (Front de Liberation Nationale) headquarters, Oujda, Morocco, March 1972.

12. Mandela in costume as a Xhosa aristocrat. (Photograph taken by Eli Weinberg in 1961. Weinberg was a member of the South African Communist Party (SACP) and the photograph was deliberately posed to project Mandela's 'African' identity at a time when the ANC and its allies were concerned about losing support to their 'Africanist' rivals.)

13. In Section B Robben Island, November 1964. This picture is one of a sequence of photographs taken during a visit to the Island by a reporter from the *Daily Telegraph*. They were the only photographs taken during Mandela's captivity that the South African authorities allowed to be published. For the visit the Section B prisoners were given sewing tasks in place of stone breaking. Mandela is wearing the shorts that were assigned to African prisoners.

14. This photograph was taken on Robben Island, in 1977, during a tour by journalists. The photographs were not released for publication. For the day Section B inmates were given light gardening work: quarry labour ceased that year. Nearest the camera is Justice Mpanza, captured in 1968 during the ANC's Rhodesian guerilla campaign. Toivo ja Toivo, the SWAPO (South West Africa People's Organization) leader, is in the middle.

15. *Time Magazine* cover published on 5 February 1990, shortly before Mandela's release. The artwork reflects the uncertainty about Mandela's physical appearance after 27 years of imprisonment.

16. With Graca Machel, Mandela's third wife, at the Live 8 HIV/AIDS benefit concert in Johannesburg, 2004.

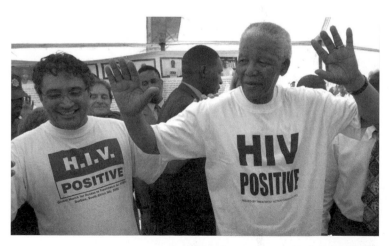

17. Post-presidential activism: Mandela photographed with HIV/AIDS activist, Zachie Achmet, Cape Town, 2001.

document entitled 'Operation Mayibuye', written months after Mandela's arrest and hastily hidden in a stove when the police arrived at Rivonia. 'Operation Mayibuye' was a plan for the launch of a guerrilla war. Operations would begin in the Transkei and the Transvaal borderlands with insurgent landings of several thousand men by submarine and aircraft. The Prosecutor, Percy Yutar, would insist that the project had already been endorsed by the ANC. This was in fact a position that would subsequently be maintained by its authors, Joe Slovo and Mbeki, although most of the other Umkhonto leaders agreed with Mandela that the document represented only a draft, that it had not been approved, and indeed that it was 'entirely unrealistic in its goals and plans'. Fortunately Mandela's co-accused prevailed upon Mbeki not to contradict such arguments in court and he did not, even when under cross-examination. Mbeki's co-author, Slovo, had left South Africa in May to secure Oliver Tambo's support for Operation Mayibuye. He told Tambo's biographer years later that Tambo was so enthusiastic about the plan that 'he did a dance around the room'.[15] Despite its impracticality—even sophisticated conventional armies find seaborne and airborne expeditionary operations challenging—Mayibuye would cast a long shadow; parts of the document resurfaced in the ANC's 'Strategic and Tactics' written by Slovo and adopted in the late 1960s, and influenced its efforts to infiltrate soldiers back into South Africa through Rhodesia. In fact, however, when the ANC finally resumed military operations in South Africa on a significant scale in the late 1970s Umkhonto we Sizwe concentrated its activities in the main cities, as it had done between 1961 and 1965.

Bram Fischer led the defence team that included ex-First World war fighter pilot and Communist Party veteran Vernon Berrange, George Bizos, and Arthur Chaskalson. It was a formidable group. The money to pay them—professionally they were obliged by the Law Society to charge fees notwithstanding their political motivations—was raised abroad, mainly by Canon John Collins. Among other fundraising events Collins organised a special auction at Christie's of artworks donated by Henry Moore, Stanley Spencer, Jacob Epstein, and Pablo Picasso. Collins' efforts enabled 'the luxury of a protracted defence' in which the lawyers' strategy would be to persuade the judge 'to get to know these "terrorists" as men'. Prolonged court proceedings would also provide time for a groundswell of international agitation to accumulate.[16] Fischer's decision to lead the defence was courageous: as a leading figure in the Communist Party he had himself been a frequent visitor to Rivonia through the course of 1962 and had met on these occasions several of the people whom the prosecution were to name as state witnesses.[17]

The defence achieved an early triumph by managing to persuade the judge to quash Yutar's indictment. The Judge, Quartus de Wet, whom Mandela had encountered previously professionally, in his view 'did not have the reputation of being a puppet of the nationalist government'.[18] Yutar's first indictment, a 'shoddy and imprecise document', the defence lawyers discovered,[19] charged the accused with actions under the Sabotage Act that preceded the law's enactment, as well as accusing Mandela of personal involvement in activities that postdated his conviction in November 1962. The state produced a second indictment and subsequently between 3 December and February presented 173 witnesses and several thousand documents including, incredibly, the escape plan that Slovo had prepared for Mandela and, more damagingly, coded messages from Tambo about the travelling arrangements of guerrilla trainees. One of the most damaging witnesses was Bruce Mtolo, a member of the Durban Regional Command who was present at Mandela's address to its members on his return to South Africa, and so was able to confirm Mandela's status as Umkhonto's commander-in-chief. Mtolo had also, later, visited Rivonia. He claimed that Mandela had warned members of the Regional Command against revealing their Communist affiliations if they went abroad in Africa; Mandela's version of this warning was that he had said that if Communists in Umkhonto visited other African countries they should not use their position to advance the interests of the party.[20] Mtolo survived Berrange's cross-examination with much of his testimony looking intact. According to the accused's attorney, Joel Joffe, Mtolo, a recidivist criminal, was an 'old hand' in the witness box, and his evidence was a skilfully 'interwoven mixture of fact and fiction'.[21] He subsequently published his memoirs. Interestingly, although he took pains in the text to discredit most of the Umkhonto leadership as self-serving and corrupt, he presented Mandela in a favourable light, noting that Mandela greeted him from the dock with a smile. Even so, as with the other Umkhonto leaders, Mandela was presented as at least an instrument if not an agent of the Communist Party's manipulation of African nationalism. While Mandela was abroad, Mtolo claimed in his book, 'there was a slight but definite swing from the leadership of Chief Luthuli towards Mandela'. This shift 'was brought about with great care by members of the Communist cells', Mtolo maintained. It was observable in the replacement of the songs sung at meetings about Luthuli by new songs, composed about Mandela.[22]

Fischer and his colleagues received a month's grace to work with the accused in preparing their defence. All were agreed to 'use the court as a platform for our beliefs'.[23] They would admit their involvement in planning and carrying out sabotage but oppose the state's contention that Umkhonto had already decided to launch guerrilla warfare and they would deny the claims of murder that appeared in the indictment; the indictment included references to several fatal attacks although there was no evidence that these were the result of Umkhonto activities. They would also insist on Umkhonto's autonomy from the ANC because they were anxious not to incriminate ANC leaders still at liberty and they would deny that Goldberg, Kathrada, Bernstein, and Mhlaba were members of Umkhonto, because in their cases Yutar's evidence concerning their presence at Rivonia at the time of the police raid or their attendance at earlier meetings was circumstantial. Hepple, with the agreement of his co-accused, had offered to turn state's evidence and on being released had fled the country. Mandela knew that his own documents were sufficient to convict him and decided to make a statement from the dock, a less restricted way of communicating his beliefs than presenting evidence for cross-examination as a witness although carrying less weight from a legal perspective, because he could not engage in argumentative exchanges with the prosecution. His assumption of the role of spokesman accorded with the public projection of his heroic role by the Communist Party as an 'African leader of a new type'.[24] Joffe, while working with him in preparing the defence case, noticed how the impact of his personality extended beyond his co-accused and their lawyers, impacting itself also on the prison officials: 'somehow Nelson was treated in a particular way—not quite with deference, for that is not the word—rather with respect'.[25] Rusty Bernstein confirmed this observation in his memoir, noting that during the trial 'several white warders turn to him for help with the essays they have to write to earn their promotion'.[26]

Mandela delivered his statement on 20 April. He read it slowly speaking for four hours to complete the text that he had prepared over the previous two weeks. At its beginning he admitted 'immediately' that he had helped to form Umkhonto. In doing so he was not, he said, under the influence of foreigners or communists, rather he was prompted by his 'own proudly felt African background'. This background included childhood memories of the tales told to him by 'the elders of my tribe', tales 'of wars fought by our ancestors in defence of the fatherland'. He reviewed the political history of the ten years that had preceded Umkhonto's formation before turning to the organisation itself. Umkhonto's members were not subject to ANC discipline, the ANC remained committed to non-violence, Mandela insisted, but even within Umkhonto the 'ANC heritage of non-violence and racial harmony was very much with us'. Consequently, in making its own plans, Umkhonto adopted an approach that 'was flexible and which permitted us to act in accordance with the needs of the times':

> . . . above all, the plan had to be one which recognized civil war as the last resort, and left the decision on this question to the future. We did not want to be committed to civil war, but we wanted to be ready if it became inevitable . . .[27]

Sabotage was a logical choice: it need not inflict loss of life and hence in a South African setting 'it offered the best hope for future race relations'. The architects of the campaign, Mandela explained, believed that South Africa's dependence on foreign capital made it vulnerable and that sabotage would 'scare away capital from the country', in the end imposing economic costs that would compel 'voters of the country to reconsider their position'. The preparations for guerrilla warfare—the training facilities that Mandela negotiated for in early 1962—were a contingency measure. Mandela then addressed the relationship between the ANC and the Communist Party, noting their separate goals while conceding their present co-operation, co-operation that was 'not proof of a complete community of interests'. Mandela's statement ended in a more personal vein. He was an African patriot, a kinsman of chiefs, and an admirer of the structure and organisation of pre-colonial African society. To be sure, he had been influenced by Marxist thought but he was not a communist, for example, he differed from the Communists to whom he had spoken in his admiration for the parliamentary system of the west, particularly in his respect for British parliamentary institutions, 'the most democratic in the world'. Umkhonto was formed by Africans and it was not fighting for a communist state. It was fighting for dignity, for decent livelihoods, and for equal political rights. Mandela's ideal remained 'a democratic and free society in which all persons live together in harmony and with equal opportunities'. It was an ideal, he told the court, against Bram Fischer's advice, for which he was prepared to die.[28]

At the end of end of his silence, Mandela refrained from turning to the gallery, 'though I felt all their eyes on me'. He sat down and it seemed to him that there was silence that lasted for many minutes, though it was probably of only 30 seconds' duration. From the gallery he heard 'what sounded like a great sigh, followed by the cries of women'.[29] This time the South African newspapers accorded his words full recognition, the *Rand Daily Mail* printing the text almost in its entirety, the first of many subsequent publications, as an anti-apartheid manifesto inside and outside South Africa. It was certainly one of the most effective rhetorical texts delivered by a South African politician, both because of its movement backwards and forwards between autobiographical confession and political prospectus and because of its powerful use of repetition: 'I have fought against white domination . . . I have fought against black domination. . . . It is an ideal which I hope to live for . . . it is an ideal for which I am prepared to die.' These were devices that would continue to characterise

Mandela's oratory throughout his political life.[30] Mandela's speech received sympathetic treatment even in the more conservative sections of the British press: it also elicited admiration in British and American diplomatic despatches.[31] In the seven weeks between Mandela's statement and his conviction there were demonstrations in European capitals and the USA, a UN Security Council call for amnesty and an all-night vigil in London's St Paul's Cathedral. Immediately after Mandela's delivery, however, Judge Quartus de Wet abruptly summoned the next witness although the court session was well past its normal daily limit.

The defence case lasted for a month: Sisulu spent five days in the witness box, successfully maintaining his key argument that Operation Mayibuye was merely a proposal and, moreover, one that would have been unlikely to succeed if implemented. Sisulu's evidence was probably decisive in persuading Justice de Wet that the accused had not committed themselves to guerrilla war. In his final verdict, however, delivered on 11 June, he found all the accused present guilty of sabotage charges with the exception of Bernstein. Winnie and Mandela's mother were present, Winnie abiding by the condition for her attendance that she should not wear Xhosa costume; once again she had ignored the advice of Mandela's village elders and neglected to take the *muti* (herbal medicine) that they had prescribed.[32] That night Mandela, Sisulu, and Mbeki informed their lawyers that they would not appeal, the risk of a death sentence notwithstanding. The risk was considerable, the lawyers advised. Mandela's view was that an appeal would weaken their stance politically: they should not rely on a state institution to upset a death sentence—'only the struggle and international solidarity could save us from the gallows'.[33] He may have been right: George Bizos had in fact been told by the British Consul, on the basis of intelligence sources, that the death sentence would not be imposed.[34] The diplomat was not completely sober at the time and even if Mandela had this information relying on it would have been a gamble. On 12 June after listening to pleas in mitigations from the novelist Alan Paton and Harold Hansen, a legal specialist in clemency arguments, Judge de Wet pronounced sentence: life imprisonment for all whom he had convicted, the maximum prison term, and especially severe on those of Mandela's co-accused against whom the charges were relatively minor. Mandela and the others were taken downstairs and escorted out of the back of the building to avoid them passing through the crowd of 2,000 assembled in front. They were locked up in Pretoria Local but at midnight they were taken from their cells, provided with sandwiches and soft drinks, and driven to a military airfield. A few hours later the prisoners from the Rivonia trial landed on Robben Island.

6

PRISONER 466/64

From August 1962, Nelson Mandela spent 27 years and six months in captivity. For more than 17 years of his sentence he was held on Robben Island, prisoner 466/64. He lived together with between 20 and 30 other prisoners convicted for political offences in Section B of a specially built one-storey block, enclosing a courtyard.

Robben Island accommodated African, Indian, and coloured political prisoners between 1962 and 1991. Numbers fluctuated; from the mid to the late 1960s there were well over 1,000 Pan Africanist Congress (PAC) and African National Congress (ANC) men on the island as well as a sprinkling of activists from other smaller organisations, and at first about the same number of common-law prisoners— that is, prisoners convicted for ordinary crimes not politically motivated offences.[1] Numbers shrank as prisoners completed their sentences although the prison population expanded again after the 1976 Soweto uprising. The first political activists to arrive were from the ANC's rival, the PAC, and PAC prisoners outnumbered the ANC group until the late 1960s. From the late 1960s until the mid-1980s most prisoners convicted under security or treason legislation were sent to Robben Island. From 1963 their captors, the warders, were exclusively white, usually Afrikaans speaking.

The political prisoners were divided into two groups. The block of single cells—that is, individual cells each housing one prisoner— separated a small number of well-known prisoners from a much larger group that were kept in 'general' dormitory-type cells. The single cells were often called the 'leadership section' although senior PAC and ANC men were also from time to time placed in general cells. All the Rivonia trial prisoners were confined in single cells. Until 1968, the general cell population also included criminals serving long sentences for common-law offences. Single cell prisoners worked and lived separately from the general cell inmates and officials did their best to prevent communication between them. The roughly square prison compound also included a hospital and a kitchen in which food for all prisoners was prepared. In Mandela's block a separate section contained isolation or punishment cells in which prisoners were kept in solitary confinement. In the single section the cells were just large enough for a tall man to lie down. Each cell had a window about one foot square, overlooking the courtyard around which the sections were constructed. The walls between the cells were two feet thick preventing any communication between them. Until 1977 prisoners normally slept on the floor. For this purpose, when Mandela arrived at Section B, he was issued with a sisal mat and three blankets. He was to sleep on the floor until the mid-1970s when the International Red Cross (IRC) persuaded the authorities to furnish the cells in Section B with beds.

From 4.30pm to 6.45am prisoners remained in their cells. Awoken at 5.30am they were meant to arise, clean their cells, and tidy their bedding. The warder would open their doors at 6.45am and Mandela and his neighbours could then empty their sanitary buckets before common-law (criminal as opposed to political) prisoners arrived with breakfast. After a few months the prisoners ate their breakfast in the courtyard and Mandela resumed his daily regime of early morning running, jogging around the courtyard perimeter for half an hour or so. After inspection there was work—repetitious manual labour—until noon. After lunch the prisoners worked again until 4.00pm. The prisoners were allowed 30 minutes to wash or shower (with cold seawater) before taking their suppers to eat in their cells. At 8.00pm, warders ordered their charges to sleep although the light in each cell remained switched on: it was never dark in Section B. Prisoners were forbidden to own watches, a simple proscription that deprived them of a basic source of self-reliance: the daily routine was marked off by bells, whistles, and the warders' commands. As soon as he moved into his cell, Mandela made himself a calendar.

When Mandela arrived, cooking was undertaken by the common-law prisoners and at best was monotonously unappetising, at worst, in the recollection of one of the Robben Island warders, 'not the sort I would feed to a dog'.[2] Breakfast comprised cold mealie pap (corn meal) porridge, protone sauce, and coffee made from burned mealie (corn) meal. Lunch was boiled corncobs and *phuzamandla*, a supposedly nutritious drink made from cornflower and yeast. Another helping of porridge enriched with the odd vegetable and, every other day, a small piece of meat constituted supper. Mandela believed that portions were often scant because the criminal chefs in the kitchen kept the more choice items for themselves. African prisoners were meant to receive 12 ounces of cornmeal a day and five ounces of meat every two days: Indians and coloureds received slightly larger quantities until 1979 when a common diet was instituted.

The Section B prisoners first worked just outside their cell corridor, in the courtyard, placed in four rows, one and a half yards apart, sitting cross-legged, in absolute silence hammering stones into gravel. The prisoners wore wire masks to protect their eyes. In January 1965, after three months of stone hammering, there was a change of assignment. Mandela's group would walk each day to a lime quarry, about 20 minutes' walk away. The work was more strenuous, because the lime had to be levered out of thin seams with picks, and the conditions were unpleasant. Until the prisoners were allowed to purchase sunglasses three years later, the glare from the limestone was painful—it damaged Mandela's eyes permanently—and, of course, it made the quarry very hot in the summer. However, the walk to and from the cell block and the nature of the work itself, which required a degree of joint effort, supplied opportunities for conversation despite its formal prohibition. Mandela and his Section B neighbours would spend almost every working day for the next 14 years in the lime quarry. The nature of the work to which they were assigned was comparable to the tasks given to all black prisoners in South African prisons. White convicts, including the political prisoners who were held at Pretoria central, were employed in workshops as carpenters or in the prisons' gardens.

Within the classificatory system used by the South African authorities, prisoners were graded with respect to their treatment and the privileges to which they were entitled, earning improvements in their status through orderly behaviour. Category D inmates such as Mandela and the other inmates were supposedly at the base of the prison hierarchy, allowed only two visits and two letters a year (only from close family members), unable to receive money or make purchases, and ineligible for study rights. In fact Mandela was treated with a degree of circumspection by the prison authorities. On the flight from Pretoria he was not manacled, unlike his fellow triallists, and on arrival at the island he was permitted to resume his University of London Bachelor of Law course. Mandela told Anthony Sampson that this treatment may have been prompted by his Transkeien royal connections; it is also possible that the Ministry of Justice was prompted by the international attention that the Rivonia trial generated. The other Rivonia prisoners had to wait until mid-1965 before they were allowed to enrol for degrees or matriculation studies through the University of South Africa and the Rapid Results College, both institutions that offered correspondence courses. Over the years most of the prisoners in Section B acquired an impressive range of academic qualifications: Eddie Daniels, arriving on the island with a Standard 8 certificate (the junior secondary completion qualification, normally obtained at the age of 16) completed his sentence with two degrees.[3]

Whatever considerations affected the senior authorities' attitude to Mandela, the warders treated him as roughly as his comrades. As was routine, the new arrivals had to strip outside the old corrugated iron jail where they were to be kept for four days until the completion of the construction of the Section B cells. Before they were handed their khaki tunics, jerseys, and shorts the naked men were searched. This was a humiliating procedure, 'no way to treat someone of my standing', Mandela commented later.[4] Normally it required prisoners to leap up and down to loosen any concealed objects, finally bending over to expose their rectums to the warders, although Mandela does not mention this in his memoir. Until 1967, the 'tausa', as this ritual was named by the prisoners, was part of the daily routine for the general section (although the political prisoners usually refused to do it), but the Section B inmates seem to have been exempt. Mandela once again protested against having to wear shorts.

After a few days in Section B he asked to see the Commanding Officer to whom he presented a list of complaints: grown men should not have to wear shorts, the cell walls were still damp, and the food was rancid. A week or so later Mandela returned to his cell after work to find a pair of long trousers. They were taken away after he insisted that before he could wear them similar clothing should be issued to others. The African prisoners in Section B would have to wait for nearly two years before they could all wear trousers. Coloured and Indian prisoners were dressed better; they were allowed trousers, socks, and underwear. For black South Africans, shorts were demeaning garments, normally worn by schoolchildren, not adults.

'Prison life settled into a routine', Mandela wrote 30 years later, 'each day like the one before, each week like the one before it, so that the months and the years blend into each other.' Narratives of this period of Mandela's life project a sense of the predictable and regimented rhythm of life in prison through concentrating on the minute details of its routine—the slight variations over time in conditions helped to emphasise its repetitive and generally uniform quality. Understandably, however, existing treatments during Mandela's life, including his own, as well as first-hand accounts by his fellow prisoners, structure their narratives by organising them around the more exceptional dimensions of prison experience. These include the various efforts, both individual and corporate, to challenge or ameliorate the prison regime as well as the occasional relief from it supplied by visitors and other kinds of contact with the outside world. Much of the time, however, prisoners lived alone, in the company of their own thoughts and memories, locked up in a small space for 15 hours a day. In this discussion of Mandela's term on Robben Island, I begin with the experiences that he shared with his comrades, considering first the ways in which he and the other men in Section B attempted to resist the prison regime. As will be evident, visitors played an important role in the success of their efforts to secure reforms. I then look at the degree to which they succeeded in exercising authority and leadership within the larger prison community and, increasingly, outside it as well. But it would be misleading to project Mandela's life on the Island only through his contributions to its heroic collective experience. More than even before, Mandela's life was solitary and introspective and domestic: an inner world constructed from recollections of family and friendship, and recorded in an intimate reflective language of letter writing quite different from his authoritative public prose in the courtroom.

As we have just seen, Mandela was prepared to assert what he took to be rights and prerogatives from the very beginning. The seven Rivonia prisoners joined a small but politically heterodox community. Its members included a PAC leader, Zephania Mothopeng, whom Mandela knew quite well, Billy Nair of Umkhonto's Durban following, George Peake, another Umkhonto saboteur, as well as a city councillor in Cape Town, and the poet Dennis Brutus, convicted for disobeying his banning restriction. There were three 'aged peasants' from the Transkei who at the PAC's behest had tried to assassinate Mandela kinsman, Kaiser Matanzima. The PAC enjoyed rather more success than its rival in assembling a rural following in the Transkei, mainly because of its popularity among Transkeien migrant workers in Cape Town. The far left was represented by Neville Alexander and Fikele Bam, adherents of the Yu Chi Chan Club, a Maoist assembly rounded up at an even earlier stage of its planned insurgency than the Umkhonto High Command. Within a few months, Umkhonto's successor High Command members were also imprisoned in Section B—Mac Maharaj, Laloo Chiba, and Wilton Mkwayi. Eddie Daniels, a member of the African Resistance Movement (ARM), was the twentieth and final person to join the original Section B group of prisoners. Mandela made friends with Daniels, a much younger man, at a time when his politically less tolerant comrades treated the fresh arrival with reserve: the ARM was a group established by Trotskyites and former members of the Liberal Party. Over the subsequent years the friendship between the two men became very close: Mandela would share his letters with Daniels and discuss family matters. Shortly after arriving Daniels fell ill, and Mandela helped him in his cell, folding bedding and emptying his sanitary bucket.

These were mainly men who were accustomed to occupying leadership positions and several of them were well educated:

Mothopeng, Mandela, Brutus, and Alexander had obtained university degrees, and Maharaj had attended the London School of Economics. They were very different from the tough but subservient felons whom the warders were used to managing. The criminals collaborated with the warders in ill treating political prisoners in the general section, especially on the 800-strong work detail that laboured at the stone quarry, the location for most of the worst brutalities recorded in prisoners' autobiographies, including the occasion when warders had buried two PAC men up to the neck for a whole day and periodically urinated upon them.[5] Casual beatings were more routine and general section prisoners were also, more occasionally, caned for insubordination,[6] a punishment that does not seem to have ever been inflicted on prisoners in Section B. Political prisoners in the dormitory cells were also vulnerable to sexual assaults, a danger mentioned in several of their autobiographies,[7] and to which there is no reference in the memoirs of Section B inmates. Any physical abuse of the Section B prisoners was more unusual despite their refusal from the start to defer to the warders' authority by calling them 'baas' (master). Shortly after his arrival, however, Alexander witnessed a 'carry on', a mass assault on the workers in the stone quarry, a reprisal for complaints about conditions, in which the warders used pick handles and batons to beat up their charges. Alexander himself was beaten with a rubber pipe that day when the 'carry on' was extended to include his group which was working nearby, collecting seaweed. He was still convalescing from a bullet wound in his stomach, received at the time of his arrest.

Understandably, Alexander tended to view warders as generally vicious. In his recollections, even Mandela, during this early particularly brutal phase, 'had already come to believe that the warders were not uniformly hostile' and that 'our occupation of the moral high ground could make it possible for us to turn some of the warders around'.[8] Mandela may have been influenced by the humanity of some of the warders that he had experienced during his first visit to the island. His views may also have been shaped by his earlier professional experiences with officials in which, as we have seen, he sometimes encountered empathy and even compassion in morally complicated adversaries. Mandela's views appear to have been shared by some of the others: in 1966 Maharaj helped a warder write an entry for a newspaper competition; in return he asked for cigarettes. Subsequently Maharaj used this favour as a source of leverage, despite moral objections from Walter Sisulu, and compelled the warder to supply them with a daily newspaper. Later on the prisoners would routinely exchange cartons of cigarettes for newspapers with warders.[9] Prisoners were forbidden newspapers; Mandela had already served a short spell in solitary confinement in the isolation section on a rice water diet after stealing the night warder's newspaper.

In the course of 1965, supervision at the lime quarry became more relaxed; the warders allowed the Section B team to talk as much as they liked as long as they continued to work. One of their guards remained obdurate and demanded silence: Mandela nominated a 'certain comrade' to accord especial respect 'to this fellow'.[10] The civility was worthwhile: one day the warder offered Mandela's comrade his half-eaten sandwich, an initiation of wary friendship which extended its embrace as he began to engage more widely in conversations with the prisoners. Warders were in fact warned not to engage the prisoners in informal exchanges; any social contact, they were told, might lead to them being 'enticed into friendship and then blackmail'.[11]

The food deliveries represented another opportunity for subverting authority. In the second half of 1965 Kathrada and Maharaj constituted a Communications Committee. They persuaded the common-law prisoners who brought in breakfast and supper to transport messages written on toilet paper and wrapped up in plastic or matchboxes and concealed in the food drums. Occasionally Mandela and the other Section B prisoners provided legal advice and assistance to common-law prisoners. Through this conduit in July 1966, the men in Section B received news of a hunger strike undertaken in protest against a reduction in rations. The Section B group joined the protest, refusing their food for several days, despite the inclusion of abundant quantities of meat and vegetables in the meals on the second day, and the intensification of the labour regime at the quarry. Mandela was summoned by Colonel Wessels, the commanding officer, to explain why the Section B inmates had joined the strike. The strike seems to have ended in victory, though not as a consequence of Mandela's representations to Wessels; the authorities offered concessions to the general section prisoners after warders themselves protested over the quality of the food served in their cafeteria. Mandela suggests in his autobiography that this was the first hunger strike by prisoners, but in fact the general section prisoners had earlier mounted two such protests, in 1963 and 1965, against particularly brutal behaviour by warders.[12]

The South African authorities denied that they held any political prisoners. In reality they accorded to security law offenders distinctive treatment, beginning with their arrest under the Sabotage Act which permitted indefinite detention in police cells before they were charged, as well as the confinement of men convicted for politically motivated offences in a specially constructed prison with no remission of sentences. More positively, the Minister of Justice from time to time also sanctioned occasional visits by journalists, representatives of the IRC and, beginning in 1967, from Helen Suzman, the only parliamentarian willing to take an active interest in the treatment of Robben Island prisoners. These occasional interruptions to prison routine began unpromisingly in November 1964 when the Section B prisoners entered their courtyard to find piles of old jerseys and sacks to sit on in place of the hammers and stones. They were told to repair rents in the clothing. Later that morning a reporter and a photographer from the British *Daily Telegraph* appeared. Mandela was allowed to speak to the reporter for 20 minutes and permitted a picture to be taken of him in conversation with Sisulu, the only picture of him in prison ever published during his captivity. When the visit was over, the men were given back their hammers and stones. A few months later Mr Henning of the American Bar Association paid a call, in the company of General Steyn, the prison commissioner. Mandela was allowed to act as the prisoners' spokesman and presented their complaints about the working conditions. The commissioner was 'courtly', doffing his hat and calling Mandela and his comrades gentlemen.

Henning was less civil: he appeared to be inebriated and he

observed that prisoners all over the world had to work and conditions at Robben Island compared favourably with American institutions (which, with respect to Section B, at least, may have been the case). Henning was a discouraging representative of his profession but Mandela's own professional body, the Transvaal Law Society were hardly more sympathetic: they tried to strike Mandela off the roll, a decision that Mandela announced he would contest, provoking a lengthy exchange of correspondence until the Society retreated. Towards the end of 1965 the Section B inmates were informed that a visit from an IRC delegate was pending. Through Mandela prisoners submitted a formal list of issues concerning food, family visits, letter censorship, studies, exercise, hard labour, and abuse from warders and once again Mandela was assigned the duty of acting as spokesman. The IRC man, Hans Sen, although Swedish resided in Rhodesia and he appeared unsympathetic, telling Mandela that mealies were a healthy alternative to bread, especially for Africans. Subsequently, however, all the prisoners in Section B received long trousers. Later IRC representatives were more assertive, obtaining better provision for studies including desks and stools and a wider range of literary material: Maharaj was even allowed to subscribe to the *Economist* until the authorities discovered that it was a news journal. From 1968, the men in Section B were allowed to subscribe to a range of magazines including *Reader's Digest* (which arrived heavily mutilated by the censor's scissors), *Huisgenoot* (a popular Afrikaans women's magazine), and *Farmer's Weekly*.[13]

Suzman's visit was preceded by a change for the worse in the quarry's management. A new senior warder, Van Rensburg, reimposed the conversation ban and charged the prisoners almost daily with breaches of prison regulations, real and imagined. The prisoners nicknamed him 'suitcase', a reference to the oversize lunch box that he brought with him and which they refused to carry for him. Bam, Maharaj, and Mandela announced the formation of a legal committee and for each charge demanded in writing 'further particulars'. Exasperated, Van Rensburg laid charges against Mandela and Bam but these were repudiated and later the prisoners heard that he had been reprimanded. One day in early 1967 Van Rensburg once again ordered the prisoners to work in silence, but the Commanding Officer, Major Kellerman, visited the quarry at lunch and counter-manded Van Rensburg's instructions. When the prisoners returned to Section B Mandela discovered that he had been assigned to another cell, number 18 at the end of the corridor. Obviously an important event was in the offing. The next day Suzman was shown into Section B: each prisoner greeted her but when she asked if they had any complaints they referred her to Mandela with whom the prison authorities hoped she would spend least time. Suzman wrote later that she was 'appalled' by the conditions that she found in the Section and she was unimpressed by Van Rensburg, not least because of the swastika that he had tattooed on his wrist.[14] She complained about the prisoners' treatment in parliament, an act of some courage given her solitary status within the House of Assembly as its only woman member and its only representative of the liberal Progressive Party. She managed to persuade Piet Pelser, the Justice Minister, to arrange Van Rensburg's transfer. Suzman visited the Island a further six times and partly as a consequence of her influence from 1967 working conditions became increasingly benign. By 1969 the prisoners were working only periodically: the warders would warn them if their senior officers were approaching so that they could pick up tools. On Sundays, instead of being locked up all day in their cells, the prisoners were allowed to spend several hours together and pro-vided with board games and cards, entitlements arising from their acquisition of higher classifications. Sometimes their food included eggs and fruit. The free association periods allowed to Section B prisoners on Sundays were of decisive importance in enabling them to develop an organised corporate life. In 1967 they were permitted to hold a memorial service for Albert Luthuli who had been killed while crossing a railway line near his home.

Despite these improvements, in January 1970 Mandela wrote a long letter of complaint to the Commissioner. Here he referred to the abusive treatment still meted out to general section prisoners, noting that 'we have always accepted that firmness and discipline is a neces-sary instruments for the preservation of law and order in a prison'. However, the letter continued, 'human beings are more likely to be influenced by exemplary conduct on the part of the officials than by brute force'. In the same restrained collegial tone, Mandela's letter also drew attention to the pointless menial tasks that they all had to perform, and the denial to them of any work that 'may encourage and develop a sense of self respect'. The Commissioner had on several occasions discouraged Mandela from acting as a representative: 'Nelson', he once exclaimed, 'you are a prisoner.' His response on this occasion was to appoint a harsh disciplinarian as Commanding Officer. Colonel Badenhorst withdrew many of the recent concessions, cutting down on study time and restricting prisoners' common recreational periods. He cancelled prisoners' visits and replaced the older warders with younger and more officious functionaries who would confiscate books and papers during suddenly arranged cell inspections. Apparently, Badenhorst instructed his subordinates that it was their 'job here to demoralise these people . . . for our race, for the white people whose country this is'.[15] Badenhorst visited the lime quarry to confirm the reports that he had heard that the prisoners were not working. Displeased with what he found there he told Mandela that he and the others should 'pull their fingers out', an expression that Mandela 'did not care for at all'.[16] That evening he lined up all the Section B inmates and reduced their classifications.

The behaviour of Badenhorst's subordinates deteriorated. In May a band of SWAPO (South West African People's Organization) insurgents led by Toivo ja Toivo arrived in the isolation section. In protest against their confinement they started a hunger strike, which the men in Section B joined. On the night of 28 May a group of drunken warders raided the Isolation section and Section B, beating up the guerrillas and insisting on searching the Section B cells. Everybody had to strip and stand with their hands raised for nearly an hour. It was a cold night and Govan Mbeki collapsed and needed to be taken to hospital in Cape Town. Shortly thereafter, Mandela managed to send a message out of the prison to the mainland; he also led a delegation of prisoners to Badenhorst to protest against the warders' actions. Badenhorst, possibly unnerved by Mbeki's collapse, received the delegation in a conciliatory manner. Next month the Commissioner arrived in the company of three judges from the Cape

Provincial Division and asked to meet a spokesman for the prisoners. Although offered the opportunity to confer with the visitors privately, Mandela insisted that Badenhorst should be present while he described the events of 28 May. Badenhorst was replaced within three months. Before leaving he summoned Mandela for a surprising reason given the earlier sentiments that he addressed to his staff: he wanted 'to wish all you people good luck', a conciliatory farewell gesture that Mandela much later recorded for posterity as a 'useful reminder that all men . . . have a core of decency'.[17]

Badenhorst's successor, Colonel Johan Willemse, was conciliatory from the beginning; he had apparently been instructed by the Commissioner to institute a more enlightened regime and he was to gain a reputation among Red Cross officials and prisoners as a reformist.[18] Mandela requested an introductory meeting and found the new Commanding Officer polite and reasonable. Even Alexander was to concede that, in Willemse, they were encountering 'a quality person'.[19] Willemse visited the quarry a few days after meeting Mandela for the first time and was taken aback by the absence of work; the prisoners paid no attention to the warders' instructions, he perceived. He told Mandela that 'there must be some discipline. It is not only good for us but good for you'. Mandela acknowledged that the Colonel was making a legitimate point and requested to organise a courtyard meeting of the men in the single cells, hitherto a prohibited event. Willemse eventually agreed and at the meeting it was resolved that Section B inmates 'would at least appear to be working' although what work they did would be at their own pace.[20] Over the next few years the prisoners would evolve their own code of behaviour: they would avoid provoking the warders while insisting on their own dignity, rudeness would be 'rebutted, firmly but politely, as far as possible'.[21] Mandela's relationship with the warders would become increasingly complicated. According to Michael Dingake, released from Section B in 1980:

With junior officers who knew their position, Nelson was charming and fatherly. Many young wardens were friendly with him, occasionally soliciting advice from him in connection with their jobs or social problems. Some brought him greetings from their parents, who wanted very much to meet him, and envied their sons who were privileged to know this great man in prison.[22]

One of these warders, James Gregory, published a ghost-written autobiography in 1995. He arrived on Robben Island in 1967, a former traffic policeman, at the time aged 24 years. His father was the descendant of Scots settlers, '*rooinek*' (red-neck) ancestry that made him the target of bullying at the Afrikaans schools he attended. Relatively better educated than many of his colleagues he was put in charge of the letter censorship office, but he also undertook guard duties in Section B over the weekends, meeting the prisoners there in a relatively relaxed environment. Having grown up on a farm, he was a fluent Zulu speaker and this attribute together with a fairly genial manner made him especially susceptible to Mandela's charm. The time of his arrival was at a time when warders as well as prisoners worked under a harshly authoritarian administration: the absence of camaraderie between older and younger officials that is evident in Gregory's narrative may have helped to soften the latter's attitudes to the men whom they guarded. As Gregory's duties included the administration of prisoners' correspondence his contact with them was necessarily not simply restricted to giving orders; letters were a crucial domain of prisoner entitlements and hence they could ask for information about their arrival. In other words information about letters represented a topic that was an exception to the general principle laid down in warders' regulations 'that the only time that we should talk to the prisoners was when we wanted them to do something'.[23] For Gregory, however, 'common sense prevailed': in reassuring his prisoners that letters had not been withheld or lost 'there was no reason why I should not be civil'.[24]

That the Section B group could maintain rules about its members' behaviour—and such conventions influenced prisoners in the general section as well—is a reflection of the degree to which the community was developing its own institutional life. From its origins in the communications system established by Kathrada and Maharaj, the senior ANC men developed an organised leadership structure. The first formation set up in 1965 was the so-called 'High Organ', originally composed of all the former National Executive members, Mandela, Sisulu, Mbeki, and Mhlaba. To diversify its composition—all the Organ's founders were Xhosas—a fifth rotating member was appointed: Kathrada, Mkwayi, and Chiba were in turn invited to join. The Organ had subordinate structures including committees appointed within the general section inmates. These bodies addressed discipline, political education, academic study, and news distribution. In each dormitory, four cell members would sleep on adjacent mats. A broader formation was established, to unite all prisoners and generally concern itself with grievances and disciplinary issues. It was itself named after Ulundi, the capital of the Zulu kingdom. Chaired initially by Mandela it included representatives of all the political organisations present on the island. One of its first undertakings was the drafting of an all-prisoner petition. Later, *Ulundi* was replaced with a series of non-partisan functional structures: examples included the Recreation and the Red Cross Committees.

At its inception the High Organ's main concern was with the regulation of day-to-day prison life among the ANC prisoners, but it soon became preoccupied with wider issues. During the late 1960s the men arrested between 1962 and 1965 in the first phase of Umkhonto activities were augmented by a trickle of fresh captives: in 1968—for example, captured members of an expedition infiltrated into Zimbabwe by the external ANC leadership joined the island community. There were occasional efforts by released prisoners to reorganise ANC groups within the country. These usually resulted in early arrests and the arrival of new prisoners. The younger men were often quite ignorant of the ANC's history and its policies and, on the initiative of Sisulu, the High Organ developed 'a course of study', known as 'Syllabus A', comprising two years of lectures on ANC history. Syllabus B, taught later, contained instruction in more general areas of theory: Mandela taught a course on political economy, 'sketching out the path from ancient communal societies to feudalism to capitalism and socialism', an approach that he considered was 'not ideological, but . . . biased in favour of socialism'.[25] The teaching of these courses was undertaken through informal discussions at the lime quarry: Mandela's 'modified Socratic method'[26] of instruction involved intensive cross-examination, an experience that could be a severe ordeal for his pupils. The programme extended its embrace to the general section: written-out versions of the lectures were smuggled out of Section B.

The ANC's intellectual life on the island did not confine itself to pedagogy. Members of the High Organ could find themselves at odds with each other over issues of strategy and political principle. Early during their sentences they continued to disagree over the merits of 'Operation Mayibuye', Mandela and Sisulu contesting Mbeki and Mhlaba's contention that a guerrilla war could be fought from bases inside South Africa, as it had in Cuba and China. 'In our view', Mandela wrote in 1976, 'the way in which guerrilla warfare started in the Portuguese territories of Angola, Mozambique and Portuguese Guinea seemed a better guide for our plans.'[27] In these territories insurgents were able to establish bases in neighbouring countries—an option denied to the ANC until Mozambique's and Angola's independence in 1974. Argument also continued about Umkhonto's performance because the eastern Cape leaders were disinclined to share Mandela's view that, by 1963, 'acts of sabotage were fizzling out' and that 'the enemy' had reduced Umkhonto 'to a shadow of itself'.[28] Mandela and Mbeki also differed sharply over another issue— whether the ANC should endorse any kind of participation in the official political life of the homelands; here the disagreement reflected the contrasting social and political backgrounds of the two men. Mbeki's birth in a Christian family of peasant modernisers in Fingoland, in the southern Transkei, and his early engagement in Marxism helped to predispose him to take a bleakly contemptuous view of patrimonial leadership in the countryside: chiefs and headmen were locked into a system of state oppression, the government's 'perfect spies', he maintained. Mbeki was convinced that the peasantry had been 'consistent in thinking along military lines' well before Umkhonto's genesis and that they represented a ready following for a revolutionary war.[29] The political tensions between the two men reflected their different personalities: Mbeki was austere, absolutist, and uncompromising. He was also less willing than the other Rivonia prisoners to accept Mandela's leadership status. Antipathy between

Mandela and Mbeki prompted a reconstitution of the High Organ in 1972, although its four original members returned to office in 1975.[30] Disagreements about contact with homeland leaders resurfaced when Mandela insisted on maintaining a friendly correspondence with Chief Mangosuthu Buthelezi, the first minister of Kwa-Zulu Natal, and an acquaintance of Mandela's from the late 1940s when Buthelezi had briefly associated himself with the ANC Youth League while attending Fort Hare.[31] Mandela had remained in touch with Buthelezi through the 1950s; Buthelezi accompanied King Cyprian Bhekkuzulu on two visits to Mandela's home and office in Johannesburg.[32] In a letter to Princess Irene Buthelezi, the Chief's wife, written in August 1969, he reminded her 'that I highly value my association with your family and I hold the Chief in high esteem'.[33] He continued to write to Buthelezi even after the Chief began publishing Mandela's letters in an effort to enhance his own political credentials as a 'liberation' politician.

Disagreements within the Rivonia group and other senior ANC veterans assumed a fresh significance in the mid-1970s when supporters of the Black Consciousness Movement (BCM) began to serve sentences on the island. The BCM emerged out of student politics at segregated universities after black student leaders broke away from the non-racial National Union of South African Students. Taking their cue from the Black Power movement in the USA, student leaders argued that a common experience of racial oppression among black, Indian, and coloured individuals supplied a basis of social identity that whites could not share; hence the struggle for liberation would be a black struggle, excluding even sympathetic whites, building its following through a message of group affirmation. BCM leaders were arrested after mounting a rally in Durban to celebrate the accession to power in Mozambique of Frente de Libertaçao de Moçambique (FRELIMO), the Mozambican liberation front. They were accommodated in single cells in Section A, sharing certain facilities with the Section B men. For the ANC elders, this new cohort of activists represented a challenge. The students were initially critical of the polite conventions that the Section B principals had evolved in their interaction with the prison authorities and they were also disinclined to defer to their political authority. They were derisive about the modest concessions that the Section B inmates had extracted from the authorities. 'They regarded us as moderates', Mandela recalled, two decades later.[34] On several occasions prison officials asked Mandela to persuade the new islanders to be more co-operative, a request that he sensibly declined. After 16 June 1976 the prison population would become younger. A secondary school protest in Soweto against the teaching of Afrikaans triggered a massive insurrection by schoolchildren and unemployed youngsters across most of the towns in South Africa; although not organised by the BCM the participants in this revolt used its phraseology and were influenced by its ideas.

It was in this setting that a fresh dispute opened up within the High Organ between Mandela and Mbeki. This time it was over whether the Communist Party and the ANC were distinct organisations and, more importantly, whether 'the Liberation Movement aspires to set up a people's democracy or a bourgeois democracy'. Mandela maintained the position that he had adopted 20 years previously, that the Freedom Charter was not a recipe for socialism, indeed that it represented 'a step towards bourgeois democracy', and that the ANC was a broad alliance of different class interests and moreover could work with all opponents of apartheid and fascism, including the BCM and even homeland political organisations. Mbeki contended that, at most, the Freedom Charter's implementation would provide space for only 'small businesses sharing a limited market' and that in the final phase of a struggle for socialism it would be the Communist Party, not the national liberation movement, that would 'lead the overwhelming majority of the population'.[35] Although Mbeki conceded that within the 'Bantustan rabble . . . there may be people who genuinely believe they are acting in the best interests of the oppressed' the ANC should eschew any kind of alliances with them. It would pay 'better dividends', Mbeki insisted, to show such people the disadvantages of 'the road they are following . . . on the basis of pointing out the correct line'.[36] As for the BCM, here one could discern 'strong links with far flung imperialist forces'.[37] Mbeki was not alone in this view: Mandela himself, in an essay written in 1976, suggested that the BCM's funding derived from American business but he also warned his colleagues 'to avoid making harsh judgements and observations about its future role', observing that 'the new movement is led by serious minded political activists who are making a definite contribution to the freedom struggle'.[38] Mandela maintained that the ANC should not risk alienating the BCM followers by aggressive attempts to recruit them, a view that seems to have prevailed within the High Organ but that was ignored among the prisoners in the general section.

Ironically, given Mandela's more conciliatory attitude to the new arrivals, Mbeki's arguments initially appeared to have more impact. This was because, within the general sections, Harry Gwala, another militant communist, had built up a personal following among the young men brought on to the Island in the wake of the Soweto uprising. Born in 1920 as the child of impoverished farm labourers, Gwala joined the Communist Party in 1940 while working as a schoolteacher in Pietermaritzburg. Later he established a network of trade unions in nearby Howick, founding a tradition of working-class politics that persisted in this centre through to the 1980s. Gwala had already served one Robben Island sentence for Umkhonto activities. Released in 1972 he was re-imprisoned in 1977 for trying to establish ANC cells. On his re-arrival back in prison he enjoyed immediate stature among the few young ANC activists in the general section. The ANC's first successful efforts to return armed activists from their east African training camps began in late 1976, partly a consequence of the efforts by released Robben Islanders in the early 1970s to resurrect recruitment networks. During his second prison term he became ill with motor neuron disease, leaving both his arms paralysed. Gwala had no more time for the BCM than Mbeki but his ferocious courage and his direct experience of recent external conditions enhanced his standing, as did his radicalism. He was critical of the older 'bourgeois' leaders and he used a language that accorded more closely to the insurrectionary mood that animated the Soweto uprising generation. To its members, Gwala's vision of a struggle that would end in a 'seizure of power' appeared more persuasive than Mandela and Sisulu's belief that in the end the ANC would compel the government to negotiate, and moreover it appeared to enjoy backing from the polemics published by the ANC's external organisation.

At its 'consultative conference' in Kabwe, Zambia in 1985, the ANC adopted a resolution that referred to a 'liberation army . . . rooted in the people, who progressively participate actively in the armed struggle both politically and militarily . . . such a struggle will lead inevitably to a revolutionary situation in which our plan and aim must be the seizure of power through a general insurrection'.[39] How full hearted the ANC's leadership's commitment to this resolution was is certainly questionable; as one shrewd observer has noted, 'by the latter part of 1986', the ANC's strategic thinkers 'were already looking over their shoulders at the possibilities of negotiations'.[40] In Section B, strategic thinking eschewed insurrectionary perspectives. Kathrada recollects that after 1976 'some overenthusiastic MK cadres came to prison with assertions that during our long years of isolation we had lost touch . . . the ANC goal was now people's democracy and socialism':

> It was at times such as these that the wisdom, cool head, realism and foresight of leaders like Mdala [old man] were indispensable. He invariably brought the polemics down to earth. He reminded us that from day one it had never been envisaged that MK could achieve a military victory over the South African army; that MK's primary aim was to engage in armed struggle alongside the political struggle and mass mobilisation; that the two together would force the enemy to the negotiation table.[41]

In 1979, the men in the general section successfully opposed a decision by the High Organ to sanction a visit to Mandela by Matanzima. Mandela himself had consented to this proposed encounter because he wanted to persuade his nephew, then the President of the recently independent Transkei, to revoke his decision to depose the Thembu king, Sabata Dalindyebo, an ANC sympathiser. He also wanted to catch up on family news, including details of his mother's funeral over which Matanzima had presided. He still felt close to his kinsman despite the political rift between them, as Kathrada noted with respect to Mandela's feelings about Matanzima, 'to change Mandela's mind about a friend is virtually impossible'.[42] After seeking advice from the general section, Mandela had refused several earlier requests for meetings from Matanzima but this one he felt would serve a beneficial purpose. The High Organ's authority and with it Mandela's own leadership position were re-established in 1980 when a rift opened among the ANC men in the general section and, unusually, the prison commanding officer allowed a meeting between them and the Section B leaders.[43] Before this, however, Mandela and Mbeki ended what had become a personal estrangement as well as a political disagreement and they started spending time in each other's company again. Kathrada was asked to produce a written summary of the main issues in their dispute and establish common ground; it concluded diplomatically that the measures spelled out in the Freedom Charter, depending on conditions at the time of liberation, might indeed enable a 'qualitative leap towards socialism', but at present it should be understood that the Charter proposed the sharing of power among all classes who had supported the struggle.

Key defections from the BCM camp to the ANC also helped to re-establish Mandela's authority, as did Mandela's own receptivity to ideas and willingness to engage with the younger men's ideas. A telling anecdote illustrating his relative accessibility to the younger men refers to a discussion that was provoked by the showing of *The Wild One*, a film about a motorcycle gang. Films began to be screened for the Section B group in 1978, another concession secured by the Red Cross. Most of the Rivonia men disapproved of Marlon Brando's unruly fraternity. Strini Moodley, one of the BCM leaders confined in the Section in 1975, insisted, however, that the bikers' rebellious spirit represented the same kind of generational revolt that characterised the 1976 school student uprising. Mandela managed to overcome his personal distaste for social disorder and, to the surprise of his comrades, agreed with Moodley. Mandela had already scored points with the BCM prisoners when just after the 1976 tumult he had proposed a new project: in future, he suggested, prisoners should refuse to stand up when spoken to by warders and they should also demand that they be addressed by their full names; the idea generated weeks of discussion within the High Organ and among the ANC prisoners in the general section before being turned down. Mandela received support from Daniels, ever 'a die hard Mandela loyalist', Kathrada recalls, and the SWAPO leader, Toivo ja Toivo, 'always ready for a fight'.[44] The same year he refused to testify as a character witness on behalf of ANC men who were being prosecuted by the authorities for their role in a brawl between the adherents of the different political organisations in the general section—to do so he felt 'would jeopardize my chances of bringing about reconciliation between the different groups'.[45]

Mandela's qualified but genuine empathy with the BCM adherents was prompted by his own memory of generational rebellion as a youth leaguer (probably as well as the sympathetic insights into them that he received during his visits from Winnie), but he also acknowledged that this group was the product of a very different culture from his own experience—they were the products of 'a milieu of rapid change and development of science and technology', he wrote to Chief Buthelezi, and among them 'education and the influence of the mass media have helped to close the generation gap' that had previously ensured deference to elders.[46] Mandela's relative willingness to listen to the BCM men was generally acknowledged. Moodley 'found him more tolerant of differing points of views than most of the others . . . never patronizing because we were a younger generation'.[47] Not all the BCM prisoners took this view. Saths Cooper, another of the BCM group, felt that, of all the Rivonia trialists, it was Sisulu who was 'the one who was able to cross divides between groups and relate to younger people in their own medium'.[48]

In his autobiography, Mandela maintained that the dispute about the relationship between the ANC and the Communist Party was ended finally through external authority: Kathrada's memorandum was sent to the ANC's headquarters in Lusaka which replied, confirming the distinct purpose of both organisations.[49] The men in Section B were able to communicate intermittently with the ANC exiles, through coded messages exchanged with their visitors (Winnie Mandela was an important medium for such exchanges), as well as through documents taken out of prison by men completing their sentences. George Bizos was also willing to take messages and, by the early 1970s, he enjoyed sufficient standing with the warders that he could lunch with Mandela at the officer's club. The High Organ was consulted about the ANC's decision at its conference at Morogoro in Tanzania in 1969 to admit Indians, whites, and coloureds to its membership, a decision that it supported (after all, the Organ treated Indian and coloured Umkhonto veterans on the Island as full ANC members). In 1971 Mandela met James April, a participant in one of Umkhonto's Rhodesian expeditions. April told Mandela about the poor conditions and abusive authority that existed in certain ANC training camps: Mandela wrote a letter to Oliver Tambo suggesting reforms. In 1974, acting on a suggestion by Daniels, Mandela again wrote to Lusaka proposing an escape plan, one of several adventurous schemes that the prisoners and their supporters, as well as South African intelligence *agent provocateurs*, contemplated in the early 1970s. In 1975, Mandela managed to correspond clandestinely with Tambo about the defection of the 'Group of Eight', a faction of ANC leaders who objected to what they perceived as the extent of the South African Communist Party's (SACP's) influence over the organisation's decision-making bodies, claiming Mandela as their leader.

To bolster its position, the ANC's mission in exile even considered for a while appointing Mandela as the organisation's president in place of Tambo, who had been acting as president since Luthuli's death. Mandela heard this news in consternation and Maharaj, on his release, took a message to Lusaka, confirming that the Islanders were agreed: they could not lead the organisation from prison. Later, Mandela wrote to Lusaka endorsing Tambo's authority: 'There is only one ANC, and that is the ANC which has its head office in Lusaka, and whose president is O.T.'[50] In 1978, SABC news broadcasts were relayed into the Section B cells.[51] From 1979, the provision of newspapers and *Time* magazine, although heavily censored, represented an additional crucial resource in enabling the island leadership to keep in touch with and respond to external events. An illuminating instance of this capacity was in November 1981, when Mandela wrote to Major Badenhorst, the prison commanding officer, requesting him to arrange the purchase of presents for his daughter's birthday. As well as a biography of Olive Schreiner the Major was to obtain 'One dairy box [not Rowntree] for about R15.00'.[52] Workers at the Wilson-Rowntree factory in East London were then on strike, led by a union that had declared its affiliation to the Freedom Charter.

The most extensive communication that the Lusaka leaders received from Mandela was his first autobiography. On his fifty-seventh birthday, in his fifteenth year in prison, Sisulu and Kathrada suggested that Mandela should write his memoirs in time for Maharaj to take out a manuscript a year later, when his release was due. Working at first at night and then during the daytime, when he convinced the warders that he was too unwell to labour in the quarry, Mandela produced a 500-page manuscript. This was condensed into tiny script by Chiba. Maharaj succeeded in hiding Chiba's version in his belongings when he left the island, and when he travelled to London subsequently he took the manuscript with him, hidden in the covers of a photograph album. Apparently Joe Slovo and Yusuf Dadoo objected to Mandela's critical treatment of the Umkhonto campaign and the work remained unpublished. Mandela's original manuscript was buried in the Section B courtyard. Its discovery by the authorities resulted in Mandela, as well as Kathrada and Sisulu, whose handwriting was obvious in the marginal comments on the text, losing study privileges—that is, the entitlement to register for external courses—for the next four years. The fragments of the manuscript unearthed by the warders are now preserved in the National Archives in Mandela's prison files.

Politics did not supply the only focus for the prisoners' intellectual and social life. Whether tigers were indigenous to Africa was one topic of controversy to which the men in Section B returned again and again, without resolution. Mandela took the view that because there was a Xhosa word for tiger the creature must once have inhabited Africa. Mandela also defended the practice of circumcision against sceptical modernists as a practice with 'salutary' health and psychological effects that also promoted 'group identification'. Later, with Ulundi encouragement and the supply of tea and biscuits from the Category A prisoners, a secret circumcision school was established in the prison hospital and initiates from the general section would wear blankets for a couple of days after the operation, 'as was the custom'.[53] Mandela's loss of study rights did not deprive of him of reading. The prison maintained a library that included, surprisingly, a volume of *Das Kapital*, and several of Nadine Gordimer's novels. Mandela read and re-read Tolstoy's *War and Peace*, identifying with General Kutusov who made his decisions through 'a visceral understanding of his men and his people'.[54] Many of the prisoners found ways of universalising their experience through their reading. For this purpose Shakespeare supplied, as Sampson notes, 'a common text'. Kathrada, for instance, took a *Collected Works* to Robben Island and from the beginning of his sentence would 'recite passages from Shakespeare daily'.[55] In many cases the prisoners drew upon the memorised heritage instilled in the missionary schools that they had attended in the 1930s. Mandela especially liked quoting W.E. Henley's 'Invictus': 'It matters not how straight the gate/How charged with punishments the scroll/I am the master of my fate/I am the Captain of my soul'. He taught it to Daniels and later, during her visits, to Winnie. Kathrada quoted the poem in one his letters in 1985.[56] This ready reference to canonical writing probably separated the older men culturally from the younger arrivals. Natoo Babenia writes disapprovingly about the BCM followers of a 'TV generation' (television was introduced in South Africa in 1976). 'They had seen too much American trash, liked it and become Americanised', Babenia complains, 'They were not of the calibre of the older generation'.[57]

In the early 1970s the authorities allowed Mandela (after repeated requests) to establish a garden in the courtyard of Section B. Mandela began operations in the same fashion as he set out to become a guerrilla general: he undertook a course of reading on horticulture. His diligence paid off; by 1975 the prisoners had harvested 2,000 chillies, 1,000 tomatoes, numerous radishes and onions, and two watermelons. He persuaded his section mates to hammer any left-over bones from their meals into powder and even for a while instituted a human waste compost pit, abandoned because of the horrible smell. Gardening as well as the facilities for volley ball and tennis, which the IRC persuaded the prison bureaucracy to permit, became increasingly central to the life of Section B when manual labour was brought to an end in 1977: by then there were just too many prisoners to supervise at work safely. Prisoners continued to be employed as gardeners and cleaners but hard labour ceased. For the inhabitants of Section B, however, the end of quarry work also left more time and energy for their interior and private lives, and it is to this dimension of Mandela's imprisonment that we now turn.

D classification prisoners were allowed visits every six months from family members whom they met under closely supervised conditions, for half an hour, separated from them by a thick glass window through which they had to listen with headphones. They could discuss only family affairs and they were forbidden from speaking in Xhosa or other African languages. Prisoners could write and receive letters, the quantities depending on their classification status. Incoming and outgoing letters were censored—often very heavily—and the authorities kept copies of outgoing letters. At the beginning of his sentence Mandela was allowed one letter every six months, only from members of his immediate family. The number of letters that he was allowed was to increase slowly—ten years later he was finally permitted to write and receive letters weekly. Winnie visited three months after his conviction, a stilted unsatisfactory encounter because both of them were discomfited by the warder's presence: on this occasion Mandela learned about his wife's second banning order which restricted her from dusk to dawn to Orlando West and consequent dismissal from her post with the Child Welfare Society. Winnie would not visit for another two years because the authorities withheld the permission that she needed to leave Johannesburg. Meanwhile she worked in a succession of badly paid clerical jobs, in shops, offices, and dry cleaning businesses, relying heavily on the charity of well- and sometimes not so well-intentioned wishers; several of her friends at this time turned out to be police informers. A more reliable source of support for Winnie was Canon Collins' International Defence and Aid Fund, which accorded to the families of the Rivonia trialists 'special treatment'.[58] Winnie made her second visit to the island during the hunger strike and on this occasion their conversation centred on their daughters' educational needs; Winnie had been sending them to an Indian school in Johannesburg which was now no longer willing to accept them—under apartheid rules Indian schools were prohibited from registering African pupils and evidently government officials had objected to the presence of the Mandela girls. Zindzi and Zeni would subsequently attend boarding schools in Swaziland, their fees paid for by Sir Robert Birley, a former headmaster of Eton and a friend of Canon Collins. On this second visit, Winnie was unable to comply with reporting obligations arising from her banning order and she was subsequently sentenced to four days in prison.

Mandela received occasional visits from other members of his family. In 1968 his mother made the trip to Robben Island, accompanied by his older children from his first marriage, Maki and Makgatho; Nosekeni Mandela died of a heart attack three months later. Mandela applied for permission to attend her funeral but this was refused although Winnie was allowed to join Matanzima and other Transkeien dignitaries at Nosekeni's graveside. Makgatho usually visited him twice a year on turning 16, the age from which visits by children were allowed. As Mandela achieved higher classification status, his visitors became more frequent and varied—in 1978, for example, Mandela received 15 visits, about half of them from Winnie. Much of the supervision of these visits was undertaken by Warder James Gregory who seems to have undertaken his duties unusually humanely, on one occasion even passing on a bar of chocolate to Winnie that Mandela had been saving for her as a Christmas present—an indiscretion that subsequently got him into trouble. Mandela normally saved his sweet ration for presents: every year he presented a bag of confectionary to Bam, with whom he shared a birthday. Mandela was unusual among the prisoners in the number of visitors that he received in the later years spent on Robben Island. As Michael Dingake noted, 'the focus of public attention was on him and so the goodwill and assistance that goes with it enabled his dedicated wife and daughters to visit him regularly'. Dingake who received just three visitors during his 15-year sentence maintained that all Mandela's comrades, 'were quite proud and happy that he, as our leader, was a focus of attention on the island in various ways, including visits'. Mandela, Dingake suggests, was in fact 'very much embarrassed' by his comparative good fortune.[59]

Correspondence represented a more reflective and intimate form of communication than visits, however, and the letters that have been preserved illuminate the introspective world of Mandela's imagination and emotions. In this world Mandela repeatedly reconstructed episodes from the first two years of his marriage, the only time that he and Winnie had been able to live as man and wife. In his cell he kept a photograph of Winnie, which he dusted very morning, a chore that he looked forward to because 'to do so gives me the pleasant feeling I am caressing you as in the old days'. He would lift the photograph 'to touch your nose with mine to recapture the electric current that used to flush through my blood whenever I did so'.[60] He kept another photograph in his cell, cut out from the *National Geographic*, of a naked woman from the Andaman islands, dancing, 'literally floating in the air . . . the left leg just above the ground and the right heel almost touching her buttock', Mandela reported jubilantly. 'Her breasts are cocked up like canons [*sic*] in the field', the letter continued, 'exactly like yours before Zeni [and] Zindzi . . . flattened them'.[61] Twenty years after their marriage he wrote: 'I wish I could drive you on a long long journey just as I did on 12/6/1958, with the one difference that this time I'd prefer us to be alone.'[62] On another of their wedding anniversaries he described for his wife his longing to embrace her 'and feel the electric shocks that your flesh rubs onto me, your navel and your heartbeat'. He dreamed about Winnie, 'perpetual dreams' that were not always comforting:

> On the night of 21/9 you and I were driving the Olds at corner of Eloff and Market when you rushed out and spewed out porridge. It was hard and old with a crust on top. Your whole body quivered as each lump came out and you complained of a sharp pain on your right shoulder. I held you tight against my body, unmindful of the curious crowd and the traffic jam. I was still quite upset when I got up but was immediately happy when I realized that it was all but a dream.[63]

In several of his dreams, Winnie is ill or in danger and he is unable to help. In one of these narratives he embraces her, but feels guilty, 'unable to look at you straight in the face'.[64] Such visions projected entirely reasonable anxieties because Winnie remained politically animated, risking and indeed receiving harsh treatment from the authorities, but at a deeper level his own consciousness of morally culpable responsibility for her vulnerability was very evident and this feeling would remain with him for the remainder of their marriage and beyond. Between 1966 and 1969 Winnie began assembling a clandestine ANC network in Soweto that extended its embrace to more than 100 people as well as developing satellite cells outside the township. The focus of this network's activities was chiefly propaganda: it produced and circulated leaflets condemning the Urban Bantu Council elections, for example. By 1969, however, Winnie and her closest associates were planning arson attacks on parked (and hence empty) railway trains.[65] In May they were arrested before they could bring these plans to fruition. From its inception the conspiracy had been closely monitored by the police: Winnie's friend and ostensible benefactress who helped her reproduce the group's leaflets, Maude Katzellenbogen, was an informer. From her arrest on 12 May, Winnie was to spend 491 days in police detention, 13 months of this period in solitary confinement. Five sleepless days and nights of nonstop interrogation induced her to sign a confession. In the end this document was not used in court because her lawyers succeeded in having the charges withdrawn in October 1970, whereupon she was once again placed under a banning order. At least one of her biographers dates a change in her personality from this period, suggesting that the aggression and even cruelty evident in her behaviour in the 1980s reflected post-traumatic stress, in which victims of abuse or torture attempt to displace their own suffering by imposing comparable mistreatment on someone else.[66] To Mandela, however, she remained the lover who dressed so carefully to please him on every visit and who 'radiated tenderness',[67] a constant companion 'that cannot be separated from self'.[68] The protective, even paternal instincts that he felt for her intensified during his imprisonment, if anything accentuated by any derogatory press reports about Winnie, cuttings of which were slipped beneath his cell door even during the time when prisoners were denied newspapers.[69] An exceptional instance of him losing his temper with the prison authorities was when Lieutenant Prins, Commanding Officer in 1975, refused a visit from Winnie and in Mandela's presence made a dismissive remark about her. Mandela told Prins that he was dishonourable and also that he was 'a bloody swine', a mild enough profanity but for Mandela a most unusual lapse of self-control.[70]

In his letters, to Winnie, Mandela constructs a idyllic domestic haven centred on her but embracing a wider set of relationships and kinsfolk: significantly he addresses her with the normal endearments of married life but also as the mother of all his children, through her and his own clan names and as 'Dadewethu', sister. In fact the extended family he longed for existed mainly in his imagination and his recollections. His older son Thembi died in 1969: Thembi had not communicated with his father for some years, taking his mother's side in the divorce. On receiving the telegram that brought this news Mandela stayed in his cell. Sisulu found him there, after missing him at the delivery of the evening meal. Sisulu said nothing but knelt by Mandela's mat and held his hand until lock up. That night, according to the duty warder, Mandela stood by his window looking out at the sky: 'he did not sleep, he did not eat, he just stood there, not moving'.[71] He later described himself as 'paralysed' and 'shaken from top to bottom'.[72] Gregory observed that for several weeks thereafter his 'anguish continued':

> I could see that he was keeping a very tight rein on his emotions. There was the hard set face, a coldness that was different from the friendly smile he would normally give. He was also cutting himself off from other ANC people. I noticed that when they were in the yard Nelson did not walk to be with them in the usual manner.[73]

Later Mandela wrote to both Evelyn and Winnie to recall Thembi visiting him at Lilliesleaf wearing his own oversize suit jacket. Some years later his younger son Makgatho stopped visiting, exasperated by his father's repeated exhortations to acquire further qualifications, a topic that also soured his relationship with Maki. Maki had an uneasy relationship with her stepmother and was reluctant to offer her the filial acknowledgement to which Mandela felt Winnie was entitled. With his younger children Mandela was gentler and more generous in his demonstrations of approval, although his expressions of his love for them could engender resentment from Winnie, who once in response to his praise for their upbringing reminded him that it was 'I, not you, [who] brought up these children whom you prefer to me'.[74] Mandela's guilt about his enforced neglect of his family responsibilities is complemented in Winnie's writing by her occasional expressions of anger at his desertion of her. To these sources of discomfort in their relationship the passing years contributed another concern, his growing age and the increasing contrast between his own physical state—'parts of my body loose and sagging' he told her in 1976—and her continuing beauty and vitality, a disparity that she was willing to speak about to journalists. 'Nelson is sixty-three now', she observed in 1982, 'and I am still like a young girl, still longing for the experience of married life.'[75]

In March 1982, Mandela was informed that Winnie had been seriously hurt in a car crash. The authorities could tell him no more and he requested a visit from her lawyer, Dullah Omar. Omar arrived on 31 March with reassuring news; Winnie's car had overturned but she was uninjured, although this information only partly dispelled Mandela's 'feeling of powerlessness and [his] inability to help her'.[76] Mandela returned to his cell only to be instructed to pack his things for his life on Robben Island was over.

7

LEADING FROM PRISON

Pollsmoor

On the evening of 31 March 1982 together with Raymond Mhlaba, Walter Sisulu, and Andrew Mlangeni, prison officials escorted Nelson Mandela to Pollsmoor prison, a few miles outside Cape Town, a modern establishment that hitherto held no political prisoners. For the next three years Mandela's new home would be Room 99, D Section, a large chamber, 30 by 50 feet equipped with beds and a separate toilet and bathroom section with two showers. Outside the room was a terrace enclosed by a high wall which after a few months the prisoners could use all day for exercise and recreation; at first, however, Mandela and his comrades were confined to the room for most of the time. Within a few weeks, they were joined by Ahmed Kathrada.

At first the men disliked their new premises. Despite more space and better washing arrangements, they resented losing their privacy, they did not enjoy spending so much time indoors, they missed the company of the other men, they disliked not having a view, and for some administrative reason they were forbidden to send telegrams— the best way of communicating urgent family business among a population largely without telephones. Outside there was only a view of the sky. The walls were newly plastered and damp; a chill Mandela contracted during his first days at Pollsmoor probably contributed to the tuberculosis with which he was diagnosed some years later. After her first visit to Pollsmoor, despite more courteous treatment and better communication facilities, Winnie felt that her husband was 'certainly worse off there than he was on the island'.[1]

The cell became all the more crowded when a sixth member

arrived, Patrick Maqubela, an Umkhonto activist captured recently in Soweto and perceived by the authorities to be a dominant personality among the African National Congress (ANC) men held at Diepkloof outside Soweto. Living in such close proximity to each other all the time was a generally unwelcome change, but in other ways the prisoners' living conditions improved. The food was better from the beginning: meat and vegetables every day. The men added the *Guardian Weekly* to their subscription list. Mandela asked for and was given 16 oil drums sliced in half and filled with top soil so that he could re-plant his garden. He still maintained his schedule of early morning exercise, arising at 4.30 for an hour of jogging and push ups, although now the authorities supplied exercise bikes and rowing machines. A television and a video machine were brought in: the older men's favourite programme became *The Cosby Show*. After negotiations, the prisoners in Room 99 were given a hot plate so that they could keep their evening meal warm after its delivery, eating it later when they wanted to. Permission was granted to enable them to buy tinned food to enliven prison rations. Mandela was allowed to use a small room, adjacent to the larger cell, as a working area. The most significant improvement was at the beginning of 1984 when he and Winnie were allowed their first contact visit, under the now familiar supervision of Warder Gregory, who spent the duration of the visit tactfully looking out of the window.[2] Gregory had been transferred to Polls-moor shortly before the prisoners travelled there and had been made responsible for all the arrangements concerning their accommodation. He was also allowed to select the officers who would guard Room 99, a job that was perceived among most prison staff as prestigious and so he had no difficulty in choosing men who could be expected to behave fairly considerately to their charges.

Why did the authorities move the prisoners? Pollsmoor was closer to the hospitals to which the older prisoners on the Island needed increasingly frequently to be taken for specialised medical attention—but the oldest prisoner in Section B, Govan Mbeki, was left behind. Both the Mandelas believed at the time that the move was calculated to decapitate the ANC's leadership structure on the Island. More generally, from the late 1970s the administration began to

disperse prisoners with the aim of reducing their organisational capacity. Officials may also have hoped that moving most of the senior
ANC leaders off Robben Island would reduce the prison's symbolic
significance for anti-apartheid campaigners. It is likely, however, that
even as early as 1982 members of the government were beginning to
anticipate the possibility of negotiating with ANC leaders. They were
quite aware of the political differences that existed between the ANC
leaders on the island and they may have hoped that, isolated from the
generally more radical younger rank-and-file prisoners and from
elderly hardliners such as Mbeki, Mandela and his comrades
might become more willing to consider an acceptable political
settlement.

In October 1980, Prime Minister P.W. Botha appointed a new
Minister of Justice (and prisons), Hendrik Jacobus ('Kobie') Coetsee.
Coetsee trained as lawyer in Bloemfontein for which he became MP
in 1968. He remained friends with a fellow law student and tennis
partner, Piet de Waal. While Coetsee moved up the echelons of the
National Party, de Waal opened a legal practice as well as taking up
farming in Brandfort, a small market town 40 miles from Bloemfontein. In 1977 Coetsee's predecessor, Jimmy Kruger, took the decision
to transport Winnie Mandela out of Soweto and relocate her in
Brandfort. She had become a vociferous champion of the schoolchildren's revolt, helping to set up in Soweto and lead a Black Parents'
Association and, in doing so, of course, helping to fuse the older
tradition of Congress or 'Charterist' resistance with the new generation of Black Consciousness insurgency. In Brandfort, Winnie soon
became a local celebrity. If anything her banishment accentuated her
iconic status and encouraged a flow of donations, which she used to
establish a crèche and various training projects in the bleak township
of Phathakele ('handle with care') that had become her new home.
She made friends with the de Waals, initially through Piet's wife,
Adele, a descendant of the revered *voortrekker* leader, Piet Retief. She
met the de Waals first when she began using Piet's legal services,
because he was the only attorney in town. Adele lent her books and
allowed her to use her bathroom, because Winnie had no running
water in her house. As was the case with his wife, Piet de Waal became

completely enraptured by Brandfort's new resident, and he began writing letters to his old tennis partner from law school, urging the minister to rescind Winnie's banning order. Encouraged by Coetsee's friendly if non-committal responses, de Waal raised a fresh topic. He asked the Minister whether there might not be a case for reconsidering Mandela's status. Coetsee was impressed and later he confessed that it was de Waal who inspired him to begin thinking about making contact with his most important prisoner.[3] In fact the authorities had begun to contemplate a conditional release for Mandela some years earlier: Kruger organised a meeting with Mandela on Robben Island in early 1976, and offered him a sentence reduction and subsequent restriction to the Transkei in return for a public acknowledgement of Matzanima's administration's legal authority. Mandela refused this and several later variations of these terms before leaving the Island, despite Kruger's entreaties to 'be reasonable'. The government, Kruger said, 'could work with you, though not with your colleagues'.[4]

In 1981, Coetsee requested the prison service to undertake a detailed analysis of Mandela's personality. The report that he received was extremely perceptive. Mandela was an 'exceptionally motivated' man. He maintained 'outstanding personal relations' and could be generally expected to behave in a 'friendly and respectful way to figures in authority'. He was not racially embittered. He was capable of recognising his own shortcomings but also believed in himself. He was philosophically pragmatic, intellectually creative, and possessed an unbelievable memory. He believed in his cause and was certain about its eventual victory—because self-discipline and initiative were the prerequisites for success. Mandela, the report concluded, 'commands all the qualities to be the Number One black leader in South Africa'. Imprisonment had served to increase his 'psycho–political posture' and enabled him to acquire an especial charisma.[5]

Aside from Mandela's personality and stature by the beginning of the 1980s, there were other considerations that were beginning to prompt the more imaginative members of Botha's administration to consider the attractions of a political settlement with ANC leaders. The imperative for radical political reform was so much more compelling than was the case two decades later when Mandela first proposed a constitutional convention.

While the African liberation movements and their allies reconstituted themselves in exile and made preparations for guerrilla warfare and in defiance of a growing chorus of international condemnation, successive National Party governments under Hendrik Verwoerd and John Vorster embarked on a much more ambitious programme of racial separation than had been contemplated by their predecessors. This involved the establishment of ethnically constituted administrations in all the historic 'native reserves', to which all Africans would be assigned as citizens as these achieved self-governing and supposedly sovereign status. The ten 'homelands', as they became known in official terminology, became increasingly overcrowded with the enforced resettlement within them of 1.4 million farm workers, former inhabitants of 'black spots' (black freehold land purchased before the 1913 Land Act which were now expropriated by the government). Several hundred thousand city dwellers were also 'endorsed out'—uprooted from their homes and deported to the homelands. Tighter 'influx control' regulated movement between homelands and the cities while a network of labour bureaus 'canalised' (the official term) workers to different employment sectors. Increasingly, apartheid planners forecasted, African urban workers would become oscillatory or permanent migrants, renewing their contracts every year, and leaving their families in the homelands. In anticipation of this outcome, the central government assumed control of African 'township' administration and in 1970 halted altogether the construction of family housing in the major cities, building instead huge dormitory-like hostels for 'bachelor' workers, segregated by sex and ethnic origin. Limitations were placed on black trade union activity and through arrests and deportations to the countryside of key office holders the most militant organisations were suppressed. 'Bantu Education' was extended to African secondary schooling through the 1960s whereas most of the elite mission schools that had produced African leadership in preceding decades either closed their doors or were absorbed into the state system. Restrictions were placed on Africans, Indians, and coloured enrolment in the major universities,

and special segregated colleges were established to train future generations of ethnic administrators. A succession of fierce anti-terrorist
laws institutionalised detention without trial and facilitated the torture of prisoners. Aided by such measures, as well as an extensive
network of informers developed over the previous decade, by 1965
the police succeeded in locating most of the clandestine networks
that the ANC and the Pan Africanist Congress (PAC) had established
after their prohibition in 1960.

During this era inflows of foreign capital as well as public
investment in such strategic industries as armaments and synthetic
petrol promoted annual gross national product (GNP) growth rates
that peaked at 8 per cent. The investment in strategic industries
was a response to the first UN resolution recommending oil and
arms embargoes on South Africa passed in 1965. In that year, the
contribution of manufacturing to the gross domestic product
(GDP) equalled the combined shares of agriculture and mining. In
1988, expressed as a proportion of the GNP, South African manufacturing, at 22 per cent, indicated a level of industrial development
comparable with India (19 per cent) or Mexico (19 per cent),
although South African factories were less sophisticated, producing
much smaller proportions of capital goods (machinery) of export
quality.

In 1976, a nationwide sequence of protests and riots by schoolchildren put South Africa's rulers on the defensive. In fact symptoms
of their vulnerability were beginning to be evident from the beginning of the decade. Growth rates contracted as production for local
markets reached its limits in a low wage economy. A decade of
African advance into semi-skilled manufacturing work—the first
Africans joined the auto-assembly lines in Port Elizabeth in 1960—
gave black labour new leverage against employers: a wave of wildcat
strikes in 1973 heralded the reconstitution of what was rapidly to
become one of the toughest and strongest trade union movements in
the developing world. Mass literacy arising from the expansion of
secondary school enrolments and the appearance in the mid-1960s
of tabloid daily newspapers aimed at township readers fostered the
formation of new political organisations. These took their inspiration

from the American Black Power movement and were led by such men as Strini Moodley and Saths Cooper, representatives of the several thousand black students attending the segregated universities. The collapse of Portuguese colonial power in nearby Angola and neighbouring Mozambique had from 1974 supplied a fresh source of militant inspiration to black activists. When the ideas of the Black Consciousness Movement percolated down to secondary schools, they found ready adherents in an educational system under increasing strain. A rash decision by the education ministry to enforce a decades-old regulation that half the curriculum should be taught in Afrikaans provoked the Soweto Students Representative Council to mount demonstrations on 16 June 1976 in the townships that bordered Johannesburg. The police fired into a crowd of 15,000 children, killing two. After the youngsters dispersed they regrouped to burn down official buildings. In the following days, the revolt spread to 50 Transvaal centres before engulfing the main centres in the eastern and western Cape. In the subsequent year of insurrectionary street battles, strikes, and classroom boycotts, at least 575 protesters died. Several thousand more crossed South Africa's borders to join the liberation organisations.

By the mid-1970s the social interests shaping Afrikaner nationalism had altered. Two-thirds of Afrikaners were now white-collar workers, mainly a consequence of preferential recruitment into the civil service and public companies. Within the business sector Afrikaner firms were now among the most advanced manufacturers, their directors increasingly discomfited by apartheid restrictions on black labour mobility. The concession of collective bargaining rights to African workers and legal recognition of black trade unions beginning in 1979 was followed by a series of other reforms that attempted to solicit support from the most urbanised Africans following the abandonment of some of the more humiliating 'petty apartheid' regulations. Such reforms reflected internal dynamics, black resistance, and the interests of local employers but they were also a response to growing external pressure that accumulated in reaction to the Soweto uprising.

Sanctions against South African trade actually preceded the

growth of an organised sanctions movement: India—at the time, still a British colony—imposed a trade boycott on South Africa in 1946 in sympathy with the Natal Indian Congress's passive resistance against land-ownership restrictions. India's share of trade with South Africa represented 5 per cent on Indian exports, a considerable sacrifice although, from the South African point of view, the effects were much less significant. As an international social movement, the sanctions campaign began with the establishment in Britain by South Africans in 1959 of Boycott South Africa (BSA). BSA's formation was prompted by a series of consumer boycotts mounted in South Africa by trade unions against particular employers and BSA chose as its first target Outspan oranges, deploying pickets outside supermarkets that stocked them. In 1960, the Anti-Apartheid Movement (AAM) constituted itself as a more permanent institutional base for Boycott's support. During the 1960s, the AAM became one of the key components in a cluster of protest organisations that provided expression and focus for a generational revolt against conventional politics by students in Britain's rapidly expanding higher educational system.

University students also pioneered the struggle against apartheid in the USA when they demonstrated outside the headquarters of Chase Manhattan in 1965, calling upon the bank to end loans to South Africa, the beginning of the divestment movement. It was to be in the USA that the sanctions movements scored its most significant victories because with its adoption, especially after 1976, by leaders in the African–American community, the anti-apartheid cause became a mainstream political concern. The first US state to legislate a divestment policy for its pension funds was Connecticut in 1982—thereafter, it was to be joined by many others. As in Britain, in the 1960s, in the USA, the public impact of the sanctions movement was a reflection of the degree to which its activities and goals became integrated with wider patterns of political mobilisation.

The 1980s call for divestment in the USA helped to reactivate the popular base of the African–American civil rights struggle. Sports sanctions were another focus of the movement, especially significant in those British Commonwealth countries that traditionally supplied partners in the international schedule of South Africa cricket and rugby teams. A 1981 tour to New Zealand by the Springboks resulted in street battles between protestors and rugby enthusiasts at every fixture in the programme. The presence of South African television cameras supplied an additional incitement to the protestors, providing them with an opportunity to project their message through a powerfully theatrical medium into South African homes. Between 1959 and 1994, the sanctions campaign represented the most widely supported single-issue protest in the world. From 1980, its cause became personified when, with the ANC's encouragement, the editor of the Johannesburg daily tabloid, *The World*, Percy Qoboza, launched the Free Mandela Campaign, a rapidly globalising movement that found in Winnie Mandela an eloquent and photogenic symbol.

In the years that succeeded Mandela's move to Pollsmoor, the government initiated further reforms, conceding executive authority to previously advisory African municipal assemblies, lifting restrictions on private sector investment in black townships, and, in 1986, repealing the system of pass laws and influx control. In the more liberal political climate that prevailed at the beginning of the 1980s, a new set of organisations based around student movements, trade unions, and township-based civic associations formed, in 1983, a United Democratic Front (UDF), proclaiming their loyalty to the 'non-racial' ideology of the ANC. The ANC's revival as a political force inside South Africa was also an effect of the resumption of Umkhonto's military operations, through lines of infiltration across the Botswana and Mozambique borders. The first focus of UDF campaigning was the boycotts that it orchestrated in reaction to elections for a 'tri-cameral' parliament. This was instituted by the government in 1984 with the addition of coloured and Indian chambers, alongside the all-white legislature with members of all three houses joining a multiracial cabinet. UDF affiliates were conspicuous in the insurrectionary climate that developed in townships in late 1984 in response to rent hikes instituted by the new councils. Township rioting, military repression as soldiers assumed control over black neighbourhoods, guerrilla warfare, and conflict between supporters of liberation movements and the adherents of homeland regimes each contributed to the bloodiest phase of South Africa's political history since the Anglo–Boer War. Between 1984 and 1994 25,000 deaths were attributed to politically motivated killing.

Coetsee may have considering a meeting with Mandela from the beginning of the decade but he bided his time until 1985. In 1984, Prime Minister Margaret Thatcher met Botha at Chequers; in her private discussion she advised the South Africans to release Mandela. Subsequently, Botha spoke to Coetsee telling him 'that we had painted ourselves into a corner'. Was there any way, Botha wondered, 'of getting us out'?[6] To obtain fresh soundings on his prisoner's political perceptions, Coetsee sanctioned two distinguished visitors to call in at Pollsmoor. The first of these, Lord Bethall, met Mandela in the governor's office. Mandela arrived with two officials: 'a six foot tall, lean figure with silvering hair', he 'could almost have seemed like any other general in the South African prison service'. Indeed, Bethall later told his readers in the *Mail on Sunday* that 'he was the most assured of them all, and he stood out as the most senior man in the room'. Mandela spoke about experiences on the Island and described his present daily routine. Every day he was out of bed at 3.30 for two hours of exercise, then reading and gardening: 'The major, here, has been tremendously helpful. He is really an excellent gardener.' He acknowledged that the CO, Brigadier Munro, did his best 'to solve our little problems'. After these pleasantries, Mandela turned to more serious matters:

> The armed struggle was forced upon us by the government. And if they want us now to give it up, the ball is in their court. They must legalise us, treat us like a political party, and negotiate with us. Until they do then we will have to live with the armed struggle. It is useless to carry on talking. . . . Of course, if there were to be talks along these lines, we in the ANC would declare a truce.[7]

In a later conversation with Louis le Grange, Minister for Law and Order, le Grange conceded that talks with the ANC were not out of the question in the future, although, at this point, the government would not be so weak as to agree to negotiations unconditionally. Let the ANC forego its guerrilla attacks and enter the political arena instead: then the government would talk to them.

And what would they talk about? To his second important caller, Samuel Dash (Chief Counsel to the US Senate Watergate Committee), Mandela spelled out the ANC's essential requirements for a political settlement: a unified South—no artificial homelands; black representation in central parliament and one man, one vote on a common roll. To be sure, black South Africans could not match the South African government militarily, but 'we can make life miserable for them', although the ANC remained committed to attacking only military personnel not civilians.[8] On 31 January, Botha made a public offer in parliament: if Mandela renounced violence he could go free. Mandela was invited to the Governor's office to receive the Hansard text. He dictated his reply to Ismail Ayob, his family lawyer, and Zindzi subsequently read his words out at a UDF rally held in a Soweto football stadium, his first public address inside South Africa for 24 years. He was a member of the ANC, and he would remain a member of the ANC until he died. Oliver Tambo was more than his brother; he was 'my greatest friend and comrade for fifty years'. He was 'surprised at the conditions the government wished to impose on me . . . for [he] was not a violent man. Let Botha show he was different from his predecessors. Let him renounce violence. Let him unban the people's organization. Certainly Mandela cherished his freedom but he cherished others' freedom more dearly. What freedom was he being offered while "the organization of the people remained banned".' Only free men can negotiate. Prisoners cannot enter into contracts. But he would return, he promised.[9]

Prisoners could speak to their adversaries without negotiating formally, however. In mid-1985, Mandela wrote to Minister Coetsee, requesting a meeting, an action that represented a decisive break with the accepted convention that 'as isolated prisoners, we would do nothing that could be construed as policy making'.[10] As he explained in 1994, 'I knew my colleagues upstairs would condemn my proposal and that would kill my initiative. . . . There are times when a leader must move out ahead of his flock, go off in a new direction.'[11] He received no reply from the Minister. Coetsee explained why later: he told the journalist Allister Sparks 'some intuition told me I shouldn't see Mr Mandela behind bars'. In December, Mandela was taken to hospital for a prostrate operation. He recuperated under very relaxed conditions—he was allowed to visit the main ward next to his private room and several of the (white) patients made reciprocal visits. One day, during this period Coetsee appeared by his bedside. The Minister had made his decision to meet Mandela impulsively after a chance conversation with Winnie, with whom coincidentally he shared a flight to Cape Town. Coetsee and Mandela's conversation was affable if wary. Mandela opened their exchange with a gentle admonishment: 'Ah, Mr Coetsee, how nice to see you. At last. I'm sorry we have not got together before.'[12] Coetsee was impressed with what he recognised as Mandela's 'old world values'. Mandela remembered Coetsee as 'very polite'. At one point in their exchange Coetsee told him 'I am interested in your being put in a situation between prison and freedom'.[13]

On his return to Pollsmoor Mandela did not rejoin his former cellmates; rather he was given three rooms on the ground floor. After a few days, Brigadier Munro sanctioned a meeting between Mandela and his comrades. The latter were indignant about his separation from them but Mandela asked them not to protest: if he was alone, he said, it would be easier for the government to approach him. He then requested a meeting with George Bizos and asked Bizos to communicate with Tambo, to inform the ANC president about Mandela's meeting with Coetsee and his plans for subsequent 'talks about talks'. Tambo replied with approval in principle: Mandela should proceed, he told Bizos on 28 February 1986. ANC officials in Lusaka had already held consultations with a senior official in the Department of Constitutional Affairs, Kobus Jordaan. In mid-1986 Mbeki's son, Thabo, the ANC's main diplomatic representative, spoke privately for a hour or so with Pieter de Lange, chair of the Afrikaner Broederbond, while both were attending a conference in New York. In May, Coetsee joined Mandela for a discussion with the Eminent Persons' Group (EPG), a body established after Commonwealth leaders disagreed about whether to impose further sanctions on South Africa. Mandela told the Nigerian visitor, General Obasanjo, that, if the authorities withdrew soldiers and police from the townships, the ANC might suspend violence as a prelude to talks. Obasanjo suggested that the release of prisoners should be linked to suspension of hostilities: Mandela conceded that this might be reasonable. After a third meeting with EPG members, Mandela asked the police commissioner, Willemse, to organise an appointment with Minister Coetsee in which they could address the possibility of talks between the government and the ANC. Coetsee responded immediately: Mandela should be brought to his home. A three-hour discussion ensued. Mandela found the minister sophisticated and receptive. At the end of the meeting he noted down Mandela's suggestion that the next step should be a discussion with Botha.

Several months elapsed. On Christmas Eve, Major Marais, the Deputy Commander of Pollsmoor, invited Mandela for a drive around Cape Town. He enjoyed several other excursions of this kind, trips that Mandela found instructive. The trips were arranged by Warder Gregory who also accompanied him, as did four more guards in a second car, armed with Uzi machine guns. The special duties that Gregory undertook on behalf of his important charge were multiplying. They included a protracted search for 'Blue Pantene', a hair tonic that Mandela had convinced himself he needed, which, in the presence of Helen Suzman, the Pollsmoor CO had promised to obtain and which had been discontinued by the manufacturers. A protracted search around Cape Town chemists unearthed some leftover stock. As his closest friends concede, humility notwithstanding, Mandela was 'not without a touch of vanity'.[14]

In his own travels around the city, Mandela was able to see at first hand 'how life had changed' since his conviction. He was also struck 'by the extraordinary wealth and ease whites enjoyed' despite the country being 'in upheaval' with 'the townships on the brink of war'.[15] He continued to hold off-the-record conversations with Coetsee, at Coetsee's home, and it was at one of these that the Minister made a formal proposal. The government would like to appoint a committee to conduct any further discussions. He, Coetsee, would chair this body, and its members would include senior prison officials (to camouflage its real purpose) and, more importantly, Dr Neil Barnard, head of the National Intelligence Service. The Committee would have Botha's support, Coetsee said. Mandela stalled; he need to speak to Sisulu and the others at Pollsmoor. He met them that evening: Sisulu was lukewarm; he wished, he said, that the government had taken the initiative 'rather than us initiating talks with them'.[16] Mlangeni and Mhlaba were enthusiastic, though. Kathrada shared Sisulu's doubts and until Mandela's release was 'never really reconciled to this action'.[17] In fact, however, Mandela's news was not altogether revelatory: the men in Room 99 had been told about their comrade's first visit to Coetsee's house by an indiscreet warder.[18] Shortly, thereafter, a smuggled note from Tambo arrived. Tambo was alarmed to learn about Mandela's separation from the other prisoners: what was going on? Mandela replied with some asperity: he was speaking to the government about one thing only, talks between the South African authorities and the ANC. At this stage he could not supply details, but the time had come for such talks and he would not compromise his comrades.

Coetsee's committee began its work in May 1988. Between May and the end of 1989 the committee held 47 sessions with Mandela. They interrupted their programme in November 1988 because Mandela was diagnosed with water on the lung and had to spend six weeks in hospital. After his convalescence in a comfortable if closely guarded private clinic on 9 December, he was installed in new quarters, not a prison cell, but rather a proper house, the deputy governor's bungalow in the grounds of the Victor Verster prison, 45 miles from Cape Town. Here Mandela would be allowed to entertain an almost unrestricted succession of visitors 'in privacy and comfort', as Coetsee informed him upon his arrival.[19] The house was comfortably furnished and the authorities even installed a well-stocked drinks cabinet although Mandela remained as abstemious as ever. Mandela used the swimming pool, though, employing a body board to manoeuvre himself out of the shallows, because he had never learned to swim properly. The bungalow's staff included a cook, Warrant Officer Jack Swart. Swart was also meant to keep the house tidy but Mandela insisted that he himself should do the washing up and continue, as he had done for the previous three decades and more, to make his own bed. He was allowed to draw upon a bank account set up by his lawyer, Ismail Ayob, to buy special supplies. His visitors included Winnie on several occasions but she would not stay, despite a message from the minister confirming that this would be permitted. She wanted no special treatment, Winnie explained; she would only stay the night with her husband when the wives of the other prisoners were afforded the same dispensation.

By now there were several parallel sets of talks continuing between officials and politicians in the government, the ANC leadership in Lusaka, as well as the dialogue that was taking place at Victor Verster. Barnard informed Mandela about his communications with Thabo Mbeki. Not all the ANC principals were convinced that a negotiated settlement was either desirable or plausible but Joe Slovo, still a key strategist and Umkhonto's chief of staff, told a journalist in March 1987 that he believed 'that the transition in South Africa is going to come through negotiation'. Although the tempo of Umkhonto activity was accelerating—its soldiers undertook several hundred operations that year and the next—Slovo probably had a better understanding than many of his comrades of the limits of what they could achieve militarily.

In preparation for meeting with the South African president, in March 1989 Mandela wrote a ten-page memorandum for Botha, then recovering from a stroke. The text provides a reasonable summary of the issues that he, Coetsee, and Barnard had been addressing over the previous year. Mandela opened by delineating his objective: to bring the government and the ANC to the negotiating table. When they met, he continued, they would find ways of reconciling two demands: black desire for majority rule in a unitary state and whites' requirement that this would not mean subjugation of the white minority. But before they could even begin to discuss this issue there were obstacles to any meeting: the government's demands that the ANC should renounce violence, abandon its communist allies, and give up its aim of majority rule. The body of the memorandum explained why these demands were unacceptable: they could not serve as preconditions for any negotiations. This was the time to overcome deadlock and Mandela hoped Botha would seize it without delay.[20]

Botha received Mandela at Tuynhuys on 5 July. They drank tea and posed for photographs, Mandela elegant in a new suit with his tie in a Double Windsor knot, specially tied for him by Major Marais, Deputy Governor at Pollsmoor, because Mandela could not meet the president 'in a hangman's noose', the unflattering simile Marais used for Mandela's own sartorial effort. As Mandela conceded to Marais, 'I have not had much use for ties in prison'.[21] After Botha solicitously served his guest his cup of tea, the two leaders conversed in a friendly fashion for 30 minutes, mainly on the subject of the 1914 rebellion by Afrikaner nationalists, and composed a bland statement for the archives. The only serious matter that Mandela raised in his conversation with Botha was the release of political prisoners, a request that Botha gently told him he could not accede to. Even so it was a promising start: unexpectedly, as Botha was normally notoriously prickly, the two men enjoyed their encounter. One month later, however, after a confrontation with his cabinet, Botha resigned. His replacement was Frederik Willem de Klerk, who had replaced Botha as leader of the National Party in January, after Botha's first stroke.

Unlike many of the National Party leaders who had hitherto been involved in contacts or communications with ANC leaders, Botha included, de Klerk was not considered a reformer or a member of the Party's more liberal wing. Able to trace his descent from seventeenth-century French Huguenot settlers, de Klerk was a third-generation Afrikaner nationalist notable and the son of a cabinet minister, related through his aunt's marriage to the second prime minister of the apartheid era, Hans Strydom, and in his early political career a protégé of Vorster, a family friend. 'Politics was in my blood', he notes in his autobiography.[22] He joined the youth wing of the National Party while a teenager and played an increasingly prominent role in various Afrikaner social movements while at university and during his early career practising company law in Vereeniging. Here he won a by-election to join parliament in 1972. After six years on the backbenches he was recruited into Vorster's cabinet as Minister for Posts and Telegraphs, an unusually early promotion. De Klerk was to remain convinced that 'the people who structured apartheid were not evil people', that in 'its idealistic form' it was a programme 'to bring political rights to all South Africans via nation states'. He knew this 'because my father was a member of the government which formulated it, and he was a good man'. He did concede to journalists interviewing him in 1994 that apartheid had failed, that 'it had just resulted in racial discrimination and minority domination'.[23] The resulting moral and practical crisis represented a matter of conscience, he conceded.

Just when this realisation became evident to de Klerk himself is not clear: in 1986 he opposed in cabinet a proposal to afford black South Africans separate representation in the national legislature and one year later was still defending residential segregation in public speeches, urging his listeners to report violations of the Group Areas Act (by then ignored by the police). As Minister of Education he had attempted to impose a racial quota system on universities (which had for some years been quietly ignoring official restrictions on black entry). What is noteworthy, however, is that in the face of vigorous opposition from many of the key white institutions de Klerk backed down and shelved his draft legislation. In his autobiography he suggests that 'the vast difference between the Verwoerdian theory of separate development and its often devastating impact upon the lives of ordinary people'[24] became clear to him between 1982 and 1985, when he was Minister of Home Affairs. Among his other duties he was responsible for administering the legal prohibitions on racially mixed marriages and 'sex across the colour line'. The laws were morally indefensible and de Klerk (who could count at least one Indian slave among his eighteenth-century ancestors) piloted their abolition through parliament. He also helped to introduce labour reforms. Writing retrospectively he claims that during the 1980s he viewed himself as a cautious reformist, favouring 'a step by step approach'. As Minister of Education, he maintains that he 'came more and more to the conclusion that there could no solution without the removal of all forms of racial discrimination'.[25] He remained, however, convinced that the 'existence of different [racial] groups . . . was a God given reality' and that their corporate identities and interests should be accommodated in any reorganised political system.[26]

As a result of his reluctance to acknowledge a damascene conversion to the cause of non-racialism, de Klerk is treated dismissively in popular histories of South Africa's transition to democracy. Certainly it is true that initially at least de Klerk's behaviour in office was prompted by pragmatic considerations. A briefing from the National Intelligence Service (NIS) helped to convince him that delaying negotiations could sacrifice leverage that could benefit white South Africans as a group if he seized the initiative early: here he took his lesson from Rhodesia in its final decade where 'when the opportunity was there for really constructive negotiations, it was not grasped'.[27] Acting on this lesson required genuine courage and moral conviction, however, and later de Klerk's willingness to take risks would prove a decisive factor in South Africa's achievement of democracy.

By this time, Mandela was in regular contact with Tambo, through a communications system established by Mac Maharaj, who had slipped back into South Africa in 1989. Through this system Mandela was able to review a document that Tambo had prepared and which the organisation released on 21 August. The ANC's Harare Declaration suggested that guerrilla operations could be suspended in return for the release of prisoners, the unbanning of the ANC, and the withdrawal of South African Defence Force soldiers from black townships. In September, Thabo Mbeki and Jacob Zuma, one of the ANC's intelligence chiefs—and an early inmate of Robben Island's general section—talked through the night in a Swiss hotel with two South African NIS officials: the ANC was prepared to negotiate on these terms. It was after this encounter that de Klerk was fully briefed about the contacts that had been developing between officials in his government and the ANC. Up to then he had been remained ignorant of the content and the frequency of these meetings. His autobiography confirms that he opposed initial government contacts with the ANC partly because of its links with the Communist Party. Unlike many of his colleagues, however, de Klerk had actually once met an important ANC leader: while chairing the Studentebond at the University of Potchefstroom in 1959 he had invited Chief Albert Luthuli to address students—the ANC president had impressed his hosts 'as a venerable old man and we respected his position as a Zulu chief'.[28]

At the beginning of October Mandela suggested to Coetsee that de Klerk should release ten prominent prisoners, including Kathrada and Sisulu (Mbeki was already at liberty, released ostensibly on health grounds one year earlier); their behaviour would be low key, he assured the minister. Kathrada and Sisulu as well as six other senior Umkhonto veterans returned home on 15 October. In November, after an extended *bosberaad* (bush conference) with his cabinet, de Klerk agreed that he and Mandela should meet, on 13 December. Once again, Mandela returned to Tuynhuys with an updated version of the memorandum that he had written for Botha.

It was for both men an encouraging encounter. As they 'cautiously sized up each other'[29] both men found the other to be a good listener. To Mandela, de Klerk also appeared willing at least to consider the possibility that the National Party commitment to 'group rights' might be negotiable. This was someone with whom the ANC 'could do business'. De Klerk told his brother afterwards that Mandela was a 'man with tremendous style . . . a politician to be reckoned with'. Significantly, however, neither of the two men's recollections of the meeting suggest that it was characterised by any warmth. De Klerk, a less emotionally demonstrative personality than his predecessor, offered neither tea nor small talk. Six weeks later, de Klerk opened parliament on 2 February 1990 with a speech that he had written out in his own handwriting, consulting only his closest advisers. In a few paragraphs, he reversed the course of South African history. The government would legalise all prohibited organisations. Political prisoners not guilty of violence would be freed. The authorities would release Nelson Mandela without conditions. Nine days later, in front of the television cameras of most of the world, Mandela walked out of Victor Verster, hand in hand with his wife.

How decisive in influencing de Klerk's decision was Mandela's initiative to begin 'talking about talks'? Of course, the South African president was influenced by a range of considerations. Especially important was the fall of the Berlin Wall which effectively ended any further prospect of Soviet support for the ANC's armed insurgency. De Klerk believed that without its eastern European allies a domesticated ANC would be a much weaker opponent.[30] He also knew that the exiles were under increasing pressure to settle with Pretoria from their hosts in Lusaka and from other governments in

South Africa. A dramatic gesture of liberalisation would probably win him strengthened diplomatic support from conservative administrations in London and Washington, the kind of support that had recently helped to broker a pragmatic liberal regime in Namibia. He was encouraged that he would enjoy such support by the warm receptions that he had received during visits to London and Washington during October. Meetings with Kenneth Kaunda in Lusaka and Joaquim Chissano in Maputo also helped to convince him that 'a window had suddenly opened'.[31] As he observed later, in November 1989, the fall of the Berlin wall 'created an opportunity for a much more adventurous approach than had previously been conceivable'.[32]

Such an approach could not be undertaken alone, however. Negotiated or 'pacted' transitions require strong adversaries and popular moral authority. By the end of 1989 it was obvious to South Africa's rulers that only their most famous captive could render any settlement legitimate. This realisation was very substantially the product of Mandela's diplomacy. In 'talking to the enemy' he had become more than the master of his fate, because he could now profoundly affect the political destiny of his compatriots.

8

MESSIANIC POLITICS AND THE TRANSITION TO DEMOCRACY

Notwithstanding the ostensible simplicity of his first appearance in public for 25 years, holding hands with Winnie and emerging through the entrance of Victor Verster on foot, Mandela's release was carefully planned. A National Reception Committee headed by Cyril Ramaphosa, the secretary-general of the National Union of Mineworkers (NUM), had been appointed by UDF (United Democratic Front) leaders and trade unionists. Unlike many of the principals in the 'Mass Democratic Tradition', Ramaphosa had not been brought up as an instinctive African National Congress (ANC) loyalist. The son of a policeman in Vendaland, he had studied law at the University of the North and while a student had joined the Black Consciousness Movement (BCM). At its formation, the NUM was not associated with the pro-ANC grouping of trade unions. As its secretary-general, Ramaphosa became the Union's chief negotiator, proving a tough and capable adversary in his confrontations with the management of the mining industry, historically the most reluctant sector of the industrial economy to concede collective bargaining rights to black workers. He joined the ANC secretly in the late 1980s but, in common with many other trade union leaders, he remained highly conscious of representing a separately and independently organised constituency. Ramaphosa and other members of the Committee needed time for preparations and Mandela had to persuade de Klerk to defer his release for 24 hours: originally the South African president wanted Mandela to be at liberty on 10 February. In the evening of 10 February, Ramaphosa and his colleagues arrived at Mandela's bungalow to help him draft a statement. Ramaphosa probably had the key influence in setting the tone of what Mandela would tell the world the next day and he was determined to make no concessions to heroic personalities. Mandela would assume his place in a movement in which his position, Ramaphosa maintained, would be 'no different from the status of any other member of the ANC'. He was 'just one of those people who may have to be considered for a leadership position'.[1]

Mandela delivered his collectively scripted statement the next day in Cape Town, from a balcony overlooking the Grand Parade. To television viewers worldwide who were expecting lyrical or celebratory prose Mandela's speech may have seemed a disappointment. Margaret Thatcher, for example, expressed dismay at 'the old ritual phrases'.[2] An American journalist who was present later described the address as 'a speech without warmth, without vision, without humanity, a speech for the warpath'.[3] De Klerk felt that 'for once, Mandela completely failed to rise to the occasion'.[4] On this occasion, however, Mandela was not addressing a global audience or even all South Africans, at least not directly. These were words of reassurance for his South African constituency, affirmation of his loyalty to his people and their cause, spoken in the idiom of modern South African political discourse, a blunt language of militancy that emphasised collective over individual experience. Speaking as 'a humble servant, of you the people', he opened his address with a series of salutations to his 'friends, comrades and fellow South Africans', paying homage to the people of Cape Town, to President Oliver Tambo, to the combatants of Umkhonto, to the South African Communist Party (SACP), to the UDF, to the Congress of South African Trade Unions, and to the 'many other formations of the Mass Democratic Movement, to the Black Sash and to the National Union of South African Students', the 'conscience of white South Africans', to 'the working class of our country', to religious communities, traditional leaders, youth, 'mothers, and wives and sisters of our nation', the world community for its contribution to the anti-apartheid struggle, and to his wife and family whose 'pain and suffering' had been so 'much greater than [his] own'.

The remainder of his address was brief. Apartheid had no future, this was recognised by the majority of South Africans, black and white. The factors that necessitated the armed struggle still existed and it would continue until a 'climate conducive to a negotiated settlement' was created. Mandela hoped that this would be soon. He remained a loyal and disciplined member of his organisation. As a leader it was his duty to place his views before the organisation and 'to allow the democratic structures to decide on the way forward'. In his talks with the government, he had not even begun discussing basic demands; his aim had been to normalise the situation. Mr de Klerk was a man of integrity, but the 'harsh reality' remained that people were still suffering under a Nationalist government. The struggle should be intensified. Sanctions should be maintained. The march to freedom was irreversible.[5]

The march to freedom still had some way to travel, however. In February 1990, de Klerk had no intention of abdicating or, in the longer term, of negotiating the National Party out of power. The South African president still believed that he could reach a settlement with his adversaries without conceding majority rule. As Mandela acknowledged later, de Klerk was 'a gradualist, a careful pragmatist' and he made his reforms with the intention of 'ensur[ing] power for the Afrikaner in the new dispensation'.[6] De Klerk's ideas on how to achieve such an objective became clearer in the weeks after Mandela's release. In various speeches de Klerk proposed a bicameral legislature in which a Senate could veto legislation approved by a House of Representatives. The House would be elected on a common roll but in the Senate all parties above a threshold of support would have equal representation. Similarly there would be an all-party cabinet with a rotating presidency which would have to make its decisions through consensus. De Klerk may have even believed that an anti-ANC coalition could prevail in an election, although in 1990 opinion poll readings confirmed to him that the ANC would win at least 60 per cent of the votes in any election.[7]

Sustaining such aspirations was the animosity between the ANC and Chief Mangosuthu Buthelezi's Inkatha Freedom Party, a movement based in the Kwa-Zulu homeland, but, unlike other homeland political organisations, a force that enjoyed considerable voluntary support outside the homeland, especially among Zulu migrant work-ers around Johannesburg. Inkatha stood for the maintenance of the Zulu monarchy as well as chiefly power, and its leaders favoured a federal political system in which regional governments would enjoy virtual autonomy. In the mid-1970s the exiled ANC leadership main-tained affable relations with Chief Buthelezi, but the relationship deteriorated as the Inkatha leader increasingly found himself in con-flict with black consciousness activists. Through the 1980s, in Natal, UDF supporters, and Inkatha adherents fought each other for control over the township communities that surrounded the major cities. Between 1990 and 1994 the tempo of violence was to accelerate, with Inkatha receiving covert support from policemen and soldiers. De Klerk would always deny knowledge of any government sponsorship of a 'third force' within the South African security establishment that had sought to accentuate ANC/UDF hostilities through *agent provo-cateur* activity, and there is no evidence to suggest that he approved such actions.

What is true, however, is that from 1990 onwards, with his know-ledge South African officials began channelling substantial funding to the Inkatha Freedom Party. Arguably, Mandela lost an important opportunity for an early reconciliation with Inkatha. Initially he wanted to arrange a personal meeting with Chief Buthelezi because, as he observed, 'he has a following and it seems to me correct to try and settle problems in which he is involved amicably'.[8] As noted above, throughout his imprisonment, Mandela had maintained a friendly correspondence with the Chief. At first, he was dissuaded from arranging a meeting by the National Executive but managed in March 1990 to obtain their sanction for a public appearance with Buthelezi at an Inkatha stronghold, Taylor's Halt. At the last moment, however, Mandela withdrew from this arrangement after Harry Gwala had angrily objected to such an encounter taking place. Gwala now headed the most bellicose faction within the Natal ANC. Other ANC leaders later conceded that Mandela's capitulation to Gwala's arguments was mistaken: intelligence chief Jacob Zuma believed that, if Mandela had publicly embraced Buthelezi at this juncture, much of the future bloodletting between ANC and Inkatha supporters might have been avoided. Mandela did meet Buthelezi in January 1991, an occasion that he used to thank the Chief for campaigning for his release and to emphasise the goals that both their organisations shared but by then the Chief was in no mood to listen: in his own speech he recited a lengthy catalogue of ANC attacks on him.

Mandela's sensitivity to militant critics such as Gwala reflected the uncertain character of his political authority at the time of his release. In directing his first words at liberty to his constituency, Mandela was making a shrewd judgement. The content of his own meetings in prison with government officials, as well as the Lusaka leadership's contact with Pretoria, had remained mostly secret—although subject to rumours and leaks. Not all the senior ANC leaders were convinced about the justifications for negotiation: in particular Chris Hani, Umkhonto's chief of staff, retained his faith that soldiers and activists could bring about an insurrectionary seizure of power, despite the public admission at the end of 1989 by Alfred Nzo, the ANC's secretary-general 'that we do not have the capacity to intensify the armed struggle in any meaningful way'.[9] Hani, a classics graduate from the University of Fort Hare and a veteran of Umkhonto's early guerrilla campaigning in Rhodesia in the 1960s, enjoyed a huge personal following as a consequence of his public profile as the ANC military's day-to-day operational commander. Between 1980 and 1982 his reputation was enhanced by his lucky escapes in a series of South African-sponsored assassination attempts. Mandela needed to convince not just his co-leadership but also the ANC's followers that he made no concessions of principle in his conversations with Coetzee's committee. Twenty-four prisoners on Robben Island even refused release: they would not leave the Island, they said, until there had been a military victory. Winning the confidence of the organisation's rank and file—the soldiers in the camps and the activists in the streets—was the first task to accomplish and would have to take priority over any serious engagement with de Klerk's constitutional proposals.

Formal negotiations would not begin for another two years. Meanwhile Mandela addressed a rally at a Soweto soccer stadium, visited Lusaka where he made a point of publicly confirming his continuing endorsement of the ANC's armed struggle, a decisive gesture in gaining the confidence of Hani, and he attended an anti-apartheid rock concert in Wembley Stadium, London, where to onlookers 'he seemed more excited by the pop singers than political leaders like Neil Kinnock'.[10] He also visited Umkhonto camps in Tanzania in April. Meanwhile, the ANC's legal specialist, Penuell Maduna, and Zuma arrived in South Africa to negotiate an indemnity law that would protect returning exiles from prosecution. In May, Mandela led ANC representatives in signing the Groote Schuur Minute in which the government undertook to amend security legislation as well as defining the categories of prisoners for release, lifting the state of emergency, and helping exiles to return. Three months later, on 7 August after a day of discussion with government negotiators, Mandela announced the ANC's suspension of its military operations, a move first suggested to the ANC's National Executive by Joe Slovo on July 19, who perceived that de Klerk needed to appease his critics on his right by demonstrating evidence that the ANC could make concessions; initially Mandela was sceptical but Slovo was persuasive, not least because of his public credentials as a guerrilla leader.[11] In fact organised ANC military activity had ceased in 1989 although the Umkhonto command maintained its underground network and continued recruiting activities. Even so, suspension was unpopular with ANC supporters, although it certainly enhanced the movement's international stature as well as the flow of European and North American financial support. It needed such resources because its chief imperative was simply to reconstruct itself as an organisation and promote at least a semblance of harmony among its three major constituents: the returning exiles, the older generation of released prisoners, and the veterans of the internal struggles led by the UDF and COSATU (Congress of South African Trades' Unions), each of which had their own competing strategic prescriptions.

In December 1990, the ANC held a 'consultative conference'. This assembly was opened by Tambo who was still recovering from a stroke that had disabled him at the end of 1989. In his speech, Tambo recommended that the organisation should modify its continuing advocacy of sanctions: the ANC could not risk at this stage alienating western governments that were already questioning the merit of maintaining these measures in place. Tambo's argument reflected National Executive consensus and his own alarm at Pretoria's success in restoring diplomatic and trade relations with European and African countries,[12] but it angered delegates who voted it down. They were critical of Mandela too for failing to consult more widely during his 'personal diplomacy'[13] with the government since his release. In closing the conference, Mandela acknowledged that leaders should 'grasp the principle that they are servants of the people' but he also rebuked his audience for their failure to express any praise for the leadership and, as for those who believed one could negotiate without secrecy, they 'do not understand the nature of negotiation'. Six months later at a formally convened national conference, Mandela returned to the theme of negotiations again, this time using the kind of language that might match the expectations of the more militant delegates: they were 'a site of struggle' that would lead 'to the transfer of power to the people'.[14] His leadership style remained a source of contention among delegates, however, with the former Robben Islander Terror Lekota rebuking Mandela amid applause for his often authoritarian efforts to impose his will, this time with specific reference to Mandela's prescription of a 30 per cent quota of female candidates in the ANC's internal elections. Even so, the delegates elected Mandela president: Tambo was too ill to continue in this role and declined to stand.

Before any constitutional negotiations could begin there needed to be agreement on who should take part and how the talks should be organised. The government wanted an all-party conference at which all would be represented equally; the ANC and its allies called for an elected assembly. Mandela brokered a compromise at the beginning of 1991: the talks should begin with an all-party meeting that would decide on an interim constitution, as well as certain more permanent principles that would be incorporated into a final constitution after the election of a constituent assembly. This was a procedure that the ANC's national executive finally agreed to in October 1991; the decision had to await the ANC's reconstitution of its internal organisation and, as well as this task, leaders were also preoccupied with the conflict between Inkatha groups and the ANC's own loyalists, some of them organised in paramilitary 'Self Defence Units'. As the 'black-on-black' warfare escalated, Mandela's relationship with de Klerk deteriorated; revelations about the murderous activities of a police unit innocuously called the 'Civil Cooperation Bureau' strengthened Mandela's feeling that he was being betrayed by a man whom in 1989 he had professed to trust. At the end of 1990, after a massacre attributed to Inkatha in Sebokeng, Mandela was still prepared 'to regard de Klerk as a man of integrity', noting that they had both 'developed an enormous respect for each other'. However, he noted, the South African president had problems in containing his security establishment and he was 'not being frank with me about that'.[15] By April 1991, however, Mandela apologised to the National Executive for misjudging de Klerk, accusing him of complicity in violent attacks on ANC-aligned communities. When Inkatha demonstrators wearing full warrior regalia surrounded the proceedings at a National Peace Accord held in the middle of Johannesburg in September 1991, Mandela denounced de Klerk for his failure to order the police to disperse the Inkatha supporters, and one month later at a Commonwealth gathering in Harare he suggested that the South African president was turning out to be 'a totally different man from what he was initially'. Writing in 1998, de Klerk maintained that during the 1980s he was 'marginalized on the State Security Council' and that throughout his presidency he remained ignorant of any secret activities by police and army units. Mandela simply did not believe such protestations, especially after official investigations indicated the scope and scale of *agent provocateur* activity. During the second half of 1990, de Klerk recalled, 'Mandela regularly telephoned me at all hours of the day and night with new accusations and allegations'.[16] His anger at de Klerk became even more openly manifest at the first plenary session of the Convention for a Democratic South Africa (CODESA).

This first assembly of CODESA was a hurried affair, arranged to meet a public deadline of beginning talks by the end of 1991 to which both the government and the ANC had committed themselves. The

occasion was intended to represent a ceremonial opening to negotiations among the nine parties present. Heads of all the delegations
read speeches in front of the television cameras, with de Klerk appearing last on the programme, as he had requested. In his remarks, de
Klerk sprang a surprise on the other delegates: he said that the ANC
had committed itself to dismantling its military wing and its failure to
do so suggested that in future it would be negotiating in bad faith—
'an organization which remains committed to an armed struggle
cannot be trusted completely when it also commits itself to peace-
fully negotiated solutions'.[17] In fact, Kobie Coetsee had the day
before warned Thabo Mbeki that de Klerk would be raising the
question of Umkhonto's continuing existence, but the message had
not reached Mandela.[18] Mandela was visibly outraged by what he
took to be de Klerk's duplicity. In fairness to de Klerk, however, there
was indeed an agreement about Umkhonto's status, the D.F. Malan
Accord, dating from February, in which the ANC pledged that, while
it would maintain its army until elections, it would provide details of
its arms and deployments and once a transitional authority was established it would subordinate its command structure to this body. The
ANC's failure to adhere to all of its provisions had already been the
subject of an angry altercation between de Klerk and Mandela on
11 September.

Mandela requested and was granted the right to respond. De Klerk
had abused the position on the programme that had been conceded
to him, he said. He had been 'less than frank' in the confidences that
he was breaking in his references to arrangements about Umkhonto's
future. Even as the head of an illegitimate minority regime, de Klerk
should be expected to uphold certain moral standards. The ANC
would surrender its weapons only to an elected government and
certainly not to a government 'which we are sure either has lost
control over the security forces or [in which] the security forces are
doing precisely what he [de Klerk] wants them to do'.[19] If de Klerk
did not know about the help that Inkatha was receiving from his own
government, then he was not to fit to lead it. He, Mandela, however,
would continue to work with him, despite his errors. It was a brutal
and high personal assault. In de Klerk's words, it 'created a rift

between us that never again fully healed'[20] despite Mandela's efforts later to repair some of the damage. The day afterwards he and Ramaphosa walked across the convention hall to shake de Klerk's hand.

It was an inauspicious beginning to the talks. The next full sessions were in mid-May; meanwhile five working groups were to address the different sets of issues. In March the government strengthened its bargaining position by organising (with reluctant ANC assent) a whites-only referendum to obtain mandate for reform, winning a majority of 68.7 per cent in the ballot in support for a broad mandate for constitutional change—urging its supporters to 'vote yes if you're scared of majority rule', and join the National party in one last trek, 'to find a real home, a true fatherland, in the new South Africa'.[21] In contrast to the dismissive treatment accorded to the referendum by Mandela's biographers, analysts of South Africa's transition to democracy view the referendum as a critical episode. Before taking negotiations any further, de Klerk needed to re-establish his own legitimacy among white South Africans, especially among those who opposed further changes. His standing had been damaged by continuing political conflict and by a succession of by-election defeats. His opponents on the right appeared to be on the ascendant. Calling the referendum represented a bold gamble and his victory in the poll was a decisive moment in the transition.[22]

In the short term, however, the referendum hardened attitudes between the main protagonists. In the months before and at the second full plenary on 15 May the differences between the two main parties focused on the issue of what size of majority a constituent assembly would need to adopt a final constitution if no consensus could be reached: the ANC were willing to allow that a bill of rights could be entrenched by a 75 per cent majority and that even ordinary clauses of the constitution could need 70 per cent support; the government's team were adamant: that all sections of the constitution should draw support from 75 per cent of the elected assembly and any future changes would need a 75 per cent majority. The government also opposed the ANC's suggestion that, in the case of deadlock after six months, a national referendum could result in the Constitution's adoption through a simple majority. Faced with government intransigence the ANC announced its withdrawal. In the aftermath of CODESA's rupture, the ANC held a special conference at which delegates voted for 'rolling mass action', strikes, and street demonstrations. The ANC would not return to the talks until the government met 14 conditions, including the establishment of an interim government of national unity and the termination of all covert activity by the security forces. This was a decision that may not have accorded with Mandela's own predispositions. De Klerk recalls that, after the initial breakdown of the discussions in CODESA's Working Group Two concerning the constitution-making procedure, he and Mandela 'met for a cup of coffee . . . both he and I were determined to keep the negotiations on course'.[23] The night before the breakdown, ANC negotiators had visited Mandela at his home, waking him up. The high majorities that the ANC had been induced into considering would award minorities a decisive influence in deciding the final constitution, yet the ANC could not afford to appear too uncompromising: Ramaphosa's inclusion of a simple majority deadlock-breaking mechanism was intended to achieve deadlock.[24]

On 16 June, the anniversary of the Soweto uprising, a national stay away closed down factories and offices through the country. On the night of the next day, a group of Zulu migrant workers, Inkatha supporters, probably assisted by rogue policemen, mounted an attack on residents in Boipatong Township, near Vereeniging, killing 38 people, including 24 women and two infants. The Boipatong massacre strengthened the moral authority of militant counsels within the ANC, especially advocates such as Ronnie Kasrils of the 'Leipzig Option' who hoped that mass insurgency by itself could bring about a collapse in the regime's support. Ciskei was chosen for the first exercise of a popular insurrection because here it was hoped that, faced with a huge demonstration of the ANC's following, the homeland security forces would disobey orders and hold their fire. Contrary to such expectations on 7 September the Ciskeien military fired 425 rounds into the ANC's procession, killing 28, wounding more than 200, and dispersing the rest. In the aftermath of this tragedy Mandela announced a halt to 'mass action' and, reportedly, censured

Kasrils. One week later, in a newspaper interview Mandela offered de Klerk a prospect of resuming talks if his government would meet three conditions: the fencing of migrant workers' hostels, the release of 200 prisoners whose political status the authorities had been disputing, and a ban on 'cultural weapons'—that is, the clubs and spears that Inkatha supporters carried when they paraded in public. De Klerk responded two days later with an invitation to a summit meeting to discuss ways of ending the violence. Mandela reciprocated with a friendly phone call, afterwards telling journalists that de Klerk 'was a very brave chap, you know, and very bright and it was worrying to hear him sounding so down'.[25]

The summit was held on 26 September. On this occasion, the government conceded all three issues and a Record of Understanding committed both sides to a resumption of the constitutional talks. The most difficult of the concessions for the government was the release of death row prisoners who included Robert Macbride, convicted for placing a bomb in a Durban bar which killed three women. Mandela was insistent, 'tough as nails' according to one witness,[26] that all three demands had to be met. In a telephone conversation Mandela warned de Klerk, to Ramaphosa's mounting alarm, against intransigency: 'Because you know in the end you are going to give in. Because if you don't we are going to humiliate you. And I will see to it that that happens.'[27] De Klerk agreed to the releases and accordingly signed a Further Indemnity Act, not, however, he claims, as a consequence of Mandela's 'bullying and blustering' but rather as a result of 'pressure from my own side'.[28] The government agreement to ban 'cultural weapons' put an end to any hopes that its members may have retained of forming an electoral alliance with Inkatha. After the Record of Understanding and with the government committed to a co-operative strategy of negotiation with the ANC, most analysts of the negotiations agree that the ANC enjoyed the upper hand; if the government had agreed to the ANC's terms in May in the end it may have obtained a more constitutionally entrenched commitment to power sharing.[29]

The groundwork for the Record had been laid down during the three months preceding it because in fact the National Party negotiators and the ANC had maintained contact discreetly, largely as a consequence of an unlikely camaraderie that had developed between the government's Roelf Meyer and Ramaphosa. Ramaphosa had emerged as an assertive and capable member of the ANC's team at CODESA, the ANC's 'most accomplished negotiator', Mandela believed,[30] a view shared by de Klerk who less flatteringly described Ramaphosa's 'relaxed manner' as belied by 'coldly calculating eyes . . . searching continuously for the softest spot in the defences of his opponents'.[31]

Another point of contact between ANC and the government was also important: in September the ANC's head of economics, Trevor Manuel, listened to a briefing from de Klerk's finance minister on the degeneration of the economy since 1990. He told Mandela what he had heard, and in Mandela's own words 'got frightened'. 'What does this mean as far as negotiations are concerned?' he asked Manuel, 'Because it appears to me that if we allowed the situation to continue . . . the economy is going to be so destroyed that when a democratic government comes to power, it will not be able to solve'. The deadlock must end, Mandela reasoned.[32] By this stage, moreover, he was keenly aware of the risk that insurgent politics represented to the prospects of a settlement. Arriving to address a meeting in Katlehong, east of Johannesburg, one of the epicentres of the warfare between ANC and Inkatha supporters, Mandela found a message awaiting him on the speakers' table: 'No peace, do not talk to us about peace. We've had enough. Please, Mr Mandela, no peace. Give us weapons. No peace.' In departing from his prepared text, he needed to draw upon his most regal manner in exercising moral authority:

> There are times when our people participate in the killing of innocent people. It is difficult for us to say when people are angry that they must be non-violent. But the solution is peace, it is reconciliation, it is political tolerance. We must accept that blacks are fighting each other in the townships . . . we must accept that responsibility for ending the violence is not just the government's, the police's, the army's. It is also our responsibility. We must put our house in order. If you have no discipline you are not a freedom fighter. If you are going to kill innocent people, you don't belong to the ANC. Your task is reconciliation. Listen to me. Listen to me.

I am your leader. I am going to give leadership. Do you want me to remain your leader? Yes? Well, as long as I am your leader, I will tell you, always, when you are wrong.[33]

By the time a new Multi-Party Negotiation Forum assembled in March 1993 the two main parties had moved considerably closer to each other. An important agent in this process was Slovo who in August 1991 had published an article in the *African Communist* proposing that, given the fact that the regime was not about to surrender as it had not been defeated, the ANC should consider a 'strategic retreat' and be willing to compromise its demand for immediate majority rule. It could consider sharing power for a fixed period, it could agree to amnesty for any of its opponents who had committed crime, and it could guarantee the jobs of civil servants. Despite engendering resistance, Slovo's proposals became the basis of the ANC's negotiating strategy, notwithstanding the doubts about 'bourgeois reformism'[34] expressed in public by Harry Gwala in Natal and comparably contemptuous reservations about 'quick fix solutions' expressed by Winnie Mandela in Johannesburg.[35] From November 1992, the ANC was prepared to countenance a coalition 'Government of National Unity' for a transitional period as well as job security for civil servants, soldiers, and policemen.

Mandela was not normally directly involved in the Forum's day-to-day bargaining, although he and other senior ANC leaders met their negotiators often, at times daily. He did take a personal part in one of the final debates, when he confronted de Klerk on 16 November 1993 over the issue of cabinet decision-making: de Klerk wanted a minority veto, Mandela insisted that he could not run a government in such a fashion and de Klerk capitulated. At this meeting it was also agreed that elections would be followed by a five-year government of national unity and that, if there was deadlock over the final constitution, this could be resolved by a 60 per cent majority.

In a more crucial context, however, in the months after the Forum started its work Mandela exercised a decisive influence. On 10 April 1993, Hani was murdered outside his home, in a middle-class white suburb in Boskburg, by an assassin commissioned by members of the right-wing Conservative Party. Hani was immensely popular and his death was followed by riots in which 70 people died. Mandela appeared on television to appeal for calm. It was a white man who had killed Hani, he noted, 'But a white woman, of Afrikaner origin, risked her life so that we may know and bring justice to the assassin.' Beyond issuing a statement of condolence, de Klerk remained silent, probably quite sensibly—as he admitted later 'this was Mandela's moment, not mine'.[36] But his silence underlined Mandela's command of national authority.

The ANC's willingness to embrace transitional constitutional arrangements, the breakdown of any prospect of alliance between the National Party and Inkatha, a consequence of the Record of Understanding, and Mandela's assumption of the role of national conciliator in the crisis that succeeded Hani's assassination were all factors that helped to induce agreement, 'sufficient consensus' as it was termed, between the principals at the talks, the ANC and the government. Mandela's personal rapport with General Constand Viljoen, leader of the Afrikaner *Volksfront*, was probably decisive in the far-right's eleventh hour embrace of the settlement: dialogue between the *Volksfront* generals and the ANC began at Mandela's home in August 1993, with Mandela telling an appreciative Viljoen: 'If you want to go to war, I must be honest and admit that we cannot stand up to you on the battlefield . . . [but] you cannot win because of our numbers and you cannot kill us all.'[37]

From the elections in April 1994, for the next five years South Africa would be governed by a coalition administration in which seats would be shared roughly proportional to their electoral support between parties with more than 5 per cent of the ballot. The elections themselves would be held under proportional representation and the electorate would be voting for a national assembly and nine regional governments demarcated by borders that, in effect, would allow at least one of the old homeland parties, Inkatha, a reasonable prospect of securing executive authority. The House of Assembly, together with the Senate, would sit as a Constituent Assembly and decide upon a final constitution which itself would have to incorporate key features of the interim constitution negotiated at the forum, including an extensive Bill of Rights. Bureaucrats, soldiers, and policemen had their jobs and pensions guaranteed and amnesty would be offered to those guilty of politically motivated killings.

Mandela's political authority was crucial in securing legitimacy for constitutional arrangements that fell well short of political expectations among the ANC's support base. An interim government of national unity was 'not power-sharing' he insisted, a position supported by Ramaphosa, who maintained that 'our idea of a government of national unity means majority rule should not be sacrificed in any way'.[38] The ANC had to compromise in other arenas as well, because by 1993 the ANC had accepted that their historical commitment to nationalising key industries would result in further capital flight: the movement's Reconstruction and Development Programme, drafted by trade unionists in 1993, related nationalisation to a policy option rather than a principled imperative. Mandela played a significant role in this realignment after returning from a World Economic Forum meeting in Davos in February 1992, convinced by listening to advice from Vietnamese and Chinese financiers. Later he told the ANC's economic commission that he had also been chastened by the warmth of the reception accorded by Davos delegates to de Klerk and Buthelezi, both of whom had spoken vigorously in favour of free enterprise.[39] Between 1990 and 1992 Mandela and other ANC leaders were acutely concerned that de Klerk might succeed in winning international support for his own version of a political settlement, a not unreasonable anxiety given de Klerk's own diplomatic successes, not just in his visits to Europe and the USA, but also in his receptions as a head of state by the governments of Nigeria and Kenya, heavyweights in pan-African affairs. Nigeria subsequently supplied the key African support for a toning down of a UN Security Council Resolution that accused de Klerk's administration of direct responsibility for the Boipating massacre. In 1992, de Klerk's successful joint nomination, together with Mandela, for the Nobel Peace Prize represented an especially telling (and for the ANC unwelcome) confirmation of his international stature. Partly with the aim of countering de Klerk's influence, Mandela visited 49 countries during 16 journeys outside South Africa from his release until mid-1992,[40] travels that accentuated ANC sensitivity to international opinion.

Meanwhile, during the settling of affairs of state, Mandela's domestic world fell apart. Winnie's own political activities were one source of strain in a marriage that, at the time of his release, he represented to the world as his emotional base, the source of his moral resilience. Winnie had been allowed to return to her old home in Orlando in 1986. The following year she established the Mandela Football Club, initially it seems as a focus for organised activity for a group of young teenagers to whom she had given shelter in the backrooms in her yard. The Club's members perceived themselves as Winnie's bodyguards, and indeed she encouraged them to assume such a function and allowed then to carry weapons when members of the group accompanied her on excursions. Increasingly, the Club began behaving in the fashion of a territorial gang, conducting turf wars with other groups of youths. It abducted adherents of rival groups and acquired a reputation for torturing its opponents. In 1988 the Mandela house was set alight by the Club's opponents, a development that prompted the formation of the Mandela Crisis Committee, a group of UDF leaders and trade unionists, including Ramaphosa.

The Footballers moved with Winnie into a house in the elite neighbourhood of Diepkloof. Their behaviour deteriorated further. A young boy, Lolo Sono, was held in Winnie's house, accused of being a spy. Winnie brought Lolo to his father's house, bruised and beaten, and said that she was taking him away. Lolo was subsequently never seen again. In December 1988 another child was kidnapped by the Football Club, this time from the Methodist Mission House in Orlando, which Winnie seemed to resent as a rival refuge for dis-affected youngsters. The priest, Paul Verryn, was on holiday and he had left the care of the children in the hands of Xoliswa Falati, a friend of Winnie's. Falati decided that one of the children in her care, 'Stompie' Seipei, was a police spy. She also maintained that he and other children were unsafe at the mission because Verryn was a homosexual. Seipei and two other boys were taken to Winnie Mandela's house. There they were beaten, in Winnie's presence. A few days later, Seipei was found in a riverbed, stabbed to death. The Mandela Crisis Committee visited Winnie and demanded to meet the other two boys whom her followers had abducted: she refused to give them up. The Crisis Committee wrote to Mandela seeking his intervention, but Mandela, loyal to his wife, maintained her innocence, although when she visited he did urge her 'to get rid of these people around you . . . it is poor judgment to have them near you'.[41] On 16 February, the Crisis Committee called a press conference and declared its 'outrage at Mrs Mandela's complicity in the recent abduction and assault of Stompei'. This was followed up with milder statements from Tambo's office, which 'with a feeling of terrible sadness' noted 'our reservations about Winnie Mandela's judgement in relation to the Mandela football club'.

At this juncture, Mandela still found it hard to believe that Winnie could be guilty of any more than bad judgement. Might not she ask forgiveness at a public press conference, he suggested to Bishop Stanley Mogoba during a visit. 'She's a wonderful girl', he wrote on 28 February, and he would 'accordingly urge patience and that you be as supportive as you always have been'.[42] Winnie underwent prosecution for her role in these events at the beginning of 1991 in a case that lasted for six months. She was exonerated of direct involvement in any assault, but convicted for authorising the abduction that had led to Seipei's death. Mandela maintained his public support for Winnie, before the trial professing to view the evidence against her as merely the outcome of the state's 'campaign to discredit my wife'. His view of the trial as essentially political caused a rupture between him and the International Defence and Aid Fund, which had been warned by officials in the European Community that its grant from the Community would be cut if it used EC funding to pay for Winnie Mandela's defence. In fact the Fund found an alternative source in an American Corporation but then found that it could not help because the Mandelas' family lawyer, Ismail Ayob, decided to charge fees well in excess of the Fund's tariff.[43]

Mandela's attitude to the trial may have shifted: at a press conference after the verdict he resisted the suggestion that he might lose faith in the South African legal system, reminding the reporters 'Once an appeal has been made, it is proper to leave the matter in the hands of the court'.[44] Even so, one year later, he would insist on

Winnie's reinstatement as head of the ANC's social welfare department from which she was dismissed in December 1992 after letters of
complaint from more than 100 ANC branches. Since 1990 he had
supported his wife's cause, using his influence to ensure her appointment or election to various positions in the ANC, beginning by
touring Orlando and making door-to-door visits to ensure her election as chairperson of the local branch of the ANC Women's League,
and with her seeking to exclude members of the Mandela Crisis
Committee from important positions. One of its members, Azhar
Cachalia, nephew of Mandela's old friend, Yusuf, received a telephoned warning from Winnie to 'stay away from Mandela . . . if you
don't you'll see what will happen'.[45] At the ANC's conference in
July 1991 he had lobbied, without success, against the election of
Ramaphosa as secretary-general.[46]

In February 1992, one month after the conclusion of the trial,
Mandela moved out of Winnie's house; after press disclosures about
her love affair with a man, 27 years her junior, who had worked with
her in the ANC's headquarters, there was little to be gained by maintaining a public pretence of private happiness. Mandela learned about
the relationship in prison and wrote to Winnie, requesting her to get
'that boy' out of the house.[47] In March, a newspaper published one of
Winnie's letters to her lover, Dali Mpofu. It described a deteriorating
situation at home: she had not spoken to *Tata* (old man/father) for
five months now. As damaging to Winnie was her reference to the
cheques that she had drawn in Mpofu's name from the Welfare
Department's bank account. She had appointed Mpofu as her deputy
in her ANC office in March 1991 and in October had taken him on a
trip to the USA to raise funds and artistic support for a projected
'Children of Africa' concert. Mandela asked George Bizos to verify
the letters with his wife; apparently Winnie, on being shown the
letters in Mandela's words, 'broke down and wept'.[48] On 17 April
1992, Mandela announced his separation from his wife, parting from
her, he said 'with no recriminations' and still 'embrac[ing] her with all
the love and affection I have nursed for her inside and outside prison'.
He would 'never regret the life Comrade Nomzamo and I have
tried to share together'.[49] But despite Winnie's efforts to achieve

reconciliation, Mandela was resolute. His last steps in his walk to freedom he would take alone, without his wife and without Tambo his partner and friend, who had died two weeks after he and Mandela had sat together at Hani's funeral.

At the beginning of her book, Mary Benson, Mandela's first biographer, posed the question: 'How is it that a man imprisoned for more than twenty three years . . . has become the embodiment of the struggle for liberation . . . and is the vital symbol of a new society?'[50] Biography itself can supply only part of the answer; usually the processes through which certain men or women become venerated in popular political culture extend well beyond the concerns that inform the analysis of a particular life. Even so, biography represents an obvious starting point in the investigation of iconographies, especially in the case of Mandela's public life, which features so conspicuously the deliberate construction of emblematic attributes by himself and others.

Mandela's own testimony supplies a most comprehensive biographical portrait of the man. *Long Walk to Freedom* is not quite autobiography, however. Part of the text is based upon the manuscript written in prison in 1975 and the rest is assembled from interviews conducted in 1994 by an American journalist, Richard Stengel. Since its publication, an illustrated coffee table edition has appeared as well as an abridged edition in basic English and translations in Zulu, Sotho, and Afrikaans, pointers to the heterodox social character of Mandela's devotees. Notwithstanding the participation of his ghost writer, it is a safe assumption that the book's 600-odd pages are a faithful reflection of Mandela's own conception of his life and personality—in Stengel's words, a mirror 'of the proud and graceful persona Mr Mandela has crafted for himself'.[51]

Even so, Mandela's autobiography reveals a complicated man. Trained in a royal household Mandela first learned his lessons about leadership by watching his guardian, Jongintaba. In the Thembu polity, decision-making was consensual—'democracy in its purest form', Mandela would describe it—in which the King's councillors would express their views until all had said all that they could say, and then the Regent himself would speak, defining the position that would most likely represent consensus. All views, notionally at least, would have an equal weight. Such a procedure contrasts with the adversarial quality of decision-making of a majoritarian democracy. 'As a leader', Mandela claims in his autobiography, 'I have always followed the principles I first saw demonstrated by the regent at the great palace.' 'A leader is like a shepherd', nudging and prodding his flock before him. Significantly he employs the metaphor of shepherding in referring to his decision to begin his talks in prison with government officials: 'There are times when a leader must move out ahead of his flock, go off in a new direction, confident that he is leading his people in the right way.'[52]

Today, Mandela likes to be called 'Madiba', his clan name, by his friends and political associates, signifying both the intimacy of kinship and the respect of ascribed status, and the name has become popularised in the South African press. Certainly, he continues to be attracted to what he perceives to be traditional notions of leadership and community, but, as his history demonstrates, in his later career he was to exercise a completely different style of leadership—one in which personal initiatives had to usurp the imperative for consensus. 'Sometimes one must go public with an idea to nudge a reluctant organisation in the direction you want it to go', he observes with reference to his unauthorised public statement in 1961 that the days of nonviolent struggle were over. And though his autobiography does not quote it, Mandela's famous remark at a later stage of negotiations, his profession of faith in the 'ordinary democracy' of majority rule,[53] adds confirmation that his understanding of African traditions supplies only one element, albeit an important one, in his political make-up. Traditions can be useful—Mandela's manipulation of custom suggests a shrewdly instrumental recognition of their role—but his narrative acknowledges that the past is another country. Returning to his Transkeian birthplace after his release from prison, he finds a landscape littered with plastic bags and a community in which pride and self-worth 'seemed to have vanished'. The argument is underlined in his discussion of his relationship with the new generation of Black Consciousness political activists who appeared on Robben Island from 1974; here he acknowledges the danger of clinging to ideas that 'had become frozen in time'. Mandela's empathy with rebellious youth is a frequent theme in his public utterances. In an angry speech delivered to 1,000 amakhosi and indunas in Kwa–Zulu Natal in 1996, Mandela reprimanded local chiefs who had helped to encourage political violence, warning them that 'they would be left behind by the real leaders emerging from the youth of the country'.[54] A few months before the 1994 election he created a furore by suggesting that the franchise should be extended to 14 year olds, a proposal that his embarrassed ANC colleagues hurriedly repudiated.

The tensions between different facets of Mandela's personality remain unresolved in his autobiography. They are evident in the different voices that tell his story. One voice is magisterial and statesman-like, the voice that emphasises the central themes of racial reconciliation and man's essential goodness ('all men have a core of decency'[55]), which runs through the text. Another voice is the less measured one recorded in the opening chapter of this book, the voice that expresses anguish of personal loss, experiences that are rendered most poignantly in the powerful recurrent image of a child putting on the clothing of his dead or absent father, an image echoed in the undressing and dressing that mark the moments of entry in Mandela's captivities. This is a voice that can subvert the impersonal heroic collective political emotions with which he attributes his public self. These are expressed on the day of his presidential inauguration: 'I felt that day, as I have on so many others, that I was simply the sum of all those African patriots who had gone before me.'[56] But as he concedes one page later, 'every man has twin obligations' and in serving his people he was prevented from fulfilling his roles as 'a son, a brother, a father and a husband'. The pain that arises from the latter recognition is generally controlled and suppressed in the book; indeed learning to control and conceal pain and its accompaniment, fear, is one of the defining qualities of manhood, he learns as a child; nevertheless it is frequently evident, no more so than in the curious mixture of the languages of bureaucratic rationality and private tribute with which he announced his separation from his wife, 'Comrade Nomzamo'.[57]

The public emotions that Mandela professes are also carefully managed. The political Mandela is at least in part the product of artifice. The third section of his book is entitled 'The birth of a freedom fighter' and its occasional deliberate use of the third person voice—'it is important for a freedom fighter to remain in touch with his own roots'—is a significant indication of Mandela's own consciousness of inventing a public identity and acting out a heroic role. There are other kinds of acting too; at several points in the narrative Mandela assumes disguises and false identities. Clothing, costume, and style are indispensable components in the different personas that Mandela assumes, nowhere more obviously than in his choice of a leopard skin *kaross* to wear in his first appearance in court after his arrest in 1962. 'I had chosen traditional Xhosa dress to emphasise the symbolism that I was a black African walking into a white man's court . . . I felt myself to be the embodiment of African nationalism.' Later, he refers to prison as 'a different and smaller arena' (to the courtroom), 'an arena in which the only audience was ourselves and our oppressors'. This awareness of an audience and his conviction of the historic destiny are both indispensable accomplices in Mandela's own crafting of his exemplary life. The links between political leadership and theatrical performance are emphasised in a reference to his role as Creone in Orestes' version of Sophocles' *Antigone*, as enacted by the prisoners on Robben Island. Significantly, several commentaries have used the metaphors of masks and masking in their analysis of Mandela's personality,[58] a term that Mandela himself used in describing the way in which in prison he concealed his anguished longing for his family.[59]

Mandela himself has an ambivalent attitude to his heroic status, recognising the merits of the ANC personalising the cause in the campaign for his release, but often affecting disdain for 'the exaltation of the president and denigration of other ANC leaders [which] constitutes praise which I do not accept'.[60] In fact, as we have seen, the ANC's development during his political life allowed plenty of scope for the influence of strong prophetic personalities. When Mandela joined the ANC, in 1942, the organisation had only recently emerged from a decade of torpor and its small following was concentrated in three cities. From its foundation in 1912 its programme had only occasionally extended beyond an annual convention of African gentry and notables. With the exception of a few communists, its leadership had been mostly at best amateur politicians; Mandela and his fellow Youth Leaguers were the first substantial cohort of African middle-class professionals to make political activism the central focus in their lives, hence their extraordinarily rapid ascent in a movement, the following of which ballooned in their wake. From his first hesitant association with the organisation shortly after his arrival in Johannesburg, it took just ten years for Mandela to emerge as its second ranking leader. The ANC's switch to militant forms of mass protest in the 1950s coincided with the development of a popular press directed at African readers and from the time of his appointment as 'National Volunteer-in-chief' in the 1952 Defiance Campaign—a civil disobedience programme that emphasised the sacrificial role of inspirational leadership—Mandela became one of South Africa's first black media personalities. Through the following decade of mobilisation politics, ANC leaders became increasingly aware of the potentialities of newspaper celebrity.

In the early 1960s there was an especial need for the ANC to develop a heroic pantheon of leaders. On the African continent its exiled representatives were encountering strong opposition from its offshoot rival, the Pan Africanist Congress (PAC), which had been rather more successful in assuming an 'authentic' African identity roughly comparable to the popular nationalist movements presided over by the charismatic and messianic leaders that were spearheading African decolonisation at that time. When the Free Mandela Committee was established at the time of Mandela's 1962 trial its organisers distributed a lapel button, bearing a portrait of the imprisoned leader wrapped in the West African toga then favoured by the continent's emergent rulers. The ultimate success of such efforts to embody the ANC's cause in a saga of individual heroism probably exceeded any of the expectations among ANC strategists in the early 1960s. In the 27 years of his confinement Mandela accumulated 12 honorary degrees, freedom of dozens of cities, and a range of awards from governments. In 1988 admirers in the Netherlands alone swamped the South African prison service with 170,000 letters and birthday cards. In the same year, 250,000 people assembled in London's Hyde

Park at the conclusion of the Free Mandela March to listen to 30 minutes of readings from Mandela's correspondence with his wife. His face appeared on postage stamps and official sculpture, and his deeds, mythical and real, were celebrated at rock concerts.

By the 1980s, Mandela could with justification claim to be 'the world's most famous political prisoner'.[61] Some of this fame arose from the popular attention that Mandela's own actions commanded: at the time of his well-publicised court appearances his story exemplified old-fashioned virtues—honour, courage, and chivalry. The explanation of this extraordinary international celebrity status cannot, however, be confined to Mandela's actions or the ANC's own efforts to foster cults of charismatic leadership, important as they were. Such endeavours were given ample assistance by: the peculiar moral appeal of South African liberation and its resonance in the international politics of anti-racism and decolonisation; the emergence of a transnational anti-apartheid 'new social movement'; Mandela's cultural adaptability as a modern folk hero; and the immortality conferred upon him by seclusion. The internationalisation of South African political conflict is obviously attributable to the existence of a uniquely institutionalised system of racism in a relatively important and accessible country in a world climate shaped by the post-war reaction against Nazism and colonialism. Anti-apartheid as a social movement drew its strength from the same forces that helped to engender a range of new political identities in mature industrial societies. But Mandela's personal qualities, which made him especially susceptible to international cult status, and the effects of his compelled isolation from everyday life, deserve more extended commentary.

'I confess to being something of an anglophile', Mandela tells us in his autobiography. The passage continues: 'When I thought of Western democracy and freedom, I thought of the British parliamentary system. In so many ways, the very model of the gentleman for me was an Englishman. . . . While I abhorred the notion of British imperialism, I never rejected the trappings of British style and manners.' On the eve of his departure from Johannesburg on a journey to address members of both houses of parliament at Westminster in 1993, he told journalists 'I have not discarded the influence which Britain and British influence and culture exercised on us'.[62] As Stengel has noticed, 'To him, the British audience is more important than either the American or the European'.[63] Relatively few 'third world' insurgencies managed to combine in their leaderships such an effective mixture of guerrilla glamour and reassuring metropolitan respectability. Like many other ANC leaders of his generation, Mandela's Anglo-Methodist schooling and his liberal literary education equipped him with a familiarity with Anglo-American culture and a capacity, consciously or otherwise, to invoke its social codes. A particularly telling example of this attribute in his personality and life history is the tragic story of his second marriage; significantly one of his first acts of rebellion was to reject a customary union arranged by his guardian. During his imprisonment, his beautiful and personable wife played a substantial role in ensuring the durability of his political authority. Notwithstanding such gestures to African tradition as the payment of *lobola*, the correspondence between Nelson and Winnie Mandela employs the informal egalitarian idioms and expresses the sexual intimacies of modern western domestic life. Mandela's very public subscription to an idyll of romantic love was a vital element in the narratives directed at western audiences.[64] More generally, his and the ANC's role as representatives of an industrialised urban community made them especially culturally intelligible in Europe and North America, all the more so given the appearance in the 1950s of an unusually talented generation of black South African writers who began to find a significant readership outside South Africa.

Mandela's incarceration and the official South African bans on the publication of his words and portraits as well as the authorities' refusal to allow photographs of him in prison, ensured that public narratives were shaped by the words and images that were available from the struggle epic that stretched from the Defiance Campaign to the Rivonia trial, a few timeless and ageless texts and pictures, which as Rob Nixon perceptively notes kept 'circulating in a heraldic fashion perfect for the needs of an international political movement'.[65] The imprisonment and isolation from public view kept the narrative and the images that accompanied it pristine, invested with the glamour of martyrdom but reinforced by the apocalyptic possibilities of a second coming. Sipho Sepamla, a poet of the 1980s' activist generation, expresses especially powerfully this vision of an assertive youthful Mandela striding his way out of prison, fist raised high in the straight-armed black power salute:

> I need today oh so very badly
> Nelson Mandela
> Out of the prison gates
> to walk broad-shouldered-among counsel
> down Commissioner
> up West street
> and lead us away from the shadow
> of impotent word weavers
> his clenched fist hoisted higher than hope
> for all to see and follow.[66]

Government strategists told an American researcher at the beginning of the 1980s that they were aware that Mandela's removal from the political stage freed him from the requirement 'to make hard, human decisions'.[67] 'Mandela is not so much a political figure as a mythical one. For this reason', opined Professor Willie Breytenbach, a key government adviser in the 1980s, 'I believe that if he should be released the key problem would be surviving long enough to play any role at all.'[68] Credo Mutwa, a self-professed 'High Witchdoctor' and an authority on indigenous culture much favoured by the old South African authorities, predicted in 1986 that Mandela's release would replace a revered hero-saviour with 'a spent force like an arrow which has spent its passion'.[69] Public opinion polling since the aftermath of the Soweto uprising consistently suggested that Mandela's personal following exceeded that of the ANC's, indicative of the extent to which the alluring enigmas created by his absence from active politics had helped to transform the guerrilla convict into a patriotic icon. When Chief Buthelezi's differences with the ANC became public, he attempted to demonstrate his membership of a more legitimate patriotic community by publishing his private correspondence with Mandela. And, although freedom did not bring all the dividends that his captors may have hoped for, it certainly detracted from the more

millenarian dimensions of the myth. During the protracted negotiations that followed Mandela's release, some South African urban
legends inverted the logic of the second coming to explain why
freedom was taking so long to arrive. A young black truck driver
informed Jeremy Cronin, a Communist Party leader, that the real
Nelson Mandela was killed in prison. 'Today's Mandela is a look-
alike. He was trained for years by the Boers and finally presented to
the public in 1990. The mission of this look-alike is to pretend to be
against the system. But in reality he is working for it.'[70]

Mandela's captivity enhanced the omnibus appeal of his authority.
Mandela biographies and hagiographies project quite different understandings of his personal greatness and its broader social meanings.
Such projections have reflected differing imperatives of various constituencies within the broad movement that he represented during his
imprisonment as well as its changing ideological predispositions.
They also testify to the ways in which his life has become emblematic
for people quite separate from the ANC's community and even
outside South Africa. Three examples must suffice.

Mandela's first biographer, Mary Benson, was secretary to the
ANC president in the 1950s and was close to many of the events that
she describes. In 1963, by which time she was living in London, she
wrote a richly textured popular history of the ANC. Her Mandela
biography was first published in 1980 as a volume in the 'PanAf Great
Lives' series. A second updated edition appeared in 1986. Limited by
its author's restricted access to sources, Benson's book concerns itself
mainly with Mandela's political career, at least until his first meeting
with Winnie. The opening chapter supplies a bare outline of its
subject's genealogy, childhood, and education. For Benson, the
important developments in the story begin after Mandela's arrival in
Johannesburg. Most of Benson's biography comprises a chronology
of public events and references to Mandela's contribution to these. Its
treatment is very general and its focus is mainly on the organisation,
not the man. Long extracts from Mandela's polemical writings and
his trial addresses occupy a large portion of Benson's text. They help
to reinforce a rather impersonal tribute with the accent on Mandela's
identity as a modern liberal democratic politician. This is the identity

that was accentuated in those public commemorations of Mandela that were directed at Europeans and North Americans. In contributing to a volume of 'literary homage', Jacques Derrida writes of Mandela as the ultimate apostle and interpreter of the rational legal traditions associated with the western enlightenment.[71]

A fuller version of Mandela's political testament, a collection of his speeches and writings, was published in London in 1965 in the Heinemann African Writers series, edited by Ruth First with an introduction by Tambo. In her foreword to the second 1973 edition, First compares the author to the then fashionable American black power heroes, George Jackson, Soledad Brother, and Angela Davis. A grainy picture of Mandela visiting an Algerian military facility adds visual confirmation to First's presentation of the ANC's 'underground political commander' as the personification of 'revolutionary power'.[72] The 'light editing' of the original material included the excision, from an article first published in 1956 about the Freedom Charter, of a passage describing the benefits that the Charter would bring to a nascent African bourgeoisie. However, even without First's editorial tidying-up, Mandela's 1950s' writings suggest a more intellectually radical figure than the pragmatic reformist projected in British and American analyses of the ANC's leadership. As we have seen Mandela's initial political experience was enriched by casual attendance at night schools organised by the Communist Party and more informal contact with its members and, although he subsequently for a while opposed communist influence within the ANC, he retained an affinity with the ideas of the left.

During the 1980s, both the exiled ANC and the internal political groups that stationed themselves in the Congress camp looked forward to a post-apartheid 'National Democracy' in which 'monopoly capital' would be displaced, a transitional stage that would precede a fully socialised society. In this context, fresh meaning was discovered in Mandela's life history. For example, within the National Union of Mineworkers, according to one of its spokesmen, after the Union's election of Mandela as its honorary Life President, 'work was done to inform workers of Mandela's history and the struggles he waged as a mineworker in Crown Mines'.[73]

In contrast to the liberal and egalitarian projections of Mandela's personality, a more deferential culture of homage developed around the Release Mandela Campaign (RMC). Here there was little room for the idea of popular sovereignty favoured by modern trade unions and civic organisations. Instead messianic obeisance to the leader was prescribed by spokesmen for the RMC during the 1980s. For Audrey Mokoena the RMC's Transvaal chairman, Mandela was 'the pivotal factor in the struggle for liberation. He has the stature and the charisma which derives from his contribution to the struggle.'[74] Mokoena's language was not atypical. Mewa Ramgobin told his audience at a Soweto RMC meeting in July 1984 that: 'I want to make bold and say in clear language that the human race must remain grateful, that the human race must go down on its knees and say thank you for the gifts it has been endowed with in the lives of the Nelson Mandelas of this country.'[75] Peter Mokaba, at the time the president of the South African Youth Congress, chaired the rally held in a Soweto stadium on 24 February 1990 to celebrate Mandela's release. He had this to say: 'Comrade President, here are your people, gathered to pay tribute to their messiah, their saviour whom the Apartheid regime failed dismally to silence. These are the comrades and the combatants that fought tooth and nail in the wilderness . . . they toiled in the valley of darkness, and now that their messiah and saviour is released, they want to be shown the way to freedom.'[76]

The attribution of Mandela with redemptive qualities of leadership reached its apogee during his visit to the USA in June 1990, four months after his release. Intended by the ANC as a fundraising trip (and most successful it was in this respect, with donations totalling US$7 million), for his African–American hosts as well as many people in his various audiences the occasion served quite different needs. As a New York newspaper report put it: 'the Mandela visit has become perhaps the largest and most vivid symbol that after many years on the edges of New York city power and politics the black community has arrived.'[77] For *Village Voice*'s Harlem correspondent 'The visit of the freedom fighter positioned us, for a minute, in the center of world politics. It made us the first family. And gave us, again, an accessible past, so that the African part of the equation suddenly had a lot more

sense'.[78] The notion of family-hood featured frequently in the comments recorded from spectators: 'We are all from Africa. This is like
family. He's a symbol of who we are.'[79] And there to welcome Mandela was the city's first black mayor, David Dinkins, there to organise
his security was the city's second black police commissioner, and
there to determine the events in his schedule were the legions of
black community leaders in Brooklyn and Harlem, 'who together
with more than 500 black churches had turned New York's African
Americans into the largest ethnic voting bloc in the city'.[80] So in
an important respect, Mandela's American journey helped to con-
solidate the leadership credentials of an African–American elite of
municipal bosses, civil rights luminaries, and show business
personalities.

But juxtaposed with the triumphalist language that accompanied
Mandela's progress was the perception that the South African visitor
supplied a missing moral dimension of authority, that his presence in
America could rekindle hope in ghetto communities affected by
social pathologies and political decay. Benjamin Chavis, the influential former director of the United Church of Christ Mission, captured
this feeling eloquently: 'We have a new Jerusalem. When he gets back
on the 'plane, we have to keep that fire alive and thank God that
Mandela has lit a fire that was extinguished in the 1960s. I think
you're going to see a lot of African Americans break out of the cycle
of hopelessness we've had.'[81] Veterans of the Civil Rights movement
repeatedly confided to journalists their conviction that Mandela's
coming 'had filled a void which had been left by the deaths of Dr
Martin Luther King and Malcolm X'.[82] This perception was widely
distributed. While waiting for Mandela's arrival, schoolteacher Mark
Reeves and his class spent 'all week studying Mr Mandela and relating
him to Martin Luther King and the Civil Rights movement'.[83] New
Yorkers 'turned him into an instant American celebrity, a civil rights
leader they could call their own'.[84] Winnie's presence evoked similar
emotions. Brushing aside the troubling controversies then surrounding Mrs Mandela in South Africa, Mrs Julie Belafonte, one of the
main organisers of the Mandela tour, told reporters 'We don't know
what happened over there . . . and in any case its irrelevant in relation

to the positive power she has displayed and the pressure she has been under. She's a wonderful role model for women.'[85]

Some 750,000 people lined the streets of New York to cheer his progress while in many other cities outside the 11 stops of his tour, programmes of festive events were arranged. Taraja Samuel, an administrator in the New York education department, 'felt a blessing from God that I could be a part of this'. Malcolm X's widow, Betty Shabazz, introduced Winnie Mandela to the congregation of Harlem's House of the Lord Church by saying: 'This sister's presence in our midst is enough. She shouldn't have to speak. To have gone through what she has gone through, and to see her so present, so composed! There must be a God. There's got to be a God.' At a meeting in Bedford Stuyvessant, Brooklyn, *Village Voice*'s correspondent, watched the sun shine through 'his silver Afro hair like a halo . . . this is a truly religious experience, a man back from the dead to lead the living, and an authentic african queen'.[86] Even the more measured official rhetoric that accompanied the tour resonated with chiliastic expectation. In his welcoming address, David Dinkins likened Mandela to a modern-day Moses 'leading the people of South Africa out of enslavement at the hands of the pharaoh'.

Mandela deftly tapped into the historical well-springs of the emotions that greeted him with gracious acknowledgement of a pantheon of appropriate local heroes. Each of his speeches included a recitation of their names: Sojourner Truth, Paul Robeson, Rosa Parks, Marcus Garvey, Fanie Lou Harries, Malcolm X, and Harriet Tobias. However, his protestations of being merely a representative of greater collective entity, the ANC, like his self-deprecatory meditations on the evanescent quality of human genius—'each shall, like a meteor, a mere brief passing moment in time and space, flit across the human stage'[87]—any such professions of mortality were drowned in the clamour arising from the procession of an African hero embodying American dreams.

In the perceptions of white South Africans, no strangers to millennial political traditions, the incarnation of Mandela as a national hero has signified the possibility of personal and communal salvation or baptism in a new 'rainbow' patriotism. Warder James Gregory's memoir, *Goodbye Bafana*, celebrates in its ingenuous fashion 'a cleans-ing process, one of ridding the anger'[88] that he experienced in his dealings with his famous prisoner. The book's title draws parallels between his relationship with Mandela and the lost innocence of a 'pre-apartheid' childhood friendship with a Zulu boy on his father's farm. As Mandela leaves prison, Gregory's mind 'returns to [his] boy-hood and to the farm where [he] played with Bafana all those years ago'.[89] In a less intrusive fashion than Gregory's often exploitative text, many others seek personally to appropriate a portion of Mandela's aura and in so doing lay to rest old demons:

> The icon of the 90s is a picture of yourself with President Mandela. . . . In homes where, during the apartheid era, the word 'struggle' was used so loosely that it could mean your wife had broken a nail or the maid hadn't pitched, Mandela's benevolent face now gazes out of large silver frames placed on study desks. He watches you from wood panelled libraries or from the walls of boardrooms. In these places the 'Me and Mandela' factor works as a talisman against the past, pushing it out of sight and into the dark recesses of time.[90]

Not content with donations to the ANC and undertaking the reconstruction of Mandela's old primary school, Bill Venter, chair-man of Altron, an electronics firm that became a major industrial company in the 1980s as a consequence of winning defence contracts, has made the birthday poem that he wrote for Mandela required reading for his employees, including it in a little red book, *Memos from the Chairman*, circulated to all staff. The poem reads: 'Your wisdom has woven a tapestry/Much more lovely than any artist's hand/With a vibrancy that only we can understand/We, who are Africa's people/ And feel the heartbeat of this land.'[91] As the new 'father of the nation', Mandela can summon expressions of loyalty from the most unexpected sources. Rejoicing in South Africa's new-found inter-national acceptability, the conservative *Citizen* newspaper noted 'the respect, almost awe' with which South Africa was now held, inform-ing its readers that 'we take even greater pride in the recognition of President Mandela's stature in the world. He is a great man who towers above other leaders, both at home, in Africa, and abroad.'[92] The more traditionally liberal *Star* profitably tapped a similar vein of sentiment when it filled a 'commercial feature' on 18 July, 1994, Mandela's birthday, with congratulatory advertisements from businesses and other organisations. After the 1994 election, Nelson Mandela maintained a series of imaginative gestures of reconciliation and empathy with white South Africa. These are discussed in more detail in Chapter 9. They included a well-publicised social encounter with the prosecutor at the Rivonia trial, Dr Percy Yutar. The latter event moved one Johannesburg journalist to refer to Mandela's 'superhuman forgiveness' more or less seriously as 'holy magnanimity', a phrase adapted from the concept of 'holy disbelief' used by the American theologian, Elizer Berkovits, to describe the loss of faith in concentration camps.[93]

What have been the political effects of this canonisation of democratic South Africa's first president? In the 1960s, charismatic heroes represented a central focus in the interpretation of African politics. David Apter described how the legitimacy of new institutions was both strengthened and weakened by Kwame Nkrumah's charismatic authority, a sacred authority that remained 'an important device by which political institutional transfer'[94] was affected. In a country in which cultural cohesion is very substantially the consequence of religious belief, 'massively Christian', sacred authority remains a critical political attribute. Liturgically inspired rhetoric has been such an important accompaniment of South African history: 'Rarely indeed in modern history has the emergence of a modern nation been guided by such strict religious oratory.'[95]

Certainly, Mandela's moral and political authority performs some of the positive functions assigned to charismatic authority by the analysts of political modernisation 30 years ago. In a country in which liberal democratic institutions and procedures are not especially popular, Mandela's identification with them may have enshrined them with a degree of legitimacy that they otherwise might have lacked. Mandela's moral endorsement of political compromise was certainly indispensable in the success of South Africa's 'pacted' political transition. Transition theory, with its focus on the choices and decisions made by political elites, is especially receptive to 'Great Men' readings of history. Within the domain of foreign policy,

Mandela's personal appeal has enabled South Africa to elicit special treatment. As Paul Neifert, a US AID representative, lamented to a House of Representatives hearing: 'Our relationship with the new South Africa has become overly personal, substituting a reckless form of hero worship for a sober analysis of long term national interest.'[96]

Mandela himself has made attempts to democratise his myth, to assert his secular authority over the more sacred dimensions of his appeal. In his autobiography he insists on his status as 'an ordinary man who became a leader because of extraordinary circumstances'. In this spirit during the ANC's election campaign, the organisation borrowed from American politics the device of a people's forum, in which members of the audience would direct questions at Mandela, standing on a podium so that they could confer with him as individualised equals, not anonymous voices from the floor. In explaining the break-up of his marriage he observes that his wife 'married a man who soon left her; that man became a myth, and then that myth returned home and proved to be just a man after all'. And though one should be wary of courtiers' tributes to their master's humility—these have been so frequently a feature of modern autocracies—in Mandela's case his unwillingness to take his authority for granted is often very evident. He was 'never sure whether young people liked him or not' he confessed when announcing the donation of his Nobel prize money to children's charities.[97] He often tells interviewers an anecdote from a private visit that he made to the Bahamas in October 1993:

> A couple approached him in the street and the man asked:—Aren't you Nelson Mandela?—I am often confused with that chap—was Mandela's mischievous response. Unconvinced, the man then whispered to his wife to inform her of their unexpected find.—What is he famous for?—his wife inquired in a hushed tone. Unsatisfied with her husband's inaudible response the woman asked Mandela outright—What are you famous for?

He concludes the anecdote: 'I hope that when I step down no one is going to ask me: what are you famous for?'[98] Perhaps it is Mandela's vulnerability as an 'ordinary man' that contributed most to reduce the sacred dimension of his appeal. His divorce hearing prompted the publication of his wife's letters to her lover, Dali Mpofu, in which, as we have noted, she referred to her husband with the dismissive diminutive, 'Tata' (father). In Mandela's evidence at the hearing he told the court this letter left him feeling 'the loneliest man'.[99] At the beginning of 1996, in trying to prepare the ground for his succession Mandela took the unusual step of publicly criticising 'the exaltation of the president, and denigration of other ANC leaders, [which] constitutes praise which I do not accept'.[100] In any case, Mandela acknowledges his own mortality: 'I don't want a country like ours to be led by an octogenarian . . . I must step down while there are one or two people who admire me.'[101]

In all this modesty there is an ambiguity, however. His preference in many of his public statements for the impersonal 'we' rather than 'I' can be read as the testimony of democratic humility—in Jacques Derrida's phrase, the presentation of 'himself in his people'.[102] This may or may not be sincere: analysts of oratory refer to a 'turnstile rhetoric . . . whereby the executive persona [only] pretends to be one of the sovereign [people]'.[103] In its most authoritarian form the leader perceives himself to be the totality of popular aspirations. The people's fora cited above did not just draw upon American electioneering; they also had a local historical resonance in the public assemblies in which chiefs customarily secured consensual popular sanction for decisions. Mandela's preoccupation with reconciliation may be just one facet of a deeper preoccupation with unity; and the politics of maintaining unity can be deeply authoritarian. Running alongside the admirable formal adherence by Mandela and his government to the tenets of liberal democracy—the ANC's respect for the independence of the constitutional court is an especially notable example of this—was a quite different discourse. Black journalists who criticise the ANC, according to Mandela, 'have been coopted by conservative elements to attack the democratic movement',[104] prominent individuals like Desmond Tutu should not criticise the ANC publicly—this 'created the impression of division within the movement'[105]—and South African politicians should emulate the example of Zimbabwe in fostering the politics of unity. The mood that such rhetoric evokes is at its ugliest when Mandela uses his personal authority to defend the misdemeanours of his subordinates, in, for example, the thunderous applause from ANC benches in parliament that followed his defence of his instructions to the security guards who fired into an Inkatha demonstration outside the ANC's headquarters.[106] The existence of such a discourse should surprise no one. In modern South Africa messianic politics has been employed to demobilise a popular insurrection in one of the world's most unequal societies and, in such a context, the institutions of liberal democracy depend upon the protection afforded by highly authoritarian forms of charismatic authority.

9

EMBODYING THE NATION

Reflecting on his dramatic interpretation in prison of the role of Creon in Sophocles' *Antigone*, Mandela acknowledged that 'you cannot know a man completely, his character, his principles, and sense of judgment [until] he's shown his colour, ruling the people, making laws . . . there's the test'.[1] Did Mandela meet such challenges? Mandela's experience of executive authority was brief, because he served only one term as president of South Africa, from 1994 until 1999. How critical are the evaluations of future political historians likely to be of Mandela's short tenure of public office?

Mandela presided over a Government of National Unity. Although, strictly speaking, this was a coalition, the African National Congress (ANC) predominated. Nearly halfway through its term, in May 1996, F.W. de Klerk and his colleagues joined the opposition benches, disappointed at their lack of influence in cabinet as well as their failure to persuade the ANC to entrench power sharing in the permanent constitution. At first, members of the cabinet worked together quite co-operatively, de Klerk concedes, although he was taken aback personally by Mandela's failure to consult him over the allocation of ANC portfolios, technically a constitutional requirement. De Klerk developed an easy relationship with Thabo Mbeki, and he and his colleagues felt that they could influence key policy areas such as education and the management of the economy. On the other hand, he was 'never asked to do more than the immediate role that the constitution had determined'[2] and he nearly resigned from the government on 15 January 1995 after Mandela attacked him with 'a tirade'[3] over indemnities extended to 3,000 senior police officers just before the election. Mandela's angry admonishment of his predecessor in front of his ministerial colleagues was followed by a private meeting concluded with smiles and handshakes but, as de Klerk noted later, the problems between the two men could only be 'papered over'[4] with Mandela's charm.

Mandela's repeated subjection of de Klerk to humiliating kinds of treatment was in conflict with his own ethical code, whatever its beneficial effects may have been in retaining for him the confidence of the ANC's popular following. Generally his biographers attribute Mandela's antipathy to de Klerk to his belief that the latter had at the very least turned a blind eye to official complicity in violence against the ANC after 1990, and in doing so had betrayed Mandela's trust in him. Perhaps, however, there were more complicated emotions affecting the two men's relationship. From their first meetings they were unable to develop anything approaching friendship: de Klerk himself refers only to 'a reasonable rapport', qualified by 'the full knowledge that we were opponents with divergent goals'.[5] Unlike most people who write about their encounters with Mandela, regardless of their social backgrounds or political predispositions, de Klerk's recollections do not include any hint of deference. Mandela may have sensed this. He certainly resented any external recognition that de Klerk could claim a share of the credit for South Africa's political transition: his discomfort was very obvious on the occasions at which they received joint awards—the Nobel Peace Prize conferment, for example. Certainly, he felt that he had good reasons for believing that de Klerk was unworthy of such recognition but, even if he had had no reason to doubt his adversary's good faith, would he have behaved differently? Mandela was a patriarchal personality conscious of his messianic stature: such leaders do not share moral authority easily.

On assuming office, Mandela announced a series of 'presidential initiatives' including free health care for mothers and children as well as a primary school feeding scheme. The Mandela administration's other achievements included impressively disciplined management of public finances in which tight controls on public expenditure eliminated a public debt of R250 billion, while at the same time redirecting resources from richer communities to poorer ones. In 1999, the government could make quite valid claims that it had undertaken serious efforts to alleviate poverty through financing the construction of nearly a million low-cost homes, extending clean water supply to millions of rural people, expanding the provision of health care in the countryside, and spending much more money on schools in black neighbourhoods. Disappointingly, however, these sorts of investments failed to reduce poverty significantly. Better housing and improved public facilities could not compensate for rising unemployment. Left-wing critics of the government argued that the liberalisation of foreign trade and Mandela's ministers' reluctance to borrow on the international capital market were partly to blame for the economy's failure to generate jobs, despite annual growth rates of nearly 3 per cent. Meanwhile business lobbies argued that social reforms were mainly to blame for unemployment, citing new industrial relations legislation and affirmative action.

Outside the arena of economic policy Mandela's government could make stronger claims about successes. Among these, the Truth and Reconciliation Commission represented an especially ambitious venture, which as well as administering amnesty through its televised public hearings supplied a forum in which the victims of human rights violations could tell their stories. The Commission's six-volume report offered a morally complicated public history, which despite angering politicians on all sides generally accorded with public perceptions.[6] A definitive Constitution was enacted in 1996. It entrenched and extended the human rights provisions of the 1993 Constitution. A Constitutional Court rapidly established its credentials as an independent and politically neutral authority. South Africa's 'path to revolution', Mandela told parliamentarians in his farewell address in 1999, would be a 'profoundly legal' journey.[7]

A sharp decline in politically motivated violence in Kwa-Zulu Natal was partly an effect of localised peace making by ANC and IFP (Inkatha Freedom Party) leaders before and after the 1994 election, partly a consequence of Inkatha's inclusion in the national administration and its predominance in the Kwa-Zulu Natal regional government, and also as a result of politically neutral public resource allocation. In April 1995, Mandela warned that he might cut off funds to Kwa-Zulu Natal because of continuing Inkatha opposition to the province's constitutional status. It was an unwise and illegal threat for him to make and provincial revenue allocation in fact remained equitable. The main credit for peace making in the province belonged to Thabo Mbeki and Jacob Zuma, as well as the second-echelon Inkatha leadership. Relations between Mandela and Mangosuthu Buthelezi remained fractious. Buthelezi had reasonable grounds to object to Mandela's failure to honour his promise, made just before the election, to invite foreign mediation in its aftermath over constitutional issues. He could not complain, however, about his own status as a senior partner in government as Minister of Home Affairs; from time to time he was appointed as acting president in Mandela's or his deputies' absences.

In general, especially at the beginning of his administration, Mandela used his powers of public appointment to send reassuring signals to former or potential adversaries, as well as taking care to achieve a balance of racial representation in his cabinet. Mandela's sensitivity to business confidence explained the reappointment of de Klerk's finance minister, Derek Keys, and after his voluntary resignation his replacement with another former banker, the comparably fiscally orthodox Chris Liebenburg. These choices as well as the selection of the similarly conservative monetarist, Chris Stals, as the governor of the Reserve Bank drew criticism from the ANC's chief whip in the House of Assembly, Bulelani Ngcuka. He suggested that Mandela might be 'leaning too much to the other side' in attempting to reassure former adversaries. Mandela's predisposition towards inclusiveness motivated a series of invitations in 1997 to the smaller parties to join his government, a 'consensual' practice maintained by his successor, Thabo Mbeki, to the detriment of vigorous opposition politics.

Mandela's inclusive 'social nationalism' in which all can join the nation if they share its values is evident in the rhetorical structure of many of his speeches, speeches that often tell a story and in doing so invite his listeners imaginatively to share emotions and experiences, a strategy of 'rhetorical induction'. It is nowhere more evident than in his address at the opening of the first parliament after the 1994 elections, when he informed his audience that a time would come 'when our nation will honour the memory of all [who] . . . gave us the right to assert with pride that we are South Africans'. And among those who would be so honoured, he continued, 'the certainties that come with age' told him that 'we shall find an Afrikaner woman who transcended a particular experience and became a South African, an African and a citizen of the world'. He went on to provide a brief biographical sketch of the Afrikaner poet, Ingrid Jonker, who committed suicide in the 1960s and, who after the 1960 Sharpeville and Nyanga shootings massacre, wrote about a child who 'is not dead . . . not dead/Not at Langa nor at Nyanga/Nor at Orlando noir at Sharpeville . . . the child is present at all assemblies and law-giving . . . this child who only wanted to play in the Sun of Nyanga is everywhere'. In quoting Jonker's poem to illustrate his argument about the new nation as the expression of 'conciliation of difference', Mandela employed 'a vivid illustration borrowed from a fiction that [was] immediately real to the audience', on both sides of the house, a poetic fiction that, because of its capacity to evoke an emotional response, represented 'subjective proof' of his arguments about a nation being reborn. In this way, the rhetorician Jean-Philippe Salazar maintains, through his appeals to moral and emotional sensitivities, Mandela's oratory may have promoted 'democratic deliberation', through constituting its audience as active participants, in the same way as a ritual incorporates those who witness it through 'inciting imitation and emulation and by arousing in individuals the consciousness of belonging to a community'.[8]

Consensual politics often has authoritarian dimensions. The new president could sound as impatient as his predecessors with media critics, in 1997, accusing newspapers of conspiring with counter-revolutionary forces to undermine democracy. This was in an uncharacteristically abrasive address to the ANC's national conference, scripted probably by Thabo Mbeki, but one year earlier, more spontaneously, Mandela had noted that 'the bulk of the mass media had set itself up as a force opposed to the ANC'.[9] Such sentiments need to be put in context: during Mandela's administration press censorship was dismantled and Mandela himself resisted any restrictive suggestions from his colleagues, even when *Hustler* magazine featured him as their 'asshole of the month', a few months after carrying photographs of one of his office staff: 'Nelson's girl, in the buff.' In general, Mandela made himself extremely accessible to journalists and remained on affectionate terms with many of them, local and foreign. Closer to home, Mandela could be less tolerant. He dropped Pallo Jordan from his cabinet in 1996 after his Minister of Posts and Tele-graphs expressed his reservations about the powers that the authorities conceded to the police in an anti-crime drive.

The same year he also dismissed Deputy Minister of the Environment, Bantu Holomisa, after Holomisa had told the Truth Commission that a member of cabinet, Stella Sigcau, had once taken a bribe from the hotelier Sol Kerzner, when she had been the ruler of the Transkei. Two years earlier, Mandela had tried to persuade Holomisa to arrange the withdrawal of charges in the Transkeien court system against Kerzner; apparently Kerzner had asked Mandela to use his influence with the Transkeien ruler in exchange for a donation to the ANC's electoral campaign. Holomisa refused but Kerzner paid his contribution anyway.[10] In 1996 both he and Jordan were offenders against a code of collegial loyalty that continued to exercise a strong influence in Mandela's sense of political propriety. Fidelity to old comrades helped to explain several especially ineffectual appointments as well as Mandela's apparent reluctance to act against the more obviously venal people in his administration. He defended a poorly timed raise in parliamentarians' salaries (just after the election) and rebuked Archbishop Desmond Tutu for his public condemnation of the pay hikes: Tutu should have raised the matter in private with him, he said. He cut MPs' pay subsequently, however.

In contrast to the ostentation of some of his colleagues, Mandela maintained a relatively simple lifestyle. He donated one-third of his salary to the charitable foundation that he had established with his share of the Nobel Peace Prize. When living in the comfortable but hardly palatial suburban home that he bought in Johannesburg's Houghton, he made his own bed and folded his own pyjamas. For holidays in Qunu he had constructed a replica of the bungalow in which he had lived at Victor Verster prison. There were no presidential cronies to constitute a privileged circle. Indeed, after the rupture of his marriage, Mandela appeared to withdraw socially even from old friends. He seemed most high spirited in the undemanding company of visiting celebrities, many of whom he charmed with his genuine warmth as well as his implausible flattery, informing Geri Halliwell of the Spice Girls, for example, of his deep admiration for her artistic accomplishments.

To what degree was Mandela's personal agency responsible for his government's performance? In general, particularly after 1996, Mandela delegated much of the day-to-day management of his administration to his deputy, Mbeki, although he retained a close commitment to personal supervision of security and intelligence matters. In the immediate aftermath of the transition, he and other ANC principals had what may seem in retrospect rather exaggerated fears about the possibility of a mutiny by an army still largely under white command. For example, after the arrest of the former minister of defence, General Magnus Malan, for his role in instigating a massacre, Mandela summoned to his office 22 political science professors from all over the country to canvass their views on the likelihood of white militarist reaction. Malan was later acquitted; the court found it impossible to establish evidence of a chain of command linking the killers to the minister's office. In the final two years of Mandela's presidency, Mbeki presided over most cabinet meetings. In the words of one journalist, Gaye Davis, from 1997 after his public announcement of his decision to govern for only one term, Mandela was 'the ultimate, rather than hands on authority'.[11] On a visit to London that year, Mandela admitted that 'the ruler of South Africa, the *de facto* ruler, is Thabo Mbeki. I am shifting everything to him.'[12] Even before then Mbeki was the principal decision-maker with respect to the detail of economic policy, especially with respect to the government's implementation of the GEAR (Growth, Employment and Redistribution) prospectus, a neo-liberal programme of macro-financial management produced by a team working under Mbeki's office. Mandela first saw a draft of GEAR very shortly before its publication, although he embraced its monetarist implications readily, making a key speech endorsing a new commitment to privatising parastatal companies. He was at this stage deeply impressed by the Malaysian experience of building an indigenous bourgeoisie through the preferential opening up of the public sector to Malay *bumiputra* (sons of the soil) entre-preneurs. By the date of Mandela's state visit to Kuala Lumpur in 1996, where he perceived 'remarkable similarities' with South Africa, his hosts and their compatriots represented South Africa's fourth largest source of investment.

Mandela was more than a figurehead president. Notwithstanding his self-deprecatory claim to Anthony Sampson that 'rather than being an asset I am more of an ornament',[13] in the first two years he governed often decisively. At cabinet meetings, according to Mac Maharaj, 'he listened impassively, taking in everything and then inter-vening'.[14] Throughout his presidency he would most weeks spend a day at the ANC offices: in the domain of a sometimes unruly party Mandela would continue to remain assertive, although he failed to impose his preference in the choice of his successor, Cyril Ramaphosa. Mandela was anxious to diversify the ethnic make-up of ANC leader-ship. He admired Ramaphosa's skills as a negotiator and he had reser-vations about Mbeki's intolerance of criticism.[15] Mbeki could be too inflexible, Mandela believed, a failing that could be explained as a consequence of his deputy having 'never played in his youth'.[16]

Although Mandela would continue to profess in public his view that 'the African National Congress is the greatest achievement in the twentieth century',[17] there were crucial occasions when Mandela employed his personal authority against the inclinations of his party successfully to reinforce national interests. For example, the Truth and Reconciliation Commission's report initially engendered a hostile response from the ANC and Mbeki attempted to delay its publication because of its 'wrong and misguided' conclusions. ANC leaders dis-liked what they perceived to be the Commission's equation of their organisation's abuses of human rights with the crimes of apartheid. Mandela endorsed the findings of the Commission in a graceful speech explaining later 'I am the president of the country. . . . I have set up the TRC [and] they have done not a perfect but a remarkable job and I approve of everything they did.'[18]

Another more minor instance of his willingness to confront his own party's predispositions was his rebuke of the ANC-chaired par-liamentary portfolio committee on defence when it recommended that the army should adopt English as its only language, a proposal, Mandela said, that could have the effect of undoing all the work that he had undertaken to promote reconciliation with Afrikaners.[19] Two years earlier, Mandela had noted that Afrikaans was an African language and that, 'for many of our people, Afrikaans is the first language that they have learned from their mothers and their fathers, the language in which they best express their deepest emotions'.[20] Afrikaner history, too, could be rendered sympathetically in an all-embracing national narrative. Laying a wreath by the statue of Anglo-Boer war guerrilla Daniel Theron, Mandela recalled that his 'own shaping as a freedom fighter' was 'deeply influenced by the work and lives of Afrikaner freedom fighters'.[21] Mandela's gestures of empathy with white South Africans—appearing at the World Cup Rugby finals dressed in a springbok jersey or meeting Verwoerd's widow to accompany her in laying flowers on her husband's grave—represented critical moments in his success in fulfilling a symbolic role as 'an embodiment of the nation that transcends ideology, party, or group'.[22] Ten days before the rugby tournament final, Mandela spoke at a meeting assembled in Soweto to commemorate the schoolchildren's uprising. On this highly charged occasion, Mandela wore a cap with the springbok emblem, a badge that for many people present at the rally would have had exclusive and objectionable associations with white South Africa. 'You see this cap I am wearing?', Mandela asked his listeners, 'This cap does honour to our boys who are playing France. I ask you to stand by them because they are our kind.'[23] Mandela's visit to Betsie Verwoerd followed a courteous exchange of letters after she had declined an invitation to a tea party that Mandela organised for the widows and wives of previous prime ministers and presidents. This gathering was held at the official presidential residence, which Mandela renamed in Afrikaans *Genadendaal* (Valley of Mercy). At the meeting with Mrs Verwoerd Mandela gently prompted her through the speech that she had prepared for the occasion (on the topic of Afrikaner self-determination) because she had forgotten to bring her spectacles.

Incorporating whites generally and Afrikaners in particular into a multiracial patriotism, in Mandela's phrase, 'a community of citizens',[24] was of course partly a practical imperative. During their exile, many ANC leaders had witnessed the effect of a sudden exodus of skilled managers and technocrats in other parts of Africa. But to the members of Mandela's generation, veterans of the 'multiracial' politics of the 1950s, building a racially united nation was a morally compelling project. Evidence of white loyalty to the new order offered for Mandela confirmation of the most important premise in his politics, that 'there are good men and women to be found in all sectors of society'.[25] Much of the loyalty that Mandela encountered and engendered was deeply personal, however. Even in the perception of such an unsentimental observer as de Klerk, Mandela 'had an exceptional ability to make everyone with whom he came into contact feel special'.[26] On meeting for a second time any of the staff in attendance at his offices or residences, he remembered their names and families and in doing so enthralled them. In the words of one bodyguard, an ex-security policeman: 'I used to do it for the money, now it's for him.'[27] More generally, the historian Hermann Giliomee suggests, 'Afrikaners were captivated by Mandela', for through his gestures of empathy he 'cast a spell' that among Afrikaners in particular and South African whites more generally 'produced a state of charismatic bewilderment'.[28]

Mandela's conciliatory behaviour did not always engender universal approval. Contributors to newspaper correspondence columns accused him of 'bending over backwards to accommodate the whites in South Africa and big business'[29] or, in a more thoughtful vein, neglecting to induce from white South Africans 'the sympathy and empathy apartheid's victims understandably craved'.[30]

In one other key area, Mandela sought to exercise decisive influence. There is a strong case for representing the foreign policy of Nelson Mandela's presidency as prompted by principle and, overall, a story of more successes than failures. Mandela delighted in personal diplomacy, telephoning heads of state in blithe disregard of international time zones and placing trusted associates in key diplomatic positions: posting his old articled clerk, Mendi Msimang, to the Court of St James and appointing his former legal secretary, Ruth Mompati, as ambassador to Switzerland. At the inception of its accession to government, the ANC placed international promotion of human rights at the centre of its foreign policy, together with respect for international law, global disarmament, and support for international organisations, as well as African and more generally southern solidarity. In Mandela's words, 'South Africa's future foreign relations [should] be based on our belief that human rights should be the core of international relations'.[31] The ANC's vision contrasted with the 'neo-realism' of South African foreign affairs professionals who emphasised the instability of the international order, South Africa's marginal status within it, and the importance of maintaining good relations with powerful industrial countries, while at the same time promoting South Africa's role as a sub-hegemonic power in Africa.

Of course, foreign policy is made by many hands and is as much the outcome of daily experience as any strategic design. Early on, Mandela's administration encountered four issues that appeared to confirm neo-realist objections to the new president's view that states should 'define national interest to include the happiness of others'.[32] The regulatory regime for the arms export trade failed, not least because of support for the industry among members of ANC's own military establishment including Defence Minister Joe Modise, although Mandela himself was prepared to defend arms sales to repressive regimes if these were traditional ANC allies. As he observed with respect to a contract with the Syrians: 'the enemies of countries in the West are not our enemies', a position that suggested a rather equivocal commitment to a human rights-centred foreign policy. Referring to Syria, Cuba, and Libya, Mandela explained: 'They are our friends and that is the moral code that I respect above everything else.'[33] On occasions, however, other considerations had to prevail. Mandela's attempt to secure diplomatic relations with both Chinas was rejected by Beijing: the incorporation of Hong Kong compelled an abrupt revision of his quixotic loyalty to Taipei, an allegiance influenced by Taiwanese donations to the ANC during the transition period. In 1998, a poorly prepared invasion of Lesotho, in support of an elected government threatened by a coup, provoked a costly insurrection in Maseru although Mandela's view that the South African action helped to establish a stable democracy looks quite defensible in the longer term. Finally, Mandela failed to evoke African or even token western support when he called for sanctions in 1996 against the Nigerian Abacha dictatorship. Infuriated by the abrupt execution of Ken Saro-Wiwa, notwithstanding his own tactful personal representations to Abacha, the South African president declared himself 'hurt and angry'. The execution, Mandela continued, was the action of 'an insensitive and frightened dictator'.[34] Such sentiments violated a cardinal principle in pan-African affairs: as his deputy, Mbeki, noted subsequently, 'African states do not turn on each other in international fora'.[35]

A series of policy reviews redefined priorities. Support for human rights ostensibly remained a key goal although an ANC research group assigned top status to efforts to secure agreement to reduce global inequalities. In future South Africa would pursue its aims through multilateral initiatives although its government 'would not always be able to act in ways to satisfy . . . the African continent'. A decision to expand foreign arms purchases signalled new recognition within official circles of the importance of military capability if South Africa was to exercise pan-African influence. In four different spheres, South African foreign policy began to acquire consistent characteristics that were to endure into the Mbeki administration.

First, South Africa embraced its role as 'a middle power'. Middle powers are medium-sized, regionally dominant states that attempt to enhance their international standing by endorsing 'multilateral solutions to international problems' through the adoption of 'compromise positions' and adherence to conventions of 'good international citizenship'. Viewed in this light South Africa's vigorous participation in transnational organisations made good sense and it reaped dividends. Its role in securing an international treaty to ban the use of personnel mines was a case in point.

At the same time, South Africa began to exploit its moral standing in the industrial world, a consequence of the international dimensions of the anti-apartheid struggle as well as Mandela's own prestige, to serve as a bridge between the north and the south. Mandela's success in brokering an arrangement in which, in return for an end to UN sanctions, the Libyans would hand over for trial the two suspects in the Lockerbie bombing represented an especially telling instance of this bridge-building predisposition. Mandela's reluctance to distance himself from old anti-apartheid allies Fidel Castro and Muammar Gadaffi, despite their maverick status, had attracted considerable international censure in western countries although it probably enhanced his stature elsewhere. South Africa invited western representatives to attend meetings of the Non-Aligned Movement, during its chairmanship of that body, and it rejected 'third world' injunctions to boycott the Davos talks. Tough bargaining extracted (arguably) important concessions for the southern African region from the five-year-long European Union trade negotiations. Despite its adoption of critical perspectives on many aspects of US foreign policy, through the creation of a bilateral Commission South Africa maintained friendly relations with the USA through the Clinton presidency into the George Bush era. Clinton claimed later that he had received guidance and comfort from the South African president throughout his impeachment hearings.

In Africa, during the later years of the Mandela presidency, chastened by Nigerian censure of its 'un-African' behaviour, officially South Africa assumed a self-effacing posture on the continent. This was in contrast to the aggressive expansion of its commercial interests, a process that evoked resentment in Kenya, Angola, and Zimbabwe. South African politicians held back from playing an assertive role in the Organization of African Unity (OAU). They stressed preventive diplomacy as their favoured means of conflict resolution. This failed badly when South African officials attempted to mediate between Mobutu and Laurent Kabila in 1997, in the short term detracting further from their influence in African affairs. In the longer term, however, sensitivity to continental protocols may have paid off. During the Mbeki presidency South Africans played a major role in designing the successor institutions to the OAU and Mbeki's colleagues brokered political settlements in The Congo itself and elsewhere. Nelson Mandela himself, after leaving office, assumed the lead role of 'facilitator' in the negotiations between December 1999 and November 2001 that led to the establishment of a national unity administration in Burundi.

Mandela's contribution to the Burundian political settlement was decisive. Violence between Tutsi and Hutu political groups claimed 350,000 lives in the 1990s, with radical Hutu groups engaged in a rebellion against an ostensibly Hutu-led government, which they perceived as susceptible to Tutsi manipulation. The Tutsi minority had predominated since independence and controlled the army and the police. External efforts to end the fighting began in 1996 with the OAU's appointment of former Tanzanian president, Julius Nyerere, as a mediator. Nyerere played a central role in negotiations until his death in 1999. Talks were interrupted by a coup d'état which reinstalled as president a former Tutsi military leader, Pierre Buyoya. Regional governments imposed a trade blockade as a sanction. Talks resumed in mid-1998 but progress was very slow, partly because complete consensus from the 19 delegations present was needed for any agreement and because Nyerere himself was not seen as disinterested by Tutsi delegates, but rather as pro-Hutu. Others present felt that Nyerere was too patient, too much of a listener.

Before attending talks Mandela made two well-publicised visits to the Burundi capital, Bujumburu, 'to meet the people'[36] and, of course, to demonstrate to local politicians his own rapport with Burundian citizens. Initially he was very keen to include in the talks armed groups, both Hutu and Tutsi, who had so far refused to attend or who for other reasons had been excluded: in the end his personal diplomacy in this vein failed—the two most important groups rejected his overtures, but his very obvious efforts to broaden the negotiation's political embrace may have helped to enhance support inside and outside Burundi for the agreement that followed. Within nine months of his appointment, Mandela had helped to persuade all 19 of the delegations to sign an accord that included transitional power-sharing political arrangements, the integration of armed rebels into a reformed military, and the establishment of a Truth and Reconciliation Commission. Mandela's key advantage over Nyerere was his ability to draw in governments from outside the region to support the negotiations. By raising the international profile of the negotiations—for example, by inviting international statesmen such as Bill Clinton to its plenary sessions—in effect Mandela raised the perceived

costs for Burundians behaving intractably. More ready to scold participants than his predecessor (and more likely to escape censure for
doing so), he drew on his own experience to encourage Burundians
to confront the issues in the conflict directly. His forceful advocacy of
ethnic power-sharing mechanisms—such as a rotating presidency—
took the issue well beyond the conventional boundaries of mediation
on conflict settlement. Mandela and the talks' main co-ordinator, Fink
Haysom, both drew on their South African experience to impose a
'sufficient consensus' procedure on the negotiations.

In this vein, difficult issues were referred to closed bilateral discussions between the most significant groups in dispute: once they had
reached concord they would take their compromise back to the plenary. 'Compromise', Mandela insisted, 'was the art of leadership' and
'you do not compromise with a friend, you compromise with an
enemy.'[37] From the point of view of many Hutu leaders, the Accord
that they signed in August 2000 certainly represented an imperfect
compromise. It left in place substantial Tutsi influence in the army in
which integration would be on a 50:50 basis rather than demo-
graphically proportional. Buyoya would retain the presidency for
another 18 months. Arguably only Mandela could have held out
the prospects of rewards for compromise through using his moral
authority to underwrite and arrange a donors' conference in Paris
hosted by President Jacques Chirac, which promised US$450 million
for reconstruction. Mandela also subsequently succeeded in inducing
an initially reluctant South African military to lead an international
peacekeeping mission.

Today the Burundian settlement survives although the rebellion
continues and thousands more have died since the Accord. Arguably
the Accord, through drawing together most of the significant groups
in the conflict, may have limited the scope of the bloodshed. Burundian politicians, apparently, concede 'that without Mandela they
would not have reached any agreement, nor so quickly'.[38] Although
one of the agreement's shortcomings was its elitist character, it is
likely that among ordinary Burundians Mandela remains a trusted
figure.

Until his departure from public office in June 1999, Mandela's stature among South Africans remained undiminished, notwithstanding the wavering levels of public approval for his government and his political organisation discerned by opinion polls. Just before the 1999 general election public satisfaction with his 'performance' as president stood at 80 per cent. This feeling was shared across racial boundaries; in a poll conducted in November 1998, 59 per cent of white South Africans believed that Mandela 'was doing his job well', despite the general antipathy to the ANC shared by most whites.[39] Even after his retirement, South Africans continued to invest their hopes for national reconstruction in Mandela's iconic status: a proposal to mint 'Mandelarands' in place of Krugerrands was motivated by the belief that such a venture would harness the savings of African–Americans in the cause of restoring the fortunes of the gold-mining industry.[40]

Mandela himself has sustained his moral authority by remaining politically assertive. From 2000, at first discreetly and later more openly, he joined forces with critics of the government's failure to implement effective measures to address South Africa's HIV/AIDS pandemic, a failure resulting partly from Mbeki's adoption of 'dissident' understandings of the illness. Mandela's own administration was itself slow in acknowledging the seriousness of the threat posed by HIV/AIDS, and failed to develop an effective strategy to address its effects. This was an omission that he regretted in a British television interview, blaming his own reluctance to speak about the disease directly on South African conventional reticence with respect to public discussion of issues related to sex.[41] After 1999, however, Mandela's identification with the Treatment Action Campaign (TAC) brought him into increasing conflict with President Mbeki's supporters both inside and outside the ANC. He expressed his reservations about the government's reluctance to sanction the prescription of anti-retroviral medication at a meeting of the ANC National Executive amid a rising clamour of derision.[42] Government policy did shift shortly thereafter, although reporters disagreed on the degree to which Mandela's advocacy was a decisive influence. In July 2002, Mandela persuaded the TAC leader Zachie Achmat to end a hunger strike in return for the government extending the provision of anti-retrovirals, embracing him in front of newsmen for a deliberately staged photo-opportunity. He subsequently 'briefed' an unusually receptive Mbeki about the content of his meeting with Achmat.[43] In 2005, Mandela's commitment to combating the AIDS pandemic became tragically personal when his second son, Makgatho, died of the illness.

Notwithstanding the apparent constancy of his popularity, the legends and narratives associated with Mandela's life undergo constant mutation. One important contributor to this process is his former wife, from whom he was finally divorced in very public proceedings in 1995. Winnie refused an amicable settlement and contested the divorce, bringing the most painful details of their domestic life into the public domain, because, in contravention of the Divorce Act, the evidence was reported in the newspapers assiduously. 'Ever since I came back from jail', Mandela told the court, 'not once has the defendant entered the bedroom whilst I was awake.' He added, 'I was the loneliest man in the world when I stayed with her'.[44] He had delayed opening the divorce proceedings, he said, because he did not want it to be thought that his decision was a consequence of Winnie's trial. He still believed in her innocence with respect to the death of Moeketsi Seipei, he maintained. Even so, not all of her behaviour was excusable. Certainly she had suffered hardships, 'but there are many women who suffered more than she did'. In her defence, Winnie had obtained an affidavit from Mandela's kinsman, friend, and political adversary, Kaiser Matanzima, suggesting that, in divorcing his wife, Mandela had ignored his obligation under customary law to subject the dispute with Winnie to mediation by tribal elders. Mandela's curt response is worth quoting: 'I respect custom, but I am not a tribalist. I fought as an African nationalist and I have no commitment to the custom of any tribe. Custom is not moribund. It is a social phenomenon which develops and changes.'[45]

In March 1999, Winnie Madikizela-Mandela ceremonially presented her wedding ring to 13-year-old Candice Erasmus, the daughter of a retired security policeman who once spied on her and who recently had joined the Madikizela–Mandela household. Sergeant Erasmus had offered testimony during the divorce on how he and his colleagues had spread false rumours about Mrs Mandela. The gift of the ring, Winnie said, was a 'symbol of reconciliation' with her former tormentors, but the occasion also marked the opening of a rhetorical offensive against her ex-husband. He was guilty, she informed journalists, 'of using Apartheid legislation which denied property rights to African women' to eject Winnie and her daughters from the home that they once shared. Winnie had been administering the house as a museum, financing the enterprise through the sale of jars of soil from the garden. Mandela's lawyers responded to Winnie's protestations by noting that the 'property was sacred to the Mandela family', because in its vicinity were buried the umbilical cords of his first children, 'in accordance with African custom'.[46] In fact, Mandela had more than met his legal obligations under his wedding contract. After the divorce Mandela had made over an *ex-gratia* payment as well as paying for Winnie's legal costs; between their separation in 1992 and divorce three years later he had given his estranged wife a total of R3 million.[47]

During the 1999 election campaign, Madikizela-Mandela travelled to America where she presented to television viewers a very different picture of her marriage to her previous testimony on the subject, one in which her one-time husband had been cold and neglectful throughout their union, interested only in his political ambitions. 'The fact I was even able to get two children from him was quite coincidental', she complained, adding that he had neglected his family throughout their marriage.[48] Returning to South Africa she urged voters to support Mandela's successor, Mbeki, at the polls, because South Africa needed, she said, a 'young man' at its helm. Despite their separation, in 1994 Mandela had appointed Winnie to a deputy minister's position in the Department of Arts and Culture, but dismissed her a year later after she had delivered a series of speeches attacking the government's commitment to racial reconciliation and its slow pace in implementing reforms. She had embarrassed her colleagues in other ways too, using public resources to promote Zindzi's business interests and investing herself in various ill-considered financial undertakings. On one occasion she hired a private jet to transport her son-in-law so that he could collect a packet of diamonds from

President Jose do Santos: on his arrival Angolan officials were non-plussed, professing no knowledge of any such arrangement.

The infirmities resulting from Mandela's age were a theme developed in the first full biography of Thabo Mbeki, in which an exhausted and querulous octogenarian president is depicted as visibly irked by the procedures of 'weaning [him] from authority . . . taking place at a quicker pace than he would have liked'. Indeed, the book's authors maintain, many of the accomplishments of Mandela's administration were in fact 'a reflection of Thabo's work'.[49] Such disparaging efforts by Mbeki's admirers are unlikely to find much official favour, however. Instead, the new ANC leadership seemed much more predisposed to emphasise Mandela's record as an 'Africanist' traditionalist, and, as such, a guiding genius, together with the new president, of a South African-led 'African Renaissance'. The ANC's preferred model of consensual democracy, 'cooperative governance', is very much in the 'organic' vein favoured by Mandela in his patriarchal meditative mode.[50] During the 1999 election, opposition hecklers at public meetings were exhorted to return 'home' to the 'family'[51] and Mandela's brief public appearances were directed mainly at securing the loyalty of chiefs in the former homelands, to whom he delivered a series of homilies on the merits of respecting age and custom, and among whom he celebrated his third wedding to Graca Machel, widow of the first Mozambican president. At these festivities, Paramount Chief Kaiser Matanzima was in prominent attendance. Graca Machel's reception as a 'full member of the Mandela clan' became the occasion of a final act of reconciliation, one in which the rift between apartheid's African collaborators and 'progressive' nationalists was symbolically closed through the incantations of a praise singer: 'Hail Dalibunga! [Mandela's praise name, given to him at his circumcision] . . . Hail Daliwonga! [Matanzima] . . . the bones of Dalindyebo, Sabatha, Ngangelizwe [Xhosa kings] are shaking now that the Thembu nation is united in this ritual.'[52]

Graca Machel, not only the widow of Mozambique's first president but for ten years a minister of education in her own country, first met Mandela in 1990. At that time she was 45 years old, employed by UNICEF and administering her own charity for child refugees. Subsequently Mandela assumed the role that Tambo played as godfather to her children. The friendship between the couple deepened several years later, and she started accompanying him on formal occasions two years before their marriage, a union that she initially resisted because she felt that it would end her own identity in public life. In contrast to his previous marriages, then, Mandela's role as suitor was a protracted one: it seems to have been rewarded by a companionship that is intelligent, considerate, and gentle. 'It was not love at first sight', Graca told journalists, but in her increasingly frequent visitor she 'came to know' a person 'who cares about the little things in life'. In their relationship, 'there were no destructive elements' for 'he's so easy to love'.[53]

Nelson Mandela's standing is likely to long outlive its subject. As white and black South African notables close ranks, modernist and traditional, in South Africa's second bourgeois republic, Mandela's many personages as well as the myths surrounding them will remain the most powerful source of ideological legitimisation at their disposal. Surprisingly, however, there is little evidence of a cult of personality. The only public statue of Mandela is located in Sandton, an upmarket shopping centre, paid for by public subscription. His image does not appear on banknotes or postage stamps, and the museum at his birthplace is low key rather than monumental, an assembly of images and objects contained in a glass box. Elsewhere Mandela's reputation as a global public hero is likely to survive the inevitable revisionist analyses of his acumen as a revolutionary leader or the shortcomings of his management of affairs of state. It is true that conventional measures of political competence can make short shrift of heroic personalities. For example, a mid-term evaluation of Mandela's government found in his performance little evidence of political talent other than 'a dogged pursuit of reconciliation' and concluded that Mandela's greatness is mainly 'a creation of the collective imagination'.[54]

There are more generous evaluations, however, that suggest that Mandela's 'celebrity branding'[55] may be an effect of the ways in which he lived his life, as much as a product of the historical circumstances that surrounded it. In a comparative study of 'moral capital',

the British political scientist John Kane has argued that innate qualities of goodness are insufficient for leaders to exercise moral influence.
Kane distinguishes moral capital or moral prestige from charisma.
Charismatic leaders rely on absolute trust and their authority is partly
magical, not entirely legal or rational. Leaders who command moral
authority achieve their position through action and behaviour,
through appearing constant to a widely shared cause, through undertaking actions that are similarly perceived to advance their cause,
through exemplifying the values that they represent in their
behaviour, and finally by the use of language and symbols that animate their followers and reach across political boundaries. Leaders
who mobilise support through the deployment of moral capital need
not be philosophical visionaries or grand strategists: they lead through
example, through scripting and acting out a narrative that embodies
the passions and aspirations of those whom they seek to attract as
followers. They may create and draw upon their moral prestige self-
consciously, as Mandela certainly did at different stages in his life, so
as to bring coherence to previously disparate social forces, and in
doing so extending exemplary influence across a range of political
constituencies.

Accordingly, Kane argues, Mandela accumulated his moral capital
through his 'skilled, dignified and powerful theatrical performances'[56]
in the service of the ANC through the 1950s and in his redemptive
leadership, and in his legal defence of armed rebellion. Mandela's
moral capital was enhanced by his comrades' and his family's evoca-
tion of a mythical personality during his imprisonment. On his
release, this intensely self-controlled personality directed his emotions, both angry and forgiving, in ways that extended his appeal well
beyond the followers of his cause, particularly during points of crisis
in the transition to democracy. As a leader in government Mandela
remained intensely conscious of the symbolic function of his role in
creating a focus for new ideas about citizenship, simultaneously
exploiting his moral power and insisting upon his ordinariness,
admitting his mistakes, even. Kane's argument is contestable: there
were certainly phases in his leadership when Mandela's authority was
more messianic than moral, closer to a Weberian charisma than the

capacity to invite reasoning trust that is implied in the notion of moral capital.

In general, however, Mandela strengthened the institutional bases of power with which he associated himself rather than substituting his authority for organised politics. This is probably his strongest achievement. As a modern democratic hero with acknowledged flaws and failings he developed a following that 'could privately resolve the problems that leaders have caused or cannot resolve'—arguably his political style engendered civic participation and democratic deliberation.[57] Neither before nor during his presidency, Mandela neither demanded nor received an entirely unconditional devotion; in power he expected his compatriots to behave as assertive citizens not as genuflecting disciples. Even to non-South Africans, Mandela's politics evoke a citizenship that is inviting and accessible because of the extent to which even the most intimate and vulnerable dimensions of his experience have become public history.

ENDNOTES

PREFACE

1. Meer, Fatima (1990) *Higher than Hope: The authorised biography of Nelson Mandela*. New York: Harper & Row. The South African edition of Meer's biography was published two years earlier: all citations to Meer's book in this volume are to the later American edition.
2. Sampson, Anthony (1999) *Mandela: The authorised biography*. London: HarperCollins.
3. Meredith, Martin (1997) *Nelson Mandela: A biography*. London: Hamish Hamilton.
4. Buntman, Fran (2003) *Robben Island and Prisoner Resistance to Apartheid*. Cambridge: Cambridge University Press.

CHAPTER I

1. Mandela, Nelson (1994) *Long Walk to Freedom*. Randburg: Macdonald Purnell, p. 11.
2. Meer, Fatima (1990) *Higher than Hope: The authorised biography of Nelson Mandela*. New York: Harper & Row, p. 10.
3. Guiloineau, Jean (2002) *The Early Life of Rolihlahla Madiba Nelson Mandela*. Berkeley, CA: North Atlantic Books, p. 9; Stengel, Richard (1995) 'The Mandela I came to know', *Readers Digest*, May; Sampson, Anthony (1999) *Mandela: The Authorised Biography* Johannesburg: Jonathan Ball, p. 6; Mandela (1994) p. 40.
4. Mandela (1994) p. 9
5. Guiloineau (2002) p. 53.
6. Callinicos, Luli (2000) *The World That Made Mandela: A heritage trail*. Johannesburg: STE Publishers, p. 23.
7. Holland, Heidi (1989) *The Struggle: A history of the African National Congress*. London: Grafton Books, p. 14.
8. Benson, Mary (1980) *Nelson Mandela*. London: Panaf Books Ltd, p. 22.
9. Meer (1990) p. 22.
10. Mandela (1994) p. 22.
11. Gordimer, Nadine (1962) 'Nelson Mandela', unpublished manuscript, in Karis, Thomas and Carter, Gwendolen. Microfilm Collection, Reel 12A 2: XM33, William Cullen Library, University of the Witwatersrand.

12. Mandela (1994) p. 36.
13. Pogrund, Benjamin (1990) *How Can Man Die Better: Sobukwe and Apartheid*. London: Peter Hlaban, p. 10.
14. Ibid, pp. 190–1
15. Mandela (1994) p. 37.
16. Ntantala, Phyllis (1992) *A Life's Mosaic*. Cape Town: David Philip, p. 67.
17. Sampson (1999) p. 19.
18. Asmal, Kader, Chidester, David and James, Wilmost (eds) (2003) *Nelson Mandela: From freedom to the future: tributes and speeches*. Johannesburg: Jonathan Ball, p. 325.
19. Suttner, Raymond (2003) 'The African National Congress underground: From the M–Plan to Rivonia', *South African Historical Journal* **49**: 134.
20. Gqubele, Thandeka and Flanagan, Louise (1990) 'Land of sweet childhood dreams', in *Weekly Mail*, 16 February.
21. Meer (1990) p. 374.
22. Callinicos (2000) p. 42.
23. Webster, Edward (2005) Letter to author, 9 September.
24. *The Star*, 1 May 1993.
25. Sampson (1999) p. 17.
26. Hammond-Tooke, David (1975) *Command or Consensus: The development of Transkeien local government*. Cape Town: David Philip, pp. 83, 187–96.
27. Cited in Macmillan, Hugh (1995) 'Return to the Malungwana Drift: Max the Zulu Nation and the common society', in *African Affairs* **94**: 50.
28. Jordan, A.C. (1973) *Towards an African Literature: The emergence of literary form in Xhosa*. Berkeley, CA: University of California Press, pp. 111–12.
29. Eve, Jeanette (2003) *A Literary Guide to the Eastern Cape*. Cape Town: Double Storey, p. 367.
30. Kratz, Corinne (2001) 'Conversations and lives', in White, Luise, Miescher, Stephen and Cohen, David William (eds), *African Words, African Voices: Critical practices in oral history*. Bloomington, IN: Indiana University Press, p. 143.
31. Mandela (1994) p. 28.
32. Joseph, Helen (1986) *Side by Side: The autobiography of Helen Joseph*. Johannesburg: Ad Donker, p. 67.
33. Bunting, Brian (1975) *Moses Kotane: South African Revolutionary*. London: Inkululeko Publications, p. 5; Mphahlele, Ezekiel (1980) *Down Second Avenue*. London: Faber & Faber, p. 14.
34. Bunting (1975) p. 5; Mokgatle, Naboth (1971) *The Autobiography of an Unknown South African*. Berkeley, CA: University of California Press, p. 11.

35. Pauw, B.A. (1963) *The Second Generation*. Cape Town: Oxford University Press, pp. 88–9.
36. Gqubele and Flanagan (1990).
37. Mandela (1994) p. 43.
38. Matthews, Z.K. (1981) *Freedom For My People*. London: Rex Collings, pp. 115–26; Pogrund (1990) p. 20.
39. Anonymous (1953) 'Nelson Mandela', in *Fighting Talk*, November, p. 9.
40. Benson, Mary (1986) *Nelson Mandela*. Harmondsworth: Penguin, p. 21.
41. Mandela (1994) p. 47.
42. Ibid.
43. Resha, Maggie (1991) *My Life in the Struggle*. Johannesburg: Congress of South African Writers, pp. 11–13.
44. Saki Shabangu, Isaac (1995) *Madiba: The Folk Hero: An historical closet drama*. Giyani: Lingua Franca Publishers, p. 3.
45. Benson (1986) p. 20.
46. Kerr, Alexander (1968) *Fort Hare, 1915–1948: The evolution of an African college*. London: C. Hurst & Co., pp. 241–6.
47. Matthews (1981) p. 67.
48. Holland (1989) p. 23; *Fighting Talk*, November 1953, p. 9.
49. Benson, Mary (1989) *A Far Cry: The making of a South African*. Harmondsworth: Penguin, p. 238.
50. *New Nation*, 7 July 1988.
51. Meer (1990) p. 102.
52. Ibid p. 30 amd p. 158.
53. Nash, Andrew (1999) 'Mandela's democracy', *Monthly Review* **50**: 11, 18–28.
54. Meer (1990), p. 102.
55. Ibid, p. 30 and p. 158.
56. Sachs, Albie (2003) 'Freedom in our lifetime', in Asmal et al. (2003) p. 54
57. Slovo, Gillian (1997) *Every Secret Thing: My family: My country*. London: Little, Brown & Co., p. 214.
58. Jensen, Robert (1999) *Transcript of Interviews at Qunu*. Austin, TX: Department of Journalism, University of Texas.
59. Meredith, Martin (1997) *Nelson Mandela: A biography*. London: Hamish Hamilton, p. 25; Sampson (1999) p. 5.
60. Mandela (1994) p. 16.

CHAPTER 2

1. Sisulu, Elinor (2002) *Walter and Albertina Sisulu: In our lifetime*. Cape Town: David Philip, p. 64.

2. Sampson, Anthony (1999) *Mandela: The authorised biography*. London: HarperCollins, p. 31.

3. Meredith, Martin (1997) *Nelson Mandela: A biography*. London: Hamish Hamilton, p. 34

4. Sisulu, Elinor (2002) 'Walter Sisulu and the ANC', public lecture, Wits History Workshop, Johannesburg, 15 May.

5. Meer, Fatima (1990) *Higher than Hope: The authorised biography of Nelson Mandela*. New York: Harper & Row.

6. *Jewish Journal*, Johannesburg, 29 October 1999.

7. Mandela, Nelson (1994) *Long Walk to Freedom*. Randburg: Macdonald Purnell, p. 81.

8. Mandela, Nelson (1993) Interview with Luli Callinicos, Johannesburg, 20 August.

9. Mandela (1994) p. 78.

10. Meer (1990) p. 27.

11. Mandela (1994) p. 72.

12. Ibid, pp. 77–8.

13. Ibid, p. 75.

14. Smith, Scott (2002) 'Tripping through Alexandra', *The Star*, Johannesburg, 3 September.

15. Ibid, p. 88.

16. Frost, Bill (1998) 'Mandela, absentee father of the struggle', in *Sunday Independent* (Johannesburg), 8 November.

17. Meer (1990) p. 40.

18. Mandela, Winnie (1985) *Part of My Soul*. Harmondsworth: Penguin, p. 68.

19. Ebarhardt, Jacqueline (1952) *A Survey of Family Conditions with Special Reference to Housing Needs, Orlando Township*. Johannesburg: City of Johannesburg Non European Affairs Department and University of the Witwatersrand, p. 13.

20. Moloi, Godfrey (1987) *My Life*, Volume 1. Johannesburg: Ravan, pp. 61–6.

21. Eberhardt (1952) p. 32.

22. St John, Robert (1954) *Through Malan's Africa*. London: Victor Gollancz, p. 225.

23. Meer, Ismail (2002) *A Fortunate Man*. Cape Town: Zebra Press, p. 80.

24. Kuper, Leo (1965) *An African Bourgeoisie: Race, class and politics in South Africa*. New Haven, CT: Yale University Press, p. 112.

25. Bantu Welfare Trust, Correspondence with Nelson Mandela, 1946–1958, South African Institute of Race Relations Papers, AD843/RJ/Pb 11.3.9, William Cullen Library, University of the Witwatersrand.

26. Kuper (1965) p. 237.
27. Union of South Africa (1954) *Population Census*, 7 May 1946, Volume 5, *Occupational and Industrial*. Pretoria: UG 41/1954, pp. 184–7.
28. Breuilly, John (1993) *Nationalism and the State*. Manchester: Manchester University Press, p. 47.
29. Kuper (1965) p. 126.
30. Mandela, Winnie (1985) p. 62.
31. Tambo, Adelaide (1997) Interview with John Carlin. Transcript from www.pbs.org/wgbh/pages/frontline/shows/mandela/interviews/tambo .html
32. Mandela, Nelson (February 1984) Letter to Princess Irene Buthelezi, 3 August 1969. Reproduced in *Clarion Call: Inhlabamkhosi*. Ulundi, Bureau of Communication, Department of the Chief Minister, Government of Kwa-Zulu, p. 9.
33. Matthews, Joe (1997) Interview with John Carlin. Transcript from www.pbs.org/wgbh/pages/frontline/shows/mandela/interviews/ matthews.html
34. Evarett, David (1992) 'Alliance Politics of a Special Type: the Roots of the ANC/SACP Alliance, 1950–1954', in *Journal of Southern African Studies* **18**(1): 22–7.
35. Mandela, Nelson (1979) Letter to Barbara Harmel, 1 October. Harmel Family Papers, South African Historical Archive, William Cullen Library, University of the Witwatersrand.
36. Meer, Ismail (2002) p. 79.
37. Edgar, Robert E. and ka Msumzi, Luynanda (eds) (1996) *Freedom In Our Lifetime: The collected writings of Anton Muziwakhe Lembede*. Athens: Ohio University Press, pp. 86–7.
38. Ibid, p. 59.
39. Meer, Fatima (1990) p. 28.
40. Meer, Ismail (2002) p. 84.
41. Erlank, Natasha (2003) 'Gender and masculinity in South African Nationalist discourses, 1912–1950', in *FS Feminist Studies* **29**(3): 653.
42. Callinicos, Luli (2004) *Oliver Tambo: Beyond the Engeli mountains*. Cape Town: David Philip, p. 142.
43. Molotsi, Peter, quoted in Callinicos (2004) p. 142.
44. Meer (1990) p. 33.
45. Karis, Thomas and Carter, Gwendolen M. (1971) *From Protest to Challenge*: Volume II: *Hope and Challenge, 1935–1952*. Stanford, CA: Hoover Institution Press, pp. 305–10.
46. Stadler, Alfred (1979) 'Birds in a cornfield: squatter movements in Johannesburg, 1944–1947', in *Journal of Southern African Studies* **5**(1): 111.

47. Ibid.
48. Mandela, Nelson (1943) 'Do we need lawyers?', in *Bulletin—Tydskrif: Transvaal African Students Association* 1(1): 5.
49. Sampson (1999) p. 44.
50. Joseph, Helen (1986) *Side by Side: The autobiography of Helen Joseph*. Johannesburg: Ad Donker, p. 67; Bernstein, Hilda (1989) *The World That Was Ours: The story of the Rivonia Trial*. London: Robert Vicat Ltd, p. 22.
51. Mandela, Winnie (1985) p. 57.
52. Hagemann, Albert (1996) *Nelson Mandela*. Johannesburg: Fontein Books, p. 23.
53. Posel, Deborah (1997) *The Making of Apartheid, 1948–1961*. Oxford: Oxford University Press, pp. 98–104.

CHAPTER 3

1. Sampson, Anthony (1999) *Mandela: The authorised biography*. London: HarperCollins, p. 52.
2. Callinicos, Luli (2004) *Oliver Tambo: Beyond the Engeli mountains*. Cape Town: David Philip, pp. 157–8.
3. Mandela, Nelson (1994) *Long Walk to Freedom: The autobiography of Nelson Mandela*. Randburg: Macdonald Purnell, p. 107; Sisulu, Elinor (2002) *Walter and Albertina Sisulu: In our lifetime*. Cape Town: David Philip, p. 80.
4. Bernstein, Lionel (1999) *Memory Against Forgetting*. London: Viking, p. 116.
5. Sampson (1999) p. 62.
6. Meer, Ismail (2002) *A Fortunate Man*. Cape Town: Zebra Press, p. 123.
7. Kathrada, Ahmed (2004) *Memoirs*. Cape Town: Zebra Press, pp. 67–8.
8. Benson, Mary (1980) *Nelson Mandela*. London: Panaf Books Ltd, pp. 47–8.
9. Mandela, Nelson (c. 1976) Unpublished autobiographical manuscripts. Department of Correctional Services Files, Nelson Mandela A5, National Archives of South Africa, Pretoria.
10. Mhlaba, Raymond (2001) *Personal Memoirs: Reminiscing from Rwanda and Uganda*. Pretoria and Cape Town: Human Sciences Research Council and Robben Island Museum, p. 79.
11. Mandela (c. 1976).
12. Mandela (1994) p. 115.
13. Johns, Sheridan and Hunt Davis Jr, R. (1991) *Mandela, Tambo and the African National Congress: The struggle against apartheid: a documentary survey*. New York: Oxford University Press, p. 39.

14. Mandela (1994) pp. 112–13.

15. Johns and Hunt Davis (1991) pp. 39–40.

16. Kathrada (2004) p. 92.

17. Suttner, Raymond (2003) 'The African National Congress Underground: From the M-Plan to Rivonia', *South African Historical Journal* **49**: 133–4.

18. Sisulu, Walter (1994) Interview with Barbara Harmel, 10 June 1994. Transcript held in the Cullen Library, University of the Witwatersrand.

19. Murray, Bruce (1997) *Wits: The open years*. Johannesburg: University of the Witwatersrand Press, p. 99.

20. Meer (2002) p. 121.

21. Matthews, Joe (1997) Interview with John Carlin. Transcript from www.pbs.org/wgbh/pages/frontline/shows/mandela/interviews/matthews.html.

22. Cachalia, Amina. Interview. Transcript from www.cbc.ca/lifeandtimes/mandela/interviews.html.

23. Turok, Ben (2003) *Nothing but the Truth: Behind the ANC's struggle politics*. Johannesburg: Jonathan Ball, p. 78.

24. Tambo, Adelaide (1997) Interview with John Carlin. Transcript from www.pbs.org/wgbh/pages/frontline/shows/mandela/interviews/tambo.html.

25. Khuzwayo, Ellen (1985) *Call Me Woman*. Johannesburg: Ravan Press, p. 139.

26. Matthews, Joe (1997) Interview with John Carlin.

27. Mandela, Nelson (1964) An autobiographical note. Written at the request of James Kantor during the Rivonia Trial.

28. Dadoo, Yusuf (1978) Quoted in Carter, David (1978) Organized non-violent rejection of the law for political ends: the experience of Blacks in South Africa, DPhil dissertation, Department of Politics, University of Durham, p. 230.

29. Mandela (1994) p. 117.

30. Meer (2002) pp. 152–3.

31. Herbstein, Denis (2004) *White Lies: Canon Collins and the secret war against apartheid*. Oxford: James Currey, p. 17.

32. Kathrada (2004) p. 99.

33. Benson, Mary (1986) *Nelson Mandela*. Harmondsworth: Penguin, p. 49.

34. Meer (2004) p. 143.

35. Meredith, Martin (1997) *Nelson Mandela: A Biography*. London: Hamish Hamilton.

36. Carter, David (1978) Organized non-violent rejection of the law for

political ends: the experience of Blacks in South Africa, DPhil dissertation, Department of Politics, University of Durham, p. 240.

37. Ibid, p. 247.

38. Mbeki, Govan (1993) Interview with Barbara Harmel and Philip Bonner, Port Elizabeth, 28 October. Transcript held at the Cullen Library, University of the Witwatersrand.

39. Stein, Sylvester (1999) *Who Killed Mr Drum? London: Corvo Books*, *p. 51*

40. Callinicos (2004) p. 209.

41. Sisulu (2002), p. 101.

42. Basner, Miriam (1993) *Am I an African? The political memoirs of H M Basner*. Johannesburg: University of the Witwatersrand Press, p. xix.

43. Holland, Heidi (1989) *The Struggle: A history of the African National Congress*. London: Grafton, p. 97.

44. Kathrada (2004) p. 103.

45. Mandela (1994) p. 129.

46. Pillay, Gerald J. (1993) *Voices of Liberation: Albert Lutuli*. Pretoria: Human Sciences Research Council, p. 28.

47. Mhlaba (2001) p. 90.

48. Mandela, Nelson (1953) Interview with Gwendolen Carter. Transcript in Thomas Karis and Gwendolen Carter Microfilm Collection, Reel 12A, 2: XM33: 94, William Cullen Library, University of the Witwatersrand.

49. Holland (1989) p. 92.

50. Matthews, Joe (1997) Interview with John Carlin.

51. Sampson (1999) p. 84.

52. Ibid, p. 85.

53. Ibid.

54. Meer, Fatima (1990) *Higher than Hope: The authorized biography of Nelson Mandela*. New York: Harper & Row, p. 59.

55. Mhlaba, Raymond (1993) Interview with Barbara Harmel and Philip Bonner, Port Elizabeth, 27 October. Transcript held at the William Cullen Library, University of the Witwatersrand.

56. Mhlaba (2001) p. 95.

57. Mkwayi, Wilton (1993) Interview with Barbara Harmel and Philip Bonner, Johannesburg, 18 October. Transcript held at the William Cullen Library, University of the Witwatersrand.

58. Meer, Fatima (1990) p. 72.

59. Resha, Maggie (1991) *My Life in the Struggle*. Johannesburg: Congress of South African Writers, p. 58.

60. Johns and Hunt Davis (1991) p. 39.

61. Mokgatle, Naboth (1975) *The Autobiography of an Unknown South African*. Berkeley, CA: University of California Press, p. 307.
62. Mandela (1994) p. 146.
63. Turok (2003) p. 78.
64. Mandela (1994) p. 177.
65. Resha (1991) p. 66.
66. Mandela (1994) p. 204.
67. Ibid, p. 208; Joseph, Helen (1986) *Side by Side: The autobiography of Helen Joseph*. London: Zed Books, pp. 69–70.
68. Hirson, Baruch (1995) *Revolutions in My Life*. Johannesburg: Witwatersrand University Press, p. 274.
69. Mandela (1994) p. 226.
70. Monroe, Richard (1984) 'Lessons of the 1950s', in *Inqaba Ya Basebenizi: Journal of the Marxist Worker's Tendency of the African National Congress* **13**: 12.
71. The CPSA was banned in 1950 and its leadership reassembled underground as the South African Communist Party (SACP). The new SACP included many but not all of the old CPSA activists.
72. Turok (2003) p. 90.
73. Mandela (1994) p. 118.
74. Mandela, Nelson. Unpublished autobiographical manuscripts.
75. Mandela (1994) p. 152.
76. Ibid, p. 220
77. Kathrada (2004) p. 131.
78. Mandela (1994) p. 223.
79. Ibid, p. 209.
80. Bernstein (1999) p. 155.
81. Mandela (1994) p. 106.
82. Bernstein (1999) p. 143.
83. Magothi, Squire (1994) Interview with Philip Bonner, Johannesburg, 6 May. Transcript held at the William Cullen Library, University of the Witwatersrand.
84. Karis, Thomas Gwendolen Carter and Gail Gerhart (1977) *From Protest to Challenge*: Volume 3: *Challenge and violence, 1953–1964*. Stanford, CA: Hoover Institution Press, pp. 245–9.
85. Turok (2003) pp. 59–60.
86. Karis et al. (1977) p. 195.
87. Hudson, Peter (1986) 'The Freedom Charter and socialist strategy in South Africa', in *Politikon: The South African Journal of Political Science* **13**(1): 78–83.
88. Johns and Hunt Davis (1991) pp. 37, 47, 57, 59.

89. Mandela, Nelson (1985) 'Freedom in our lifetime', in *Sechaba Commemorative Publications, Selected Writings on the Freedom Charter, 1955–1985*. London: African National Congress, p. 25.

90. Karis et al. (1977) pp. 787–90.

91. Bernstein (1999) p. 146.

92. Johns and Hunt Davis (1991) p. 45.

93. Kathrada (2004) p. 56.

94. Johns and Hunt Davis (1991) p. 37.

95. Ibid, pp. 40–1.

96. Meredith (1997) pp. 127–9.

97. Sampson (1999) p. 99.

98. Karis et al. (1977) p. 39.

99. Johns and Hunt Davis (1991) p. 48.

100. Ibid, p. 68.

101. Mandela (1994) p. 248.

102. Meredith (1997) p. 104.

103. Derrida, Jacques (1987) 'The laws of reflection: to Nelson Mandela in admiration', in Derrida, Jacques and Mustapha Tlili (eds), *For Nelson Mandela*. New York: Seaver Books, p. 36.

104. Holland (1989) p. 83.

105. Murray (1997) pp. 54–6.

106. Meredith (1997) pp. 103–4.

107. Mandela, Nelson (1993) Interview with Luli Callinicos, 20 August.

108. Ibid.

109. Resha (1991) pp. 67–9.

110. Clingman, Stephen (1998) *Bram Fischer: Afrikaner revolutionary*. Amherst, MA: Massachusetts University Press, p. 201.

111. Mandela, Winnie (1988) *Part of My Soul*. Harmondsworth: Penguin, p. 58.

112. Sampson (1999) p. 101.

113. Meer, Fatima (1990), p. 79; Meredith (1997) p. 108.

114. Gilbey, Emma (1994) *The Lady: The life and times of Winnie Mandela*. London: Vintage Books, p. 95.

115. Tambo, Adelaide. Interview with John Carlin.

116. Gilbey (1994) p. 42.

117. Mandela, Winnie (1988) p. 60.

118. Ibid, p. 60.

119. du Preez Bezdrob, Anne Marie (2003) *Winnie Mandela: A life*. Cape Town: Zebra Press, p. 69.

120. Mandela, Winnie (1988) p. 59.

121. Gilbey (1994) p. 43.

122. Mandela, Winnie (1988) p. 65.
123. Resha (1991) p. 154.
124. Ibid, p. 93.
125. Meer, Fatima (1990) p. 158.
126. Mandela (1994) p. 99.
127. Johns and Hunt-Davis (1991) p. 50.
128. Meer, Fatima (1990) p. 156.
129. Mandela, Nelson (1980) Letter to Denis Healey, 1 January. Department of Correctional Services Files, Nelson Mandela A5, National Archives of South Africa.
130. Mandela, Winnie (1988) p. 58.

CHAPTER 4

1. Magubane, Bernard, Bonner, Philip, Sithole, Jabulani, Delius, Peter, Cherry, Janet, Gibbs, Pat and April, Thomoza (2004) 'The turn to armed struggle', in *South African Democracy Education Trust, The Road to Democracy in South Africa*: Volume 1: *1960–1970*. Cape Town: Zebra Press, p. 118.
2. Ngubane, Jordan (1963) *An African Explains Apartheid*. New York: Frederick A. Praeger, p. 169.
3. Sampson, Anthony (1999) *Mandela: The authorised biography*. London: HarperCollins, p. 141.
4. Karis, Thomas, Carter, Gwendolen and Gerhart, Gail (1977) *From Protest to Challenge*: Volume 3: *Challenge and Hope*. Stanford: Hoover Institution Press, p. 358.
5. Dingake, Michael (1987) *My Fight Against Apartheid*. London: Kliptown Books, p. 65.
6. Sampson (1999) p. 142.
7. Pogrund, Benjamin (2000) *War of Words: Memoirs of a South African Journalist*. New York: Seven Stories Press, p. 96.
8. *Contact* (Cape Town), 6 April 1961.
9. Karis et al. (1977) p. 377.
10. Ngubane (1963) p. 172.
11. *New Age* (Cape Town) 30 March 1961.
12. Harrison, Nancy (1985) *Winnie Mandela: Mother of a nation*. London: Victor Gollancz, p. 122.
13. Mandela, Nelson (1978) *No Easy Walk to Freedom*. London: Heinemann African Writers, p. 21.
14. Mandela, Nelson (1994) *Long Walk to Freedom*. Randburg: Macdonald Purnell, p. 245.

15. Sampson (1999) p. 144; Gilbey, Emma (1994) *The Lady: The life and times of Winnie Mandela*. London: Vintage Books, p. 58.

16. Pogrund (2000) pp. 96–7.

17. Kuper, Leo (1956) *Passive Resistance in South Africa*. London: Jonathan Cape, p. 15.

18. Sampson (1999) p. 143.

19. Slovo, Joe (1995) *Slovo: The unfinished autobiography*. Johannesburg: Ravan Press, p. 150.

20. Mhlaba, Raymond (1993) Interview with Barbara Harmel and Philip Bonner, Port Elizabeth, 27 October 1993. Transcript held at the William Cullen Library, University of the Witwatersrand.

21. Mandela (1994) p.225.

22. Pogrund (2000) p. 99.

23. Sampson (1999) p. 148.

24. Meer, Fatima (1988) *Higher Than Hope: The authorized Biography of Nelson Mandela*. New York: Harper & Row, p. 168.

25. Callinicos, Luli (2004) *Oliver Tambo: Beyond the Engeli mountains*. Cape Town: David Philip, p. 281.

26. Turok, Ben (2003) *Nothing but the Truth: Behind the ANC's struggle politics*. Johannesburg: Jonathan Ball, p. 123.

27. Ibid, p. 115.

28. Magubane et al. (2004) p. 53.

29. Mbeki, Govan (1993) Interview with Barbara Harmel and Philip Bonner, Port Elizabeth, 28 October 1993. Transcript held at the William Cullen Library, University of the Witwatersrand.

30. Gilbey (1994) p. 60; Sampson (1999) p. 154.

31. Suzman, Helen (1993) *Memoirs: In no uncertain terms*. London: Sinclair Stevenson, p. 52.

32. Bunting, Brian (1975) *Moses Kotane: South African Revolutionary*. London, Inkululeko Publications, pp. 268–9.

33. Matthews, Joe (1994) Interview with Philip Bonner, Cape Town, 18 August 1994. Transcript held at the William Cullen Library, University of the Witwatersrand.

34. Meer, Ismail (2002) *A Fortunate Man*. Cape Town: Zebra Press, p. 224.

35. Meer, Fatima (1988) p. 171.

36. Mandela (1994) p. 272.

37. Turok, Ben (1974) *Strategic Problems in South Africa's Liberation Struggle*. Richmond, Canada: Liberation Support Movement Press, p. 45.

38. Mandela, Nelson (1976) Unpublished autobiographical manuscripts. Department of Correctional Services Files, Nelson Mandela A5, National Archives of South Africa.

39. Turok (1994) p. 49.
40. Meer, Fatima (1971) 'African nationalism—some inhibiting factors', in Adam, Heribert (ed.), *South Africa: Sociological perspectives*. Oxford: Oxford University Press, pp. 140–3.
41. Meredith, Martin (1997) *Nelson Mandela: A biography*. London: Hamish Hamilton, p. 208.
42. Mandela (1994) p. 262.
43. Matthews, Joe. Interview with Philip Bonner.
44. Mandela, Nelson (1961) Notes on Che Guevara's Guerilla Warfare, Exhibit R25, *Rivonia Trial Records*, Brenthurst Library, Johannesburg, 8.
45. Mandela, Nelson (1961) Untitled annotations, Exhibit R15, *Rivonia Trial Records*, Brenthurst Library, Johannesburg, 7.
46. Sampson (1999) p. 156.
47. Kathrada, Ahmed (2004) *Memoirs*. Cape Town: Zebra Press, p. 148.
48. Ibid, p. 142.
49. Turok (2003) p. 127.
50. Karis et al. (1977) p. 717.
51. Magubane et al. (2004) p. 83.
52. Matthews, Joe. Interview with Philip Bonner.
53. Mandela (1962) Diary, entry for 3 January–13 July 1962, Exhibit R17, *Rivonia Trial Records*, Brenthurst Library, Johannesburg, entry for 8 January 1962.
54. Mandela (1962) Diary, entry for 8 January 1962.
55. Sithole, Jabulani and Mkhize, Sibongiseni (2000) 'Truth or lies? Selective memories, imagings, and representations of Chief Albert John Luthuli in recent political discourses', in *History and Theory* **30**: 72–80.
56. Mandela (1962) Diary, entry for 27 February 1962.
57. Sampson (1999) p. 166.
58. Mandela, Nelson (1962) Maroc Diary, Exhibit R16, *Rivonia Trial Records*, Brenthurst Library, Johannesburg, entry for 21 March 1962.
59. Mandela, Diary, entry for 3 January–13 July 1962, entry for 11 May 1962.
60. Herbstein, Denis (2004) *White Lies: Canon Collins and the secret war against apartheid*. Oxford: James Currey, p. xx.
61. Sampson (1999) p. 168.
62. Ibid, p. 187.
63. Ibid, p. 170.
64. Harrison (1985) p. 129.
65. Mandela, Nelson (1962) PAFMECSA, Exhibit R13, *Rivonia Trial Records*, Brenthurst Library, Johannesburg, 1962.
66. Kathrada, Ahmed (1988) 'My hero, my friend', in *Nelson Mandela: Our*

greatest asset, special supplement to *Independent Newspapers*, Johannesburg, 17 July: p. 8.

67. Mandela (1994) p. 300.

68. Ibid.

69. Kasrils, Ronnie (1998) Ar*med and Dangerous: From undercover struggle to freedom*. Johannesburg: Jonathan Ball, p. 50.

CHAPTER 5

1. Mandela, Nelson (1994) *Long Walk to Freedom*. Randburg: Macdonald Purnell, pp. 303–4.

2. Sampson, Anthony (1999) *Mandela: The authorised biography*. London: HarperCollins, p. 172.

3. Mandela (1994) p. 304.

4. Sampson (1999) p. 173.

5. Slovo, Joe (1995) *Slovo: The unfinished autobiography*. Johannesburg: Ravan Press, p. 160.

6. Johns, Sheridan and Hunt Davis Jr, R. (1991) *Mandela, Tambo and the African National Congress: The struggle against Apartheid*. New York: Oxford University Press, pp. 111–13.

7. Karis, Thomas, Gwendolen Carter and Gail Gerhart (1977) *From Protest to Challenge*: Volume 3: *Challenge and Violence, 1953–1964*. Stanford, CA: Hoover Institute Press, pp. 726–32.

8. Mandela, Nelson (1976) Unpublished autobiographical manuscripts. Department of Correctional Services Files, Nelson Mandela A5, National Archives of South Africa.

9. Meredith, Martin (1997) *Nelson Mandela: A biography*. London: Hamish Hamilton, p. 225.

10. Ibid, p. 227.

11. Kathrada, Ahmed (2004) *Memoirs*. Cape Town: Zebra Press, p. 17.

12. Karis et al. (1977) p. 742–3.

13. Meredith (1997) p. 229.

14. Sampson (1999).

15. Callinicos, Luli (2004) *Oliver Tambo: Beyond the Engeli mountains*. Cape Town: David Philip, p. 290.

16. Bizos, George (2004) Quoted in Denis Herbstein, *White Lies: Canon Collins and the secret war against Apartheid*. Oxford: James Currey, p. 83.

17. Clingman, Stephen (1998) *Bram Fischer: Afrikaner revolutionary*. Amherst, MA: University of Massachusetts Press, p. 304.

18. Joffe, Joel (1995) *The Rivonia Story*. Bellville: Mayibuye Books and the University of the Western Cape, p. 29.

19. Ibid, p. 34.
20. Ibid, p. 88.
21. Ibid, p. 92.
22. Mtolo, Bruno (1966) *Umkhonto we Sizwe: The road to the left*. Durban: Drakensberg Press, pp. 39–40.
23. Mandela (1994) p. 346.
24. *African Communist*, October 1962.
25. Joffe (1995) p. 127.
26. Bernstein, Lionel (1999) *Memory against Forgetting*. London: Viking, p. 306.
27. Karis et al. (1977) pp. 771–96.
28. Ibid.
29. Mandela (1994) p. 354.
30. Grint, Keith (2000) *The Arts of Leadership*. Oxford: Oxford University Press, p. 271.
31. Sampson (1999) p. 194.
32. du Preez Bezdrob, Anne Marie (2003) *Winnie Mandela: A life*. Cape Town: Zebra Press, p. 124.
33. Kathrada, Ahmed (1990) 'My hero, my friend', in *Nelson Mandela: Our greatest asset*, special supplement to *Independent Newspapers*, Johannesburg, 17 July, p. 4.
34. Sampson (1999) p. 195.

CHAPTER 6

1. Buntman, Fran (2003) *Robben Island and Prisoner Resistance to Apartheid*. Cambridge: Cambridge University Press, p. 19.
2. Gregory, James (1995) *Goodbye Bafana: Nelson Mandela, my prisoner, my friend*. London: Headline Books, p. 124.
3. Kathrada, Ahmed (2004) *Memoirs*. Cape Town: Zebra Press, p. 226.
4. Gilbey, Emma (1994) *The Lady: The life and times of Winnie Mandela*. London: Vintage Books, p. 66.
5. Dlamini, Moses (1984) *Robben Island Hell Hole*. Trenton, NJ: Africa World Press, p. 26.
6. Naidoo, Indres (1982) *Island in Chains: Prisoner 885/63*. Harmondsworth: Penguin Books, p. 123.
7. Dlamini (1984) p. 23; Babenia, Natoo (1995) *Memoirs of a Saboteur*. Bellville: Mayibuye Books and University of the Western Cape, p. 125.
8. Sampson, Anthony (1999) *Mandela: The authorised biography*. London: HarperCollins, p. 216.

9. Kathrada (1996) Interview with Patrick O'Malley, 26 March. Transcript from www.omalley.co.za.

10. Mandela, Nelson (1994) *Long Walk to Freedom*. Randburg: Macdonald Purnell, p. 404.

11. Gregory (1995) p. 130.

12. Solani, Noel and Nieftagodien, Noor (2004) 'Political imprisonment and resistance in South Africa: the case of Robben Island, 1960–1970', in *South African Democracy Education Trust, The road to democracy*: Volume 1, *1960–1970*. Cape Town, Zebra Press, p. 405

13. Kathrada (2004) p. 44.

14. Suzman, Helen (1993) *Memoirs: In no uncertain terms*. London: Sinclair Stevenson, p. 154.

15. Gregory (1995) p. 136.

16. Mandela (1994) p. 444.

17. Ibid, p. 448.

18. Buntman (2003) p. 199.

19. Sampson (1999) p. 226.

20. Mandela (1994) p. 449.

21. Neville, Alexander. Quoted in Sampson (1999) p. 244.

22. Dingake, Michael (1987) *My Fight Against Apartheid*. London: Kliptown Books, p. 221,

23. Gregory (1995) p. 155.

24. Ibid.

25. Mandela (1994) p. 455.

26. Dingake (1987) p. 215.

27. Mandela, Nelson (1976) Unpublished autobiographical manuscripts. Department of Correctional Services Files, Nelson Mandela A5, National Archives of South Africa.

28. Ibid.

29. Mbeki, Govan (1992) *The Struggle for Liberation of South Africa: A short history*. Cape Town: David Philip, pp. 88–9.

30. Buntman (2003) p. 97.

31. Mhlaba, Raymond (2001) *Raymond Mhlaba's Personal Memoirs: Reminiscing from Rwanda and Uganda*. Pretoria and Cape Town: Human Sciences Research Council and Robben Island Museum, p. 139.

32. Mandela, Nelson (1966) Letter to Chief Mangosuthu Buthelezi, 4 November. Reproduced in *Imhlabamkhosi: Clarion Call*. Ulundi: Bureau of Communication, Department of the Chief Minister, Government of Kwa Zulu, February 1984, p. 7.

33. Mandela, Nelson (1969) Letter to Princess Irene Buthelezi, 3 August, in *Imhlabamkhosi: Clarion Call*, February 1984, 8–9.

34. Mandela (1994) p. 471.
35. Mbeki, Govan (1991) *Learning from Robben Island: The prison writings of Govan Mbeki*. Cape Town: David Philip, p. 182.
36. Ibid, p. 186.
37. Ibid, p. 187.
38. Mandela, Nelson (2001) 'Whither the Black Consciousness Movement: An assessment' in Maharaj, Mac (ed.), *Reflections in Prison*. Cape Town: Struik Publishers, p. 38.
39. Legassick, Martin (2002) *Armed Struggle and Democracy: The case of South Africa*, Uppsala: Nordiska Afrikainstitutet, p. 46.
40. Ibid.
41. Kathrada, Ahmed (1998) 'My hero, my friend', in *Nelson Mandela: Our greatest asset*, special supplement to *Independent Newspapers*, Johannesburg, 17 July, p. 6.
42. Kathrada (2004) p. 268.
43. Buntman (2003) p. 100.
44. Kathrada (1998) p. 5
45. Mandela (1994) p. 474.
46. Sampson (1999) p. 277.
47. Meer, Fatima (1990) *Higher than Hope: The authorized biography of Nelson Mandela*. New York: Harper & Row, pp. 273–4.
48. Sisulu, Elinor (2002) *Walter and Albertina Sisulu: In our lifetime*. Cape Town: David Philip, p. 263.
49. Mandela (1994) p. 415.
50. Callinicos, Luli (2004) *Oliver Tambo: Beyond the Engeli mountains*. Cape Town: David Philip, pp. 354–7.
51. Kathrada, Ahmed (2001) *Letters from Robben Island*. Cape Town: Struik Publishers, p. 97
52. Mandela, Nelson (1981) Letter to Major Badenhorst, 18 November. Department of Correctional Services Files, Nelson Mandela A5, National Archives of South Africa.
53. Mandela (1994) p. 415.
54. Ibid, p. 479.
55. Kathrada (2001) p. 38
56. Ibid, p. 191.
57. Babenia (1995) p. 194.
58. Herbstein, Denis (2005) *White Lies: Canon Collins and the secret war against apartheid*. Oxford: James Currey, p. 174.
59. Dingake (1987) p. 164.
60. Meer (1990) p. 339.
61. Mandela, Nelson (1976) Letter to Winnie Mandela, 26 February.

Department of Correctional Services Files, Nelson Mandela A5, National Archives of South Africa.

62. Meer (1990) p. 349.

63. Ibid, p. 352.

64. Ibid, p. 353.

65. Houston, Gregory (2004) 'The post-Rivonia ANC/CP underground', in *South African Democracy Education Trust, The road to democracy*: Volume 1: *1960–1970*. Cape Town: Zebra Press, p. 654.

66. du Preez Bezdrob, Anne Marie (2003) *Winnie Mandela: A life*. Cape Town: Zebra Press, p. 217.

67. Meer (1990) p. 345.

68. Ibid, p. 346.

69. Harrison, Nancy (1985) *Winnie Mandela: Mother of a nation*. London: Victor Gollancz, p. 170.

70. Mandela, Nelson (1975) Memorandum. Department of Correctional Services Files, Nelson Mandela A5, National Archives of South Africa.

71. Gregory (1995) p. 192.

72. Mandela (1969).

73. Gregory (1995) p. 194.

74. Sampson (1999) p. 254.

75. Ibid, p. 304.

76. Mandela (1994) p. 497.

CHAPTER 7

1. Mandela, Winnie (1988) *Part of My Soul*. Harmondsworth: Penguin, p. 142.

2. Gregory, James (1995) *Goodbye Bafana: Nelson Mandela, my prisoner, my friend*. London: Headline Books, p. 300.

3. Sparks, Allister (1994) *Tomorrow is Another Country*. Sandton: Struik, p. 20.

4. Mandela, Nelson (1994) *Long Walk to Freedom*. Randburg: Macdonald Purnell, p. 507.

5. Sampson, Anthony (1999) *Mandela: The authorised biography*. London: HarperCollins, p. 300.

6. Ibid, p. 336.

7. Johns, Sheridan and Hunt Davis Jr, R. (1991) *Mandela, Tambo and the African National Congress: the struggle against apartheid*. New York: Oxford University Press, p. 168.

8. Ibid, p. 172.

9. Ibid, p. 215.

10. Kathrada, Ahmed (1998) 'My hero, my friend' in *Nelson Mandela: Our greatest asset*, special supplement to *Independent Newspapers*, Johannesburg, 17 July, p. 6.

11. Mandela (1994) pp. 458–9.

12. Gregory (1995) p. 346.

13. Sparks (1994) p. 25.

14. Kathrada (1998) p. 8.

15. Mandela (1994) p. 521.

16. Ibid, p.523.

17. Kathrada, Ahmed (2004) *Memoirs*. Cape Town: Zebra Press, p. 322.

18. Ibid, p. 321.

19. Gregory (1995) p. 405.

20. Meredith, Martin (1997) *Nelson Mandela: A biography*. London: Hamish Hamilton, pp. 387–9.

21. Gregory (1995) p. 448.

22. de Klerk, F.W. (1998) *The Last Trek, A New Beginning: The autobiography*. London: Macmillan, p. 11.

23. Walmeir, Patti (1997) *Anatomy of a Miracle: The end of apartheid and the birth of the new South Africa*. Harmondsworth: Penguin.

24. de Klerk (1998) p. 74.

25. Ibid, p. 97.

26. Ibid, p. 108.

27. Meredith (1997) p. 397.

28. de Klerk (1998) p. 31.

29. Ibid, p. 157.

30. Guelke, Adrian (2005) *Rethinking the Rise and Fall of Apartheid: South Africa and world politics*. Basingstoke: Palgrave Macmillan.

31. de Klerk (1998) p. 161.

32. Guelke (2005) p. 157.

CHAPTER 8

1. Sampson, Anthony (1999) *Mandela: The official biography*. London: Harper-Collins, p. 430.

2. Ibid, p. 409.

3. Waldmeir, Patti (1997) *Anatomy of a Miracle: The end of apartheid and the birth of the new South Africa*. Harmondsworth: Penguin, p. 201.

4. de Klerk, F.W. (1998) *The Last Trek, A New Beginning: The autobiography*. London: Macmillan, p. 169

5. Reddy, E.S. (1990) *Nelson Mandela: Symbol of resistance and hope for a free South Africa*. New Delhi: Sterling Publishers, pp. 7–13.

6. Mandela, Nelson (1994) *Long Walk to Freedom*. Randburg: Macdonald Purnell, p. 569.

7. de Klerk (1998) p. 191.

8. Meredith, Martin (1997) *Nelson Mandela: A biography*. London: Hamish Hamilton, p. 423.

9. Sampson (1999) p. 426.

10. Ibid, p. 414.

11. Meredith (1997) p. 417.

12. Rantete, Johannes (1998) *The African National Congress and the Negotiated Political Settlement in South Africa*. Pretoria: J.L. van Schaik, p. 195.

13. Mandela (1994) p. 581.

14. Sampson (1999) p. 125.

15. Meredith (1997) p. 429.

16. de Klerk (1998) p. 202.

17. Strand, Per (2000) Decisions on democracy: the politics of constitution-making in South Africa, 1990–1996. Uppsala: PhD dissertation, Department of Government, Uppsala University, p. 124.

18. Strand (2000) p. 124; Waldmeir (1997) p. 250; de Klerk (1998) p. 225.

19. Strand (2000) p. 125.

20. de Klerk (1998) p. 225.

21. Waldmeir (1997) p. 273.

22. Jung, Courtney, Lust-Okar, Ellen and Shapiro, Ian (2005) 'Problems and prospects for democratic settlements: South Africa as a model for the Middle East and Northern Ireland', in *Politics and Society* **33**(2): 277–326.

23. de Klerk (1998) p. 240.

24. Strand (2000) p. 247.

25. Meredith (1997) p. 476.

26. Sparks, Allister (1994) *Tomorrow is Another Country*. Sandton: Struik, p. 182.

27. Meredith (1997) p. 476.

28. de Klerk (1998) p. 252.

29. Strand (2000) pp. 249–51.

30. Mandela (1994) p. 583.

31. de Klerk (1998) p. 238.

32. Waldmeir (1997) p. 302.

33. Meredith (1997) p. 495.

34. Ibid, p. 478.

35. Ibid, p. 480.

36. de Klerk (1998) p. 276.

37. Meredith (1997) p. 493.

38. Strand (2000) p. 168.

39. Turok, Ben (2003) *Nothing but the Truth, Behind the ANC's Struggle Politics.* Johannesburg: Jonathan Ball, p. 300.

40. Pfister, Roger (2003) 'Gateway to international victory: the diplomacy of the African National Congress', in *Journal of Modern African Studies* **41**(1): 65–8.

41. Gregory, James (1995) *Goodbye Bafana: Nelson Mandela, my prisoner, my friend.* London: Headline Books, p. 236.

42. Sampson (1999) p. 379.

43. Herbstein, Denis (2005) *White Lies: Canon Collins and the secret war against apartheid.* Oxford: James Currey, p. 321.

44. Johnson, Shaun (1998) 'Marks of the man', in *Nelson Mandela: Our greatest asset,* special supplement to *Independent Newspapers,* Johannesburg, 17 July: 12.

45. Meredith (1997) p. 413.

46. Ibid, p. 445.

47. Ibid, p. 458.

48. Ibid, p. 464.

49. Mandela (1994) p. 592.

50. Benson, Mary (1986) *Nelson Mandela.* Harmondsworth: Penguin.

51. Stengel, Richard (1995) 'The Mandela I came to know', in *Reader's Digest,* May.

52. Mandela (1994) p. 458.

53. Jung, Courtney and Shapiro, Ian (1995) 'South Africa's negotiated transition: democracy, opposition and the new constitutional order', in *Politics and Society* **23**: 2.

54. Sole, Sam (1966) 'Angry Mandela reads the riot act', in *Sunday Independent* (Johannesburg), 17 March.

55. Mandela (1994), p. 249.

56. Ibid, p. 614.

57. Ibid, p. 590.

58. Braude, Claude (1966) 'We need to share Mandela's hidden pain to lay past abuses to rest', in *Sunday Independent,* 3 March.

59. Meer, Fatima (1990) *Higher than Hope: The authorised biography of Nelson Mandela.* New York: Harper & Row, p. 334.

60. Nyatsumba, Kaiser (1966) 'Mandela raps praise singers', in *The Star* (Johannesburg), 28 February.

61. Johns, Sheridan and Hunt Davis Jr, R. (1991) *Mandela, Tambo and the African National Congress: The struggle against apartheid.* New York: Oxford University Press, p. ix.

62. Carlin, John (1994) 'Love affair with Britain', in *The Star,* 1 May.

63. Stengel, Richard (1994) 'The Mandela I came to know', in *The Spectator* (London), 19 November.

64. See, for example, Harwood, Ronald (1987) *Mandela*. London: Channel 4 Books.

65. Nixon, Rob (1994) *Homelands, Harlem and Hollywood: South African culture and the world beyond*. London: Routledge, p. 178.

66. Sepamla, Sipho 'I need' in Meer, Fatima (1990), p. vii. (Reproduced with permission.)

67. Davis, Steve (1987) *Apartheid's Rebels: Inside South Africa's hidden war*. New Haven, CT: Yale University Press, p. 50.

68. Erasmus, Chris (1988) 'Mandela: The options', in *Inside South Africa*, September.

69. Mutwa, Credo (1986) *Let Not My Country Die*. Pretoria: United Publishers International, pp. 162–4.

70. Uys, Stanley (1993) 'The ANC generation gap that haunts Mandela', in *The Guardian Weekly* (London), 23 April.

71. Derrida, Jacques (1987) 'The laws of reflection: Nelson Mandela in admiration', in Derrida, Jacques and Tlili, Mustapha (eds), *For Nelson Mandela*. New York: Seaver Books,.

72. Mandela, Nelson (1973) *No Easy Walk to Freedom*. London: Heinemann, pp. v–vii.

73. 'The Charter on the Mines', *SASPU National* (Johannesburg), supplement on the Freedom Charter, Last Quarter 1987, p. 5.

74. 'Heed Free Mandela Movement, Government urged', a press cutting used as Exhibit D 30, *State vs Mewa Ramgobin*, Supreme Court of South Africa, Pietermaritzburg, 1985.

75. Speech at Release Mandela Committee meeting, Soweto, 8 July 1984, Schedule A, Indictment, *State vs Mewa Ramgobin*, p. 19.

76. From the transcript of the rally reproduced in Shabungu, Isaac Saki (1995) *Madiba: The Folk Hero*. Giyani: Lingua Franca Publishers, p. 107.

77. Gottleib, Martin (1990) 'Mandela's visit, New York's pride', in *New York Times*, 25 June.

78. Jones, Lisa (1990) 'Nelson and Winnie in the black metropolis', in *Village Voice* (New York), 3 July.

79. 'Waiting joyously for an African Godot', in *New York Newsday*, 21 June 1990.

80. Gottleib (1990).

81. Applebone, Peter (1990) 'American blacks talk of change after Mandela', in *New York Times*, 1 July.

82. 'Mandela takes his message to rally in the Yankee Stadium', in *New York Times*, 22 June 1990.

83. *New York Newsday*, 21 June 1990.

84. Alessandra (1990) 'Pride and confusion mix in talk on education', in *New York Times*, 21 June.

85. Tierney, John (1990) 'Meeting New York on her own', in *New York Times*, 23 June.

86. Jones (1990).

87. Mandela, Nelson 'Opening address to the joint session of the US House of Congress, 26 June 1990', in Reddy (1990) p. 83.

88. Gregory (1995) p. 434.

89. Ibid, p. 489.

90. Sampson, Liz (1997) 'Me and My Mandela', in *Sunday Life* (Cape Town), 19 January.

91. Gevisser, Mark (1996) 'Grown fat on total onslaught contracts, Bill Venter meets Mandela on the road to Damascus', in *Sunday Independent*, 15 December.

92. Editorial (1999) *The Citizen* (Johannesburg), 15 January.

93. Braude, Claudia (1997) 'Yutar and holy disbelief', in *Weekly Mail and Guardian* (Johannesburg), 27 March.

94. Apter, David (1972) *Ghana in Transition*. Princeton, NJ: Princeton University Press, p. 323.

95. Salazar, Phillipe-Joseph (2002) *An African Athens: Rhetoric and the shaping of democracy in South Africa*. Mahwah, NJ: Lawrence Erlbaum Associates, p. 16.

96. Russell, Alec (1996) 'Mandela magic leaves the world lost for words', in *Daily Telegraph* (London), 5 July.

97. Waugh, Esther (1994) 'Mandela gives Nobel money to children', in *The Star*, 11 March.

98. Battersby, John (1996) 'Mandela meditates on the ironies of fame', in *Sunday Independent*, 24 November.

99. 'I won't be your bloody fool, Dali, wrote furious Winnie', in *The Star*, 20 March 1996.

100. *Sunday Times* (Johannesburg), 25 February 1996.

101. 'Presidential accolades for nation-building citizens', in *The Star*, 11 November 1996.

102. Derrida (1987) p. 26.

103. Salazar (2002) p. 35.

104. 'Mandela fires newsmen', in *The Star*, 14 November 1996.

105. 'Mandela hits out at Tutu, chief whip', in *The Star*, 27 September 1994.

106. Vilikazi, H.M. (1995) 'Leaders' moral quality must rise', in *The Star*, 12 June.

CHAPTER 9

1. Brink, Andre (1999) 'Mandela: a tiger for our time', in *Mail and Guardian* 4 June: 16–23.
2. de Klerk, F.W. (1998) *The Last Trek, A New Beginning: The autobiography*. London: Macmillan, p. 356.
3. Ibid, p. 350.
4. Ibid, p. 352.
5. Salazar, Jean-Phillipe (2002) *An African Athens: Rhetoric and the shaping of democracy in South Africa*. Mahwah, NJ: Lawrence Erlbaum Associates. This text contains the full commentary of Mandela's speech.
6. Gibson, James (2004) *Overcoming Apartheid: Can truth reconcile a divided nation?* Cape Town: Human Science Research Council.
7. *The Star*, 29 March 1999.
8. Salazar (2002) pp. 9, 21–7, 171–2.
9. Meredith, Martin (1997) *Nelson Mandela: A biography*. London: Hamish Hamilton, p. 528.
10. Holomisa, Bantu (1996) Interview with Patrick O'Malley, 1 November. Transcript at www.omalley.co.za.
11. *Mail and Guardian*, 1 July 1997
12. Mervin Gumede, William (2004) *Thabo Mbeki and the Battle for the Soul of the ANC*. Cape Town: Zebra Press, p. 62.
13. Sampson, Anthony (1999) *Mandela: The authorised biography*. London: HarperCollins, p. 550.
14. Ibid, p. 510.
15. Mervin Gumede (2004) pp. 49–54.
16. Sampson (1999) p. 545.
17. *The Star*, 24 April 1997.
18. *Mail and Guardian*, 11 June 1999.
19. *The Star*, 16 February 1998.
20. *The Star*, 19 September 1996.
21. *The Star*, 7 March 2002.
22. Frederickson, George (1990) 'The making of Mandela', in *New York Review of Books*, 27 September: 28.
23. Waldmeir, Patti (1997) *Anatomy of a Miracle: The end of apartheid and the birth of the new South Africa*. Harmondsworth: Penguin, p. 269.
24. *The Star*, 18 July 1998.
25. *The Star*, 11 May 2004.
26. de Klerk (1998) p. 346.
27. Sampson (1999) p. 497.

28. Giliomee, Hermann (2003) *The Afrikaners: Biography of a people*. London: Hurst & Co., p. 648.
29. Ndekera, Ntsimane (1997) Letter in *Mail and Guardian*, 30 March.
30. Mahabane, Itumuleng (2004) 'Beyond the figurehead', in *Mail and Guardian*, 19 March.
31. Sampson (1999) p. 556.
32. Barber, James (2004) *Mandela's World*. Oxford: James Currey, p. 93.
33. *The Star*, 5 May 1997.
34. Sampson (1999) p. 557.
35. Barber (2004) p. 115.
36. Bentley, Kristina A. and Southall, Roger (2005) *An African Peace Process: Mandela, South Africa and Burundi*. Cape Town: Human Sciences Research Council, p. 73.
37. Ibid, p. 71.
38. Ibid, p. 192.
39. Electoral Institute of Southern Africa, Institute for Democracy in South Africa and Markinor, *Opinion 1999*, Survey Data held at the Electoral Institute of Southern Africa, Johannesburg.
40. *Business Report* (Johannesburg), 5 March 1999.
41. *The Star*, 4 March 2003.
42. Mervin Gumede (2004) p. 170–1.
43. *Sunday Independent*, 1 December 2002.
44. Meredith (1997) p. 539
45. Ibid.
46. *The Star*, 17 April 1999.
47. *Mail and Guardian*, 22 March 1995.
48. *The Star*, 1 June 1999.
49. Hadland, Adrian and Rantao, Jovial (1999) *The Life and Times of Thabo Mbeki*. Cape Town: Zebra Press, pp. 98, 149
50. Nash, Andrew (1999) 'Mandela's democracy', in *Monthly Review* **50**: 11.
51. *Sunday Times*, 31 January 1999.
52. *The Star*, 10 April 1999.
53. *The Star*, 6 March 1998.
54. Beresford, David 'Mandela's greatness is from being here', in *Mail and Guardian*, 7 November 2004.
55. *The Star*, 1 November 2001.
56. Kane, John (2001) *The Politics of Moral Capital*. Cambridge: Cambridge University Press, p. 126.
57. Grint, Keith (2000) *The Arts of Leadership*. Oxford: Oxford University Press, p. 420; Salazar (2002) p. 40.

CHRONOLOGY

1918, 18 July	Nelson Mandela is born at Mvezo, on the Mbashe river, Transkei
1926, January	Begins attending school in Qunu and is given an English name, Nelson
1928	Mandela's father, Henry Gadla Mphakanyisa Mandela, dies. Nelson accepted as a ward by the Thembu Regent, Jongintaba Dalindyebo, and travels to Mqhekezweni to live at the Regent's Great Place
1934	Initiation and circumcision
1935, January	Enrols at Clarkebury School
1937, January	Enrols at Healdtown School to complete senior certificate
1939, February	Enrols for BA degree at Fort Hare University
1939, 4 September	South African declaration of war on Germany
1940, November	Expelled from Fort Hare after refusing to serve on the Student Representative Council (SRC)
1941, April	Sells two of Jongintaba's oxen and travels to Johannesburg with Justice, Jongintaba's son
1941, April	Works briefly as a company policeman at Crown Mines, Johannesburg
1941	Meets Walter Sisulu, who finds Mandela clerical employment and the prospect of an articled clerkship with a legal firm, Witken, Sidelsky & Eidelman. Registers to complete his degree through correspondence. Lives in Alexandra
1941	Starts attending African National Congress (ANC) meetings with Guar Radebe
1942	Joins ANC
1942	Moves from Alexandra to stay with fellow clansman at the Witwatersrand Native Labour Compound
1942, December	BA Graduation at Fort Hare

1943, February	Enrols for part-time LLB studies at the University of the Witwatersrand and begins articled clerkship
1943	Joins 'The Graduates' discussion group and develops friendship with Oliver Tambo
1943, August	Marches with Alexandra Bus Boycotters
1944, April	Elected onto the ANC Youth League (CYL) Executive at the League's foundation meeting
1944	Marries Evelyn Mase, first cousin of Sisulu. Moves in with Evelyn's sister and her husband in a company house at City Deep Mine
1944	Completes articles and begins full-time study at Wits
1945	Birth of first son, Thembekile Madiba Mandela
1946, January	The Mandelas move into their own rented house in Orlando West, Soweto
1946	Provides legal advice to James Mpanza's 'Sofazonke' movement
1946, 12–16 August	African mine-workers' strike
1947, December	Elected on to the Provincial Executive of the Transvaal ANC and opposes Communist Party of South Africa (CPSA)/Indian Congresses/ ANC 'Votes for All' campaign
1948	Birth and death, nine months later, of first daughter Makaziwe Mandela
1948, 26 May	(Afrikaner) National Party wins general election
1949, January	Refuses to sign a TANC/TIC (Transvaal ANC/Transvaal Indian Congress) joint statement on the Durban riots
1949, November	Fails to persuade Dr A.B. Xuma to endorse the CYL's Programme of Action
1949, December	Fails exams at Wits Law School and subsequently has to complete legal training through the professional association
1950, February	Joins the ANC's National Executive Committee (NEC)
1950, April	Leads opposition to the CPSA's call for a May Day protest against the Party's impending

	prohibition. Disrupts CPSA meeting in Newtown, Johannesburg
1950, 1 May	Witnesses police baton charge in Orlando West
1950, May–June	Helps organise ANC/SAIC (South African Indian Congress) 26 June 'Day of Mourning'
1950, 26 June	Birth of second son, Makgatho Lewanika Mandela
1950, September	Elected president of the ANCYL
1951, 17 June	Participates in ANC NEC meeting that decides to invite other organisations to discuss joint protests against unjust laws
1952, January	Passes attorney's professional examinations and joins Hyman Basner's legal practice
1952	Travels to Bloemfontein to obtain Dr James Moroka's signature to the ANC demand for repeal of unjust laws
1952, 26 June	Arrested and detained for two nights while witnessing curfew breakers in central Johannesburg on first day of the ANC's Defiance Campaign
1952, August	Opens own legal office at Chancellor House, Johannesburg
1952, mid-August	Arrested and charged under the Suppression of Communism Act
1952, October	Elected president of the Transvaal Provincial ANC (TANC)
1952, November	Convicted after trial under Suppression of Communism Act and receives suspended 20-month prison sentence
1952, December	Elected deputy president of the ANC
1952, December	Banned, confined to Johannesburg, and forbidden to attend meetings for six months
1953	Communist Party reorganises clandestinely and renames itself as the South African Communist Party (SACP)
1953, June	Helps lead opposition to Sophiatown removals, participating in weekly meetings in Sophiatown
1954	Birth of first surviving daughter, Pumla Makaziwe Mandela

1954, December	Fails to persuade fellow ANC NEC members to opt for a limited boycott of Bantu Education
1955, 8 February	Dissuades Freedom Volunteers from resisting first removals in Sophiatown
1955, 25 June	With other NEC members reads and approves draft Freedom Charter on the eve of the Congress of the People
1956, 5 December	Arrested and charged with treason
1957, January	Evelyn moves out of 8115 Orlando West with her furniture and children
1958, 14 June	Marries Winifred Nomzano Zanyiwe Madikizela
1958	Participates in the ANC leadership's decision to abandon a three-day stay away after the first day of the strike
1958, October	Persuades ANC Women's League (ANCWL) anti-pass law protesters to apply for bail
1959, 5 February	Birth of third daughter, Zenani Mandela
1960, 21 March	Mandela spends night at Joe Slovo's house discussing Congress Alliance response to the Sharpeville massacre
1960, 28 March	Mandela burns his reference book in Orlando before invited journalists
1960, 8 April	Prohibition of the ANC and Pan-Africanist Congress (PAC)
1960, 30 March	Arrested and detained under State of Emergency regulations
1960, August	Testifies and is cross-examined at the Treason Trial in Pretoria
1960, 31 August	Released from detention
1960, September	Tours country to explain NEC decision to maintain secret ANC organisation while dissolving the Youth and Women's Leagues
1960, 23 December	Birth of fourth daughter Zindziswa ('Zindzi') Mandela
1961, January–February	Tours country to co-ordinate preparations for All-in-Africa Conference. Visits Maseru,

	Basutoland for discussions with Ntsu Mokhehle
1961, 23 March	ANC National Working Committee (NWC) decides that Mandela should 'go underground' after All-in-Africa Conference
1961, 25 March	Addresses All-in-Africa Conference, Pietermartizburg to call for a national constitutional convention
1961, 29 March	With fellow accused acquitted of treason. During next two months lives in SACP-organised accommodation and visits main cities to lead planning of a strike aimed to coincide with South Africa's declaration of a republic
1961, 29 May	Monitors first day of planned three-day stay at home from 'safe house' in Soweto
1961, 30 May	Announces the end of the stay away, on its second day
1961, early June	Agrees with Sisulu to propose the adoption of violent tactics at an upcoming meeting of the ANC's NWC
1961, late June	Mandela argues the case for the ANC using violence at a two-day meeting of the ANC's NWC. The NWC agrees to put the decision to a full NEC meeting
1961, July	Mandela attends an NEC meeting at Stanger, Natal, attended by Chief Luthuli and persuades those present to sanction the establishment of Umkhonto we Sizwe
1961, July–August	Mandela lives in Yeoville apartment of SACP member, Wolfie Kodesh
1961, September	Moves to another safe house in Norwood
1961, October	Moves to Lilliesleaf Farm, Rivonia, disguised as a gardener. Attends planning meetings of Umkhonto's High Command and participates in recruitment and early experiments with explosives. Visits Cape Province and Natal to help establish regional command structures
1961, 16 December	Umkhonto we Sizwe begins sabotage campaign

1962, 4 January	After decision that Mandela should attend Pan-African Freedom Movement of East, Central and West Africa (PAFMECSA) conference Mandela travels to Natal to consult with Chief Luthuli
1962, 10 January	Leaves Johannesburg and crosses Bechuana border
1962, 29 January	After visits to Tanganyika, Sudan, and Nigeria, arrives at the PAFMECSA meeting in Addis Ababa, Ethiopia
1962, February and March	In north Africa, including a visit to the FLN's (Front de Liberation Nationale's) ALN (Armée de Liberation Nationale) headquarters at Oujda, Morocco, 18–21 March
1962, April–June	Travels through West Africa with Tambo
1962, June	Spends three weeks in London
1962, 28 June	Begins military training in Ethiopia
1962, mid-July	Mandela receives telegram from Sisulu asking him to return to South Africa
1962, 24 July	Arrives at Lilliesleaf Farm and attends ANC NWC meeting to report on his travels
1962, 26 July	Travels to Durban and during the next week meets Chief Luthuli, as well as members of the Natal Umkhonto Regional Command
1962, 5 August	Arrested outside Pietermaritzburg
1962, 6 August	In Johannesburg, Mandela is charged with incitement and leaving South Africa illegally
1962, July–October	Mandela held at Fort Prison, Johannesburg
1962, 13 October	Opening of Mandela's trial in Pretoria
1962, 7 November	After Mandela's plea in mitigation he is sentenced to three years' imprisonment. He is taken to Pretoria Central prison. Refuses to wear shorts and spends several weeks in solitary confinement before joining other prisoners. Sits next to PAC leader Robert Sobukwe while sewing mailbags
1963, May	Mandela is taken to Robben Island
1963, mid-July	Taken to Pretoria to join Umkhonto leaders arrested at Rivonia

1963, 9 October	Charged under Sabotage and Suppression of Communism Acts with responsibility for acts of sabotage as well as the promotion of guerrilla warfare and the planning of an armed invasion
1964, 20 April	Delivers statement from the dock
1964, 12 June	Sentenced to life imprisonment. Taken in a military aeroplane to Robben Island
1964, November	Visited by *Daily Telegraph* reporter and photographer
1965, January	Mandela, with other Section B prisoners, begins work at lime quarry
1965	Visited by Mr Henning, representative of the American Bar Association
1965	Mandela helps establish and joins High Organ
1965, after June	Section B prisoners establish Communications Committee
1965, about November	Visit from Hans Sen of the International Red Cross (IRC)
1966, about June	African prisoners in Section B allowed to wear long trousers
1966, July	Mandela participates in hunger strike
1968	After representations from the IRC, Section B prisoners allowed to subscribe to a limited list of magazines
1969, 12 May	Winnie Mandela arrested and held under Terrorism Act for 491 days
1969, July	Death of first son, Thembekile (Thembi) Mandela
1970, January	Mandela addresses letter of complaint to the Commissioner of Prisons
1970, June	Mandela protests against behaviour of the prison's commanding office, Colonel Badenhorst. Badenhorst is replaced
1970, 14 September	Winnie Mandela released
1975, July	Begins writing his autobiography. Completes text one year later
1976, 16 June	Start in Soweto of country-wide schoolchildren's uprising
1976	Meets Minister of Justice, Jimmy Kruger, who

	offers him a conditional reduction of sentence; Mandela refuses offer
1977	Prison authorities end daily manual labour
1977, 17 May	Winnie Mandela banished to Brandfort
1982, 31 March	Mandela, Sisulu, Raymond Mhlaba, and Andrew Mlangeni moved to Pollsmoor prison
1983, 20 August	Formation of the United Democratic Front (UDF)
1984, January	First 'contact visit' with Winnie Mandela
1985, 31 January	P.W. Botha offers Mandela conditional freedom. Zindzi Mandela reads Mandela's rejection of the offer to a mass meeting in Soweto
1985, mid	Mandela writes to the Minister of Justice, Kobie Coetsee, requesting a meeting
1985, December	Meets Coetsee while recuperating in hospital from an operation. On return from hospital Mandela confined separately from former cell mates. Requests meeting with lawyer George Bizos and writes letter to Tambo informing him about his intention to meet members of the government
1986, 16–19 May	Meets members of the Commonwealth Eminent Persons' Group
1986, 24 December	Mandela is driven around Cape Town. Through 1987 has several meetings with Minister Coetsee
1988, May	Mandela begins a series of 47 meetings with a special committee constituted by Minister Coetsee
1988, November	Hospitalised after diagnosis of tuberculosis
1988, 9 December	Moved to bungalow in the grounds of Victor Verster prison
1989, 2 February	Following a stroke, Botha resigns as leader of the National Party
1989, 5 July	Meets President Botha
1989, 14 August	Botha resigns as president and is replaced by F.W. de Klerk
1989, 13 December	Meets President de Klerk

1990, 2 February	President de Klerk announces unbanning of ANC and other prohibited organisations, release of political prisoners and suspension of death penalty
1990, 11 February	Release
1990, 2 March	Mandela reappointed as deputy president of the ANC, effectively the leader of ANC because of Tambo's illness after a stroke
1990, 2–4 May	First formal talks with government produce agreements on indemnities for returning exiles and on release of prisoners
1990, 6–7 August	At second round of talks, ANC announces suspension of armed struggle
1991, 5 July	Mandela elected ANC president at national conference
1991, 12 February	D.F. Malan Accord—ANC undertakes to inform the government about Umkhonto's deployments
1991, 22 December	Mandela and de Klerk clash over the issue of Umkhonto's activities at the opening session of Congress for a Democratic South Africa (CODESA)
1992, 17 April	Mandela announces his separation from Winnie
1992, 15 May	ANC withdraws from CODESA and subsequently decides upon a campaign of 'mass action' in support of its demands that the government meet 14 conditions before any resumption of negotiations
1992, 26 September	ANC and government sign a Record of Understanding and resume formal negotiations
1993, 10 April	Mandela appears on television to call for calm in aftermath of the assassination of Chris Hani
1993, 10 December	Attends award ceremony in Oslo as joint winner with de Klerk of Nobel Peace Prize
1994, 27–8 April	ANC wins 62.6 per cent of the poll in general election
1994, 10 May	Inauguration as president
1996, March	Divorces Winnie
1998, 18 July	Marries Graca Simbine Machel

1999, 2 June	ANC wins 66.36 per cent of poll in its second general election and Mandela ends his term as president
1999, December	Assumes role of 'facilitator' in Burundian peace negotiations
2005, 6 January	Death of Mandela's second son, Makgatho

FURTHER READING

South African history is represented in rich veins of both academic and popular writing, each shaped by conflicting political traditions, nationalist (Afrikaner and African), liberal, and Marxist, as well as more recent 'postmodern' and feminist approaches. Two useful surveys that combine balance, accessibility, and sophistication are Robert Ross's *Concise History of South Africa* (Cambridge: Cambridge University Press, 1999) and William Beinart's *Twentieth Century South Africa* (Oxford: Oxford University Press, 2001). The historical background to Mandela's childhood can be explored in Noel Mostert's *Frontiers: The epic of South Africa's creation and the tragedy of the Xhosa people* (London: Jonathan Cape, 1993). The most comprehensive overview of South African history during the apartheid era is Dan O'Meara's *Forty Lost Years* (Athens: Ohio University Press, 1996). The later chapters of Herman Giliomee's *The Afrikaners* (London: Hurst & Co., 2003) represent the best published account of apartheid's development.

Each biography of Mandela has its strengths. When researching his authorised biography, *Mandela*, Anthony Sampson obtained access to South African official records and in consequence his treatment of the prison period is particularly illuminating. Martin Meredith's *Nelson Mandela* contains compelling insights about Mandela's politics during the 1950s and especially well-informed commentary on the transition to democracy, between 1990 and 1994. Fatima Meer's affectionate earlier tribute, *Higher than Hope*, reproduces a well-chosen selection of Mandela's letters. A fascinating portrayal of Winnie Madikizela Mandela's life is in Emma Gilbey's *The Lady* (London: Vintage Books, 1994); Gilbey's treatment is highly critical and draws partly upon police sources.

Saul Dubow supplies a succinct review of the ANC's development since its foundation in 1912 in *African National Congress* (Stroud: Sutton Publishing Inc., 2000). More detail—perhaps more than most readers would wish for—is available in my own *Black Politics in South Africa since 1945* (London: Longman, 1983), and the ANC's chronology is documented most authoritatively in the five-volume *From Protest to Challenge Series*, edited by Thomas Karis, Gwendolen Carter, and Gail Gerhart, published between 1972 and 1997 (Stanford, CA: Hoover Institution Press and Pretoria: University of South Africa Press). For up-to-date treatments of the ANC's first decade of armed insurgent politics, see the essays in the South African Democracy Education

Trust's *The Road to Democracy in South Africa*: Volume 1: *1960–1970* (Cape Town: Zebra Press, 2004). More left-wing traditions in South African politics, including the Communist Party's early evolution, are addressed in Allison Drew's *Discordant Comrades: Identities and loyalties on the South African left* (Pretoria: University of South Africa Press, 2002). Well-researched treatments of the South African Communist Party's (SACP's) history since 1960 include Eddy Maloka's *The South African Communist Party in Exile* (Pretoria: Africa Institute, 2002) and Stephen Ellis and Tsepo Sechaba's *Comrades Against Apartheid: The ANC and the Communist Party in exile* (London: James Currey, 1992). Insider accounts of the Communist Party range from Michael Harmel's disciplined official history of the Party written under a pseudonym, A. Lerumo, *Fifty Fighting Years* (London: Inkululeko Publications, 1971) to the more iconoclastic indiscretions of Ben Turok's *Nothing but the Truth: Behind the ANC's struggle politics* (Cape Town: Zebra Press, 2003). Vladimir Shubin offers a unique perspective from the vantage point of a Soviet sympathiser, well informed about official contacts between Moscow and the SACP as well as about the ANC: *ANC: A view from Moscow* (Bellville: Mayibuye Books, 1999).

Many of Mandela's friends, associates, and adversaries have either written their own life stories or been the subjects of biographies. Ahmed Kathrada's *Memoirs* (Cape Town: Zebra Press, 2004) are exceptional for their intelligence and readability and were for me a crucial source in writing about Mandela's imprisonment. Luli Callinicos' biography of Oliver Tambo, *Oliver Tambo: Beyond the Engeli mountains* (Cape Town: David Philip, 2004) is outstanding in its genre and indispensable for any understanding of the ANC's post-Second World War history. Lionel Bernstein's *Memory Against Forgetting* (London: Viking, 1999) is written with grace and candour by a key figure in the politics of the ANC's alliances with the Communist Party during the 1950s. F.W. de Klerk's *The Last Trek: A new beginning* (London: Macmillan, 1998) offers an unusually dispassionate assessment of Nelson Mandela's political style and his text is informative about his own motives and intentions during the political settlement.

The popular insurrectionary movement that developed inside South Africa in the wake of the Soweto uprising of 1976 is described and analysed in detail and in depth in Tony Marx's *Lessons of Struggle* (New York: Oxford University Press, 1992), Ineke van Kessel's *Beyond Our Wildest Dreams* (Charlottesville, VA: University of Virginia Press, 2000), and Jeremy Seekings' *The UDF: A history* (Cape Town: David Philip, 2000). Allister Spark's *Tomorrow is Another Country* (Sandton: Struik, 1994) is an exciting and discerning narrative about the negotiations that brought Mandela and his movement into power by one of South Africa's most respected journalists. For more academic projections of the transition, read: Richard Spitz and Matthew Chaskalson, *The Politics of Transition: A hidden history of South Africa's negotiated settlement*, Timothy D. Sisk, *Democratization in South Africa: The elusive social contract* (Princeton, NJ: Princeton University Press, 1995), and Adrian Guelke, *Rethinking the Rise and Fall of Apartheid* (Basingstoke: Palgrave Macmillan, 2005).

Finally, the achievements and shortcomings of Mandela's administration, as well as the government of his successor, Thabo Mbeki, are debated in the following: Patrick Bond, *Elite Transition: From Apartheid to Neo-Liberalism in South Africa* (London: Pluto Press, 2000), Hein Marais, *South Africa: Limits to Change: The Political Economy of Transition* (London: Zed Books, 2001), Tom Lodge, *Politics in South Africa from Mandela to Mbeki* (Oxford: James Currey, 2003), and William Mervin Gumede, *Thabo Mbeki and the Battle for the Soul of the ANC* (Cape Town: Zebra Press, 2004).

INDEX